TODAY IN
NEW ZEALAND
HISTORY

TODAY IN NEW ZEALAND HISTORY

Neill Atkinson,
David Green,
Gareth Phipps
and Steve Watters

EXISLE PUBLISHING

First published 2017
This edition published 2020

Exisle Publishing Pty Ltd
226 High Street, Dunedin, 9016, New Zealand
PO Box 864, Chatswood, NSW 2057, Australia
www.exislepublishing.com

A CiP record for this book is available from the National Library of New Zealand.

ISBN 978-1-77559-428-4

Designed by Nick Turzynski of redinc. book design
Typeset in Garamond Premier Pro 11/14
Printed in China

This book uses paper sourced under ISO 14001 guidelines from well-managed forests and other controlled sources.

10 9 8 7 6 5 4 3 2 1

Disclaimer
While this book is intended as a general information resource and all care has been taken in compiling the contents, neither the authors nor the publisher and their distributors can be held responsible for any loss, claim or action that may arise from reliance on the information contained in this book.

Published in partnership with Manatū Taonga — Ministry for Culture and Heritage and the Alexander Turnbull Library — National Library of New Zealand Te Puna Mātauranga o Aotearoa.

CONTENTS

INTRODUCTION

On 1 January 1859 hundreds of Wellingtonians crowded aboard the steamer *Wonga Wonga* to visit New Zealand's first permanent lighthouse at Pencarrow Head. The light was a godsend for mariners, and its construction on a rocky, windswept headland was a notable achievement; equally remarkable was the identity of its first official keeper, Mary Bennett, who remains New Zealand's only female lighthouse keeper.

Dates matter, and they are often a starting point for our engagement with history. For most New Zealanders, days like 6 February or 25 April are laden with significance. They are recognised as markers of important moments in our past; they inspire pride, connection, reflection, or perhaps controversy. Whatever we think about their origins, the attention they get or the ways in which they are marked, they mean something, just like the Fourth of July, Bastille Day or 9/11. Some dates hold a sombre or sinister place in the nation's collective memory: 22 February (the second Canterbury earthquake), 12 October (Passchendaele), 5 November (Parihaka) or 24 December (Tangiwai). Others highlight more uplifting moments, like Rutherford's Nobel Prize (10 December 1908), Hillary's ascent of Everest (29 May 1953) or New Zealand's golden hour at the Rome Olympics (2 September 1960).

This book presents a series of snapshots of New Zealand historical events organised by date, from 1 January to 31 December, with some dates featuring two events. They range from the dramatic headline moments mentioned above to the hopefully less familiar and sometimes downright quirky — from Jockey Y-fronts (16 March 1940) and a Nazi sabotage hoax (29 March 1942) to the Greymouth beer boycott (29 September 1947) and a parachuting Santa (20 November 1937). In addition, Born on this Day boxes scattered throughout the text provide brief biographical details on more than 70 figures of significance to New Zealand history.

The content has been produced by the Ministry for Culture and Heritage, whose Research and Publishing Group prepared the text, in partnership with the Alexander Turnbull Library, which provided the majority of the illustrations. Many of these stories were originally published on the Ministry's NZHistory website (www.nzhistory.govt.nz), which has presented a Today in History calendar feature for more than a decade. The original text was reshaped for this publication, and a number of new events have been added; the web content has in turn been refreshed and augmented. Other material, especially the Born on this Day details, has been drawn from the Ministry's Te Ara encyclopedia (www.teara.govt.nz), which incorporates the Dictionary of New Zealand Biography.

The stories presented here are intended to inform, entertain and encourage curiosity and further inquiry, not to provide a comprehensive history of New Zealand. Any 'today in history' approach has limitations. Most obviously, the Gregorian calendar — a 16th-century Catholic–European solar calendar, which was adopted in Britain in 1752 and has become the de facto international standard — was brought to New Zealand aboard European ships. As a result, the earliest event in this book is Abel Tasman's ill-fated encounter with Māori in Golden Bay in December 1642 (the Dutch Republic had adopted the Gregorian calendar in 1582); most of the events prior to the 1840s focus on the activities of European sailors, traders and missionaries — or in one case, a cricket match (see 20 December). Māori had their own understanding of time based on Maramataka, a traditional lunar calendar that divided the year into 12 months of 29½ days each (a lunar calendar is around 11 days shorter than a solar calendar).

A date-based approach also privileges historical events that can be confidently pinned to a single day — elections, battles, new laws, arrivals, appointments, disasters and sports events. It inevitably favours novelty, the 'shock of the new', rather than what followed; the word 'first' features prominently in the following pages. It is a less useful tool for illustrating the more complex, incremental trends and forces that have shaped our society over time. For example, we feature New Zealand's landmark women's suffrage legislation of 1893, and highlight the achievements of the first woman doctor, lawyer, university graduate, juror, mayor and MP. But the format cannot easily capture the longer-term changes in women's employment, political participation or social status that lay behind such events, nor the achievements and struggles of the many who followed in the footsteps of those trailblazers.

The same is true of many other key developments in New Zealand history, such as urbanisation (including the dramatic story of post-Second World War Māori urbanisation), the emergence of Auckland as the country's economic powerhouse, the evolution of a sense of national identity (and the myths associated with it), changing employment patterns, declining family sizes, the ageing population or more recent demographic change brought about by migration. Sometimes specific events can be used to highlight more significant long-term shifts. The first export shipment of frozen meat aboard the *Dunedin* on 15 February 1882, for example, was not in itself a major event — after all, the experiment might easily have failed — but its success paved the way for a trade that was to become the cornerstone of the 20th-century New Zealand economy. Similarly, when the Waitangi Tribunal was established — initially to consider contemporary rather than historical claims — on 10 October 1975, few could have predicted the impact it would have on New Zealand society over the following four decades.

Within the limitations of the format we have sought to avoid an overly simplistic 'triumphs and tragedies' approach, and provide representative coverage across decades, regions, themes and topics. Nevertheless, the selection has an inherent randomness, and a number of interesting events have had to be omitted simply because they clashed with others occurring on the same date, or because the subject matter was covered in other, similar stories. A broader range of events, including in some cases more than two on a single day, can be found on the Ministry's NZHistory website, which provides links to other information on that site, on Te Ara and elsewhere online. Interested readers are encouraged to explore other historical sources and approaches, and the Further Reading section provides a selection of print and online publications, including valuable recent general overviews such as *Tangata Whenua* and *A History of New Zealand Women*.

NEW ZEALAND'S FIRST LIGHTHOUSE LIT

Pencarrow Head lighthouse, near Wellington Harbour, was lit for the first time amid great celebration. After years of inadequate solutions, Wellington finally had a permanent lighthouse — a New Zealand first. Equally notable was the lighthouse's first keeper, Mary Bennett, who had looked after Pencarrow's temporary light since her husband's death in 1855 — she remains New Zealand's only female lighthouse keeper.

During the day, many settlers visited their new lighthouse on the SS *Wonga Wonga*. The 10 a.m. excursion carried about 65 people. The afternoon excursion, which left at 4 p.m., was much more crowded.

When the *Wonga Wonga* anchored off Pencarrow about 7 p.m. nearly 40 people, including officials, went ashore and walked up to the lighthouse, where engineer Edward Wright gave a tour.

Wellington's provincial superintendent, Isaac Featherston, had the honour of lighting the light for the first time. Although those on the *Wonga Wonga* were initially concerned at the apparent inefficiency of the light, their disappointment soon gave way to pleasure as a brilliant light came into view.

BORN ON THIS DAY

Margaret Cruickshank,
1873–1918,
first woman doctor

Pencarrow Head lighthouse,
c. 1900.

FIRST OFFICIAL AIRMAIL FLIGHT TO SAN FRANCISCO

2 January
1938

The first official New Zealand airmail to the United States left Auckland for San Francisco on Pan American Airways' *Samoan Clipper*. The Sikorsky S-42B flying boat was piloted by Captain Ed Musick — then regarded as the world's most famous pilot — and carried 25,000 items of mail.

After crossing the International Date Line, Musick arrived in Pago Pago, American Samoa, where it was still 1 January. At his next stop, an uninhabited atoll 1700 kilometres south of Hawaii, he was met by a schooner with supplies. On 3 January, the *Samoan Clipper* arrived in Honolulu, where the mail was transferred to a Martin M-130 flying boat, which arrived in San Francisco on 6 January.

Disaster struck on the return trip. Shortly after taking off from Pago Pago on 11 January, Musick reported an oil leak in one of his engines; as he attempted to dump fuel for a safe landing, the plane caught fire and exploded. There were no survivors. In 1939 a headland on the eastern side of the Tamaki River was renamed Musick Point in the pilot's honour.

Flying boats, Mechanics Bay, Auckland, December 1937–January 1938.

1930

FIRST NEW ZEALAND-MADE 'TALKIE' SCREENED TO PUBLIC

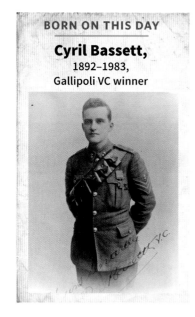

*C*oubray-tone News, the work of the inventive Edwin (Ted) Coubray, had its first public screening at Auckland's Plaza Theatre. Filmed on location around the city, footage included the funeral of Catholic Bishop Henry Cleary, workers on Queen Street and the Auckland wharves, and scenes from 'The Romance of Maoriland', which captured poi, haka and waiata performances.

After a private screening of Coubray's newsreel a week earlier, the *Auckland Star* commented:

> *While the film does not reach the perfection in sound of American or British 'talkies', it must not be branded as 'amateurish.' The makers have not the same equipment as is available for foreign producers.*

Film-maker Coubray began developing his own sound-on-film system following the arrival of 'talkies' in New Zealand in early 1929. After six months' experimentation, and at a cost of £3000 (over $280,000 today), the Coubray-tone sound system was operational. This entirely New Zealand-made enterprise was the first of its kind in Australasia.

After six months' experimentation, and at a cost of £3000 . . . the Coubray-tone sound system was operational.

Coubray brothers at work, December 1929.

HILLARY LEADS NEW ZEALAND PARTY TO SOUTH POLE

Sir Edmund Hillary's New Zealand team became the first to reach the South Pole overland since Robert Falcon Scott in 1912, and the first to do so in motor vehicles.

The New Zealand contingent was part of a larger Commonwealth Trans-Antarctic Expedition (TAE) led by British adventurer Vivian Fuchs, which planned to undertake the first crossing from one side of Antarctica to the other.

After helping establish Scott Base on Ross Island during the summer of 1956–57 (see 20 January), and laying food and fuel depots for Fuchs' party, Hillary and his four-man team set out for the Pole on modified Massey Ferguson tractors. It was an arduous slog through snow ridges, soft snow and dangerous crevasses, but Hillary reached the Pole 16 days ahead of Fuchs.

Hillary's so-called 'dash to the Pole' caused controversy as it took place without the express permission of the TAE, and against the instructions of the committee co-ordinating New Zealand's contribution. While his devil-may-care approach appealed to many, some viewed it as an arrogant attempt to outplay Fuchs. The success of the venture, however, ultimately overshadowed any ill feeling.

It was an arduous slog through snow ridges, soft snow and dangerous crevasses . . .

Sir Edmund Hillary on a tractor bound for Cape Crozier.

5 January
1977

OCCUPATION OF BASTION POINT BEGINS

BORN ON THIS DAY

Gottfried Lindauer,
1839-1926,
artist

L ed by Joe Hawke, the Ōrākei Māori Action Committee occupied Takaparawhā (Bastion Point reserve), a promontory overlooking Auckland's Waitematā Harbour. Ngāti Whātua maintained the land had been unjustly taken from them and were angered by plans to subdivide it for a private housing development.

In April 1977, a disused warehouse was re-erected on the site as Arohanui Marae, but facilities were rudimentary and in winter the exposed promontory was a bleak place to live. In February 1978, the government offered to return some land and houses to Ngāti Whātua if the iwi paid $200,000 in development costs. The occupiers stayed put, but on 25 May — 506 days after they had arrived — a large force of police moved in to evict them, arresting 222 protesters and demolishing buildings.

When the jurisdiction of the Waitangi Tribunal was widened to cover retrospective issues, Joe Hawke's Ōrākei claim was the first historical claim to be heard. The Tribunal's 1987 report recommended the return of land to Ngāti Whātua, and the following year the government agreed (see 1 July).

Ngāti Whātua occupation of Bastion Point.

GODFREY BOWEN SETS WORLD SHEEP-SHEARING RECORD
6 January 1953

At Akers Station at Ōpiki, Manawatū, Godfrey Bowen set a new world record, shearing 456 full-wool ewes in nine hours. Bowen helped establish sheep shearing as a legitimate sport and was one of the first people inducted into the New Zealand Sports Hall of Fame in 1990. In the years after the Second World War, Godfrey and his brother Ivan revolutionised the wool industry through their improved shearing methods — the 'Bowen technique' — which added value to the national clip and helped lift the profile of shearing. After breaking the world record, Godfrey became chief shearing instructor for the New Zealand Wool Board. In 1954 he helped establish two university courses on the subject. In 1960 he was made an MBE for services to the sheep industry. Godfrey Bowen taught the Bowen technique in many countries around the world. In 1971 he and local farmer George Harford opened the Agrodome near Rotorua. This 'theme park dedicated to the New Zealand farm' set the benchmark for rural tourism ventures.

Godfrey Bowen shearing at Ōpiki, Manawatū, 1953.

BUMPY LANDING FOR TASMAN'S FIRST SOLO FLYER

Australian Guy Menzies' flight from Sydney ended awkwardly when he crash-landed in a swamp at Harihari on the West Coast. But his heroic effort helped to lift spirits on both sides of the Tasman against the backdrop of the Depression.

The first successful trans-Tasman flight had been completed in 1928 by the illustrious Australian aviator Charles Kingsford Smith and his crew aboard the Fokker tri-motor *Southern Cross* (see 11 September).

The 21-year-old Menzies took off from Sydney in *Southern Cross Junior*, a single-engined Avro Avian biplane. He carried neither a wireless nor food; 'his luggage was one spare collar, a razor, and a toothbrush.' He encountered rough weather over the Tasman and was driven well south of his intended destination, Blenheim. Shortly before 3 p.m., Menzies mistook a swamp near Harihari for flat ground and crash-landed his aircraft, which flipped upside down. He walked away with only a few scratches.

While his arrival was less dignified than Kingsford Smith's, Menzies took more than 2½ hours off his compatriot's time, completing the flight in 11 hours 45 minutes.

Guy Menzies' Avro Avian aeroplane in a swamp at Harihari.

HAAST BEGINS WEST COAST EXPEDITION

In January 1863, geologist Julius von Haast led an expedition in search of an overland route from the east to the west coast of the South Island. He found a suitable route from the upper Makarora River, crossing the Southern Alps by the mountain pass now known as Haast Pass.

Although prospector Charles Cameron is credited with 'discovering' the pass, Haast was rewarded by having it named after him. His expedition reached the pass on 23 January. After crossing it, they travelled downstream, reaching the coast on 20 February. On an earlier expedition, Haast had discovered the extent of the Grey River coalfields and found traces of gold in several rivers.

Haast was one of a number of European scientists who surveyed and explored New Zealand's landscape during the 19th century. Between the late 1830s and the 1870s, Ernst Dieffenbach, Ferdinand von Hochstetter and Haast covered much of the country, recording its animals and geology. As Canterbury Provincial Geologist from 1861, Haast led comprehensive surveys of the province, sprinkling German names over the landscape as he went.

View of Haast Pass looking north from Fish River by Julius von Haast, 1866.

DEATH OF KATHERINE MANSFIELD
9 January 1923

Internationally acclaimed author Katherine Mansfield revolutionised 20th-century English short-story writing. She died from tuberculosis in France, aged just 34. Katherine Mansfield was the pen name of Kathleen Mansfield Beauchamp. Finding New Zealand too provincial, she sailed to London in 1908 and never returned. Despite this, she never lost her ties to the country of her birth, the setting for some of her best-known stories. Mansfield inspired mixed reactions in London literary circles — Virginia Woolf admitted to being jealous of her writing, but the poet T.S. Eliot described her as 'a thick-skinned toady' and 'a dangerous woman'. She had a stormy relationship with editor and writer John Middleton Murry, whom she eventually married. After her death, Murry prepared her remaining writings for publication, a labour of love that did much for her international reputation. While Mansfield's output was small — five collections of stories, and reviews, journals, letters and poems — her works have inspired biographies, radio and television programmes, plays, operatic works and films. The house in Thorndon, Wellington where she was born is one of New Zealand's most-visited heritage sites.

Katherine Mansfield at Menton, France, 1920.

PIONEER AVIATORS VANISH OVER THE TASMAN

New Zealanders George Hood and John Moncrieff disappeared during a 'gallant if somewhat ill-organised attempt' to complete the first flight across the Tasman Sea. They took off from Richmond, Sydney, in a single-engined Ryan monoplane, the *Aotearoa*, in the early hours of 10 January. The 2335-kilometre flight to Trentham, just north of Wellington, was expected to take 14 hours.

This attempt at aviation history captured the public's attention. By late afternoon, 10,000 people had joined the aviators' wives, Laura Hood and Dorothy Moncrieff, at Trentham Racecourse to welcome them. They waited in vain. Radio signals were picked up for 12 hours, but then contact was lost. The aviators were never seen again.

Later that year Australian Charles Kingsford Smith and his three-man crew achieved what Hood and Moncrieff had died attempting when they landed the *Southern Cross*, a Fokker tri-motor, at Wigram, Christchurch (see 11 September). Guy Menzies completed the first solo Tasman crossing, in a single-engined plane, in 1931 (see 7 January).

Laura Hood and Dorothy Moncrieff at Trentham Racecourse, waiting for their husbands to arrive.

1846

RUAPEKAPEKA PĀ OCCUPIED BY BRITISH FORCES

The battle at Ruapekapeka ('bats' nest'), a sophisticated pā built by the Ngāpuhi chief Kawiti, ended the Northern War. Debate soon raged as to whether the fortress had been deliberately abandoned or captured.

The Northern War erupted in March 1845. Ruapekapeka gave the new governor, George Grey, an opportunity to establish his authority following the failure of his predecessor, Robert FitzRoy, to win a decisive victory.

As well as 1300 British troops and navy personnel, Grey had 400 allied Māori (Ngāpuhi rivals of Hōne Heke and Kawiti led by Tāmati Wāka Nene). The British trudged for three weeks across rugged country. When they reached Ruapekapeka in early January 1846, they outnumbered their opponents by four to one.

On 10 January, a bombardment created three small breaches in the palisade. Next morning the pā was found to be nearly empty. The British chased its few occupants towards nearby bush — and a possible ambush, which they were able to avoid.

Following the battle, the Māori antagonists made peace, leaving Grey little choice but to pardon rather than punish the 'rebels'.

Painting of Ruapekapeka pā by Lieutenant-Colonel Cyprian Bridge, 1846.

QUEEN ELIZABETH II OPENS PARLIAMENT

A crowd of 50,000 greeted Queen Elizabeth II, resplendent in her coronation gown, when she opened a special session of the New Zealand Parliament in its centennial year. This was the first time a reigning monarch had opened New Zealand's Parliament.

The Queen and her husband, Prince Philip, had arrived in New Zealand shortly before Christmas 1953. Throughout their tour, large and enthusiastic crowds met them at every stop. About three in every four New Zealanders saw the Queen as she visited 46 towns and cities and attended 110 functions. At Tīrau, a community of 600 people in south Waikato, a crowd of 10,000 turned up for a glimpse of the young monarch.

Another notable first during this tour was Queen Elizabeth's Christmas broadcast from Auckland, the first time this broadcast was made outside Britain. The Queen ended it with a message of sympathy for the people of New Zealand in the wake of the Tangiwai rail disaster of the previous night (see 24 December).

The Queen speaking in Parliament, 1954.

'TORPEDO BILLY' MURPHY WINS WORLD FEATHERWEIGHT BOXING TITLE
13 January 1890

By defeating Irish-born American Ike Weir at San Francisco, Murphy became the first New Zealander to win a world professional boxing title. Until Joseph Parker won the World Boxing Organisation's version of the heavyweight title in 2016, Murphy was the only New Zealand-born boxer to have held a recognised world professional title. Born in Auckland in 1862, Thomas William Murphy ('Torpedo Billy') began boxing as a teenager before moving to Australia in 1887. Two years later, he moved to the United States. Weir dominated the early rounds of the title fight, but Murphy knocked him down five times in the thirteenth before knocking him out in the fourteenth. When Murphy returned to New Zealand, he was deemed to have forfeited his title. It continued to be recognised in New Zealand and Australia until he lost to Australian Albert Griffiths in September 1890 in Sydney. Murphy later returned to the United States. By the time he hung up his gloves in 1907 he had fought 112 times for 65 wins, 32 losses and 15 draws. Murphy died in 1939 and was made an inaugural member of the New Zealand Sports Hall of Fame in 1990.

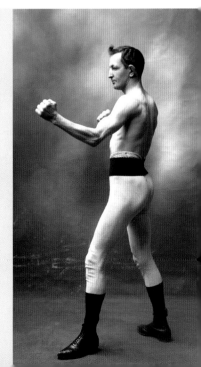

Thomas William Murphy ('Torpedo Billy'), c. 1905.

14-YEAR-OLD FINDS NEW ZEALAND'S OLDEST FOSSILS

In 1948, a 14-year-old Nelson schoolboy discovered the oldest fossils ever found in New Zealand. Malcolm Simpson was a member of the party that accompanied University of Otago geologist Noel Benson on an expedition to Cobb Valley, near Motueka. During the trip, Simpson hammered off some fresh limestone containing indistinct fossils and passed it to Professor Benson, who initially considered the fossils to be indistinguishable molluscan remains.

After returning to Dunedin, Benson discovered the samples contained trilobites — a fossil group of extinct marine arthropods. Intrigued, he sent them to the Geological Survey of Great Britain for identification. Three months later, an excited Benson telephoned Simpson to let him know that they were Cambrian fossils from the Paleozoic era (542–251 million years ago) — making them the oldest rocks yet found in New Zealand.

In 1998, on the fiftieth anniversary of the find, the Geological Society of New Zealand awarded Simpson the Wellman Prize for his contribution to palaeontology.

Trilobite limestone found by Malcolm Simpson.

VIETNAM WAR PROTESTERS GREET UNITED STATES VICE-PRESIDENT
15 January 1970

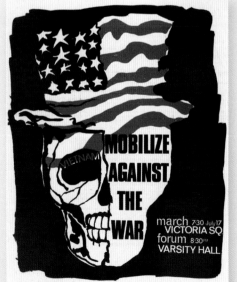

United States Vice-President Spiro Agnew's three-day visit to New Zealand sparked some of the most violent anti-Vietnam War demonstrations seen in this country. Many protesters and some media accused the police of excessive force against demonstrators. New Zealand was Agnew's last stop on a 25-day, 60,000-kilometre, 11-nation goodwill tour of Pacific and Asian countries. His wife, Judy, Apollo 10 astronaut Eugene Cernan, 10 journalists, aides and Secret Service agents accompanied him. The presence of a high-ranking American politician attracted the attention of the anti-war movement, who saw the New Zealand government as bowing to the US over participation in the war. Over 500 protesters greeted the Vice-President in Auckland. The following evening protests continued outside a state dinner for Agnew. Up to 700 protesters assembled outside his hotel and shouted anti-war slogans at guests as they arrived. There were 200 police on hand and a series of scuffles broke out. Around 11.45 p.m. the police moved against the demonstrators, making 11 arrests. The protests attracted widespread media attention here and in the United States.

Mobilisation poster produced by the Committee on Vietnam, Wellington, 1966.

WOMEN'S AUXILIARY AIR FORCE FOUNDED

The Women's Auxiliary Air Force (WAAF) was formed to enable the Royal New Zealand Air Force (RNZAF) to release more men for overseas service during the Second World War. Within 18 months, authorities also created a Women's Auxiliary Army Corps and a Women's Royal Naval Service. The WAAF contributed to the war effort by easing personnel shortages. Initially, women served as cooks, mess-hands, drivers, clerks, equipment assistants, medical orderlies and typists. By the end of the war, they were working in a variety of trades.

In April 1941 an initial draft of 200 women, led by Superintendent Kitty Kain, arrived at RNZAF Station Rongotai in Wellington. WAAFs went on to serve at every major air force station in New Zealand, as well as in Fiji and on Norfolk Island.

Women did not hold service ranks until 1942, when the WAAF officially joined the RNZAF. They subsequently held ranks equivalent to those of men. At its peak in 1943, the WAAF numbered more than 3600, and around 4750 women passed through its ranks. More than 100 achieved commissioned officer rank, mainly in encoding and decoding work and administration.

BORN ON THIS DAY
Ormond Burton,
1893–1974,
soldier, pacifist, writer

The Style for You is Air Force Blue!

−JOIN THE **WAAF**

At its peak in 1943, the WAAF numbered more than 3600, and around 4750 women passed through its ranks.

Cover of WAAF recruitment booklet.

NEW ZEALAND CONSTITUTION ACT COMES INTO FORCE

Governor Sir George Grey issued a proclamation to bring the New Zealand Constitution Act (UK) of 1852 into operation, establishing a system of representative government for the colony.

The act created a General Assembly made up of an appointed Legislative Council and a House of Representatives elected every five years by males aged over 21 who owned, leased or rented property of a certain value. It also created six provinces with elected superintendents and provincial councils. By British standards, the property qualification was modest, allowing most male settlers to vote.

On 5 March, Grey issued a further proclamation setting out regulations for registration and voting, and outlining the boundaries of the 24 electoral districts, which were to return 37 general and 87 provincial members.

New Zealand's first general election was held between July and October 1853, but Grey was criticised for calling the provincial councils to meet before the General Assembly, giving provincialism a five-month head start on central government. The General Assembly did not meet until 24 May 1854 (see 24 May), 16 months after the Constitution Act had come into force.

Extract from the New Zealand Constitution Act published in several successive issues of the *Taranaki Herald* from 8 December 1852.

THE NEW ZEALAND CONSTITUTION ACT.

ENGLISH VERSION.

" THE NEW ZEALAND CONSTITUTION ACT, 1852."—
15 and 16 VICTORIA, CAP. 72, SEC. 71.

Her Majesty may cause Laws of Aboriginal Native Inhabitants to be maintained.

Passed 30th of June, 1852.

SECTION 71.—And Whereas it may be expedient that the Laws, Customs, and Usages of the Aboriginal or Native Inhabitants of New Zealand, so far as they are not repugnant to the general principles of Humanity, should for the present be maintained for the Government of themselves, in all their relations to and dealings with each other, and that particular districts should be set apart within which Laws, Customs, or Usages should be so observed. It should be lawful for Her Majesty, by any Letters Patent to be issued under the Great Seal of the United Kingdom from time to time to make Provisions for the purposes aforesaid, any repugnancy of any such Native's Laws, Customs, or Usages, to the Law of England or to in any part thereof, in any wise notwithstanding.

'MONTEGO BAY' HITS NO. 1

Upper Hutt's Jon Stevens made back-to-back no. 1 singles when 'Montego Bay' bumped 'Jezebel' from the top of the New Zealand charts.

Stevens became the pin-up boy of New Zealand pop with his double success during the summer of 1979–80. His first single 'Jezebel' reached no. 1 in early December 1979. 'Montego Bay', a cover of Bobby Bloom's 1970 hit, gave Stevens a rare double. It topped the charts for seven weeks. More success followed with the release of his debut album, *Jezebel* (1980), which cemented Stevens' position as New Zealand's premier solo male artist of the time.

Like many New Zealand musicians, Stevens crossed the Tasman to try his luck in Australia. In 1985, he was a founding member of Australian rock band Noiseworks, which enjoyed success on the Australian charts before disbanding in 1992. He then had two highly acclaimed stints playing Judas in Australian productions of *Jesus Christ Superstar*. Following the death of INXS frontman Michael Hutchence, Stevens had a spell as the singer's replacement in the early 2000s.

Cover of Jon Stevens'
Jezebel album.

1845

HŌNE HEKE CUTS DOWN THE BRITISH FLAG – AGAIN

The first Māori to sign the Treaty of Waitangi, Ngāpuhi chief Hōne Heke Pōkai soon became disenchanted with the consequences of colonisation. He expressed his outrage by repeatedly attacking the flagstaff on the hill above Kororāreka (Russell).

Hōne Heke chopping down the British flag is an enduring image in New Zealand history. Traditional Pākehā interpretations portrayed him as a 'rebel' who was finally subdued by 'good Governor' George Grey. In reality, questions of authority in the north remained unresolved well after the mid-1840s, years in which the Bay of Islands also lost its political and economic importance.

Te Haratua, Heke's right-hand man, first attacked the flagstaff in July 1844. The British re-erected it, but it was levelled twice in January 1845. A fourth attack on the flagstaff on 11 March signalled the outbreak of war in the north.

The Northern War was no simple matter of Māori versus British — two Ngāpuhi factions squared off against each other. Heke and Te Ruki Kawiti fought both the Crown and Ngāpuhi led by Tāmati Wāka Nene. The fighting ended in a stalemate in January 1846 (see 11 January).

Heke cutting down the flagstaff at Kororāreka, painted by Arthur McCormick, 1908.

SCOTT BASE OPENS IN ANTARCTICA
20 January 1957

Captain Harold Ruegg, Administrator for the Ross Dependency, opened Scott Base, New Zealand's permanent Antarctic research station, during a ceremony on Ross Island. Ruegg gave a short speech to a small crowd, which included Sir Edmund Hillary, Admiral George J. Dufek, and other officers from McMurdo Station, the nearby American logistical support base. Appropriately, as the base was named after the British explorer Robert Falcon Scott, the New Zealand flag was then raised on a flagstaff used by Scott at Hut Point in 1903. The base was established to support the privately run Commonwealth Trans-Antarctic Expedition (TAE) of 1955–58. It was to accommodate both the New Zealand party of the TAE and a group of New Zealand scientists attached to the expedition who also contributed to the International Geophysical Year. These parties were the first to winter over at Scott Base. By agreement with the Ross Sea Committee of the TAE, the base became the property of the New Zealand government at the completion of the expedition.

The Mess (D Hut) at Scott Base, January 1957.

AMERICAN ACROBAT PARACHUTES FROM BALLOON

'Professor' Thomas Baldwin descended by parachute from a balloon floating high above South Dunedin. The American acrobat had worked up a circus act using a trapeze and a hot-air balloon before making his first parachute jump a few years earlier, and subsequently toured the world as a paid entertainer. A pioneer balloonist and aviator, he later designed airships and aircraft.

Baldwin's first planned ascent from the Caledonian Ground was abandoned because the wind was too strong. Two days later, thousands turned up to watch his second attempt, in which he reached at least 1000 feet before leaping out of the balloon clutching his parachute, which inflated after a heart-stopping period of free-fall. A sail on the side of the parachute allowed him to steer away from danger. The act of detaching the parachute opened a hole through which gas escaped from the balloon, bringing it back to earth. Baldwin landed safely in a paddock beside the Hillside Railway Workshops.

A few days later, a local boy jumped off the roof of his house clutching an umbrella, which proved to have inferior aerodynamic properties to Baldwin's parachute — he broke his arm.

Two days later, thousands turned up to watch his second attempt, in which he reached at least 1000 feet before leaping out of the balloon clutching his parachute . . .

Thomas Baldwin in later life.

1840

EUROPEAN SETTLERS ARRIVE IN WELLINGTON

The New Zealand Company's first settler ship, the *Aurora*, arrived at Petone to found the settlement that would become Wellington.

Named after the first Duke of Wellington, the victor of the Battle of Waterloo, the new town was part of the New Zealand Company's systematic model of colonisation developed by Edward Gibbon Wakefield. Central to his scheme were packages of land comprising a town acre (0.4 hectares) and an accompanying 100 country acres (40 hectares). There were 1100 one-acre town sections in the plan for Port Nicholson.

Implementation of this design was problematic. Flooding forced the abandonment of the original site for the town at Pito-one (Petone), while land sale uncertainties dogged the makeshift community after it moved across the harbour to Thorndon and Te Aro.

By the end of the year, 1200 settlers had arrived in Wellington. Wakefield had hoped to make the settlement the capital of New Zealand. He was disappointed when Governor William Hobson chose Auckland instead, but Wellington eventually became the capital in 1865.

Plan of Wellington, 1840.

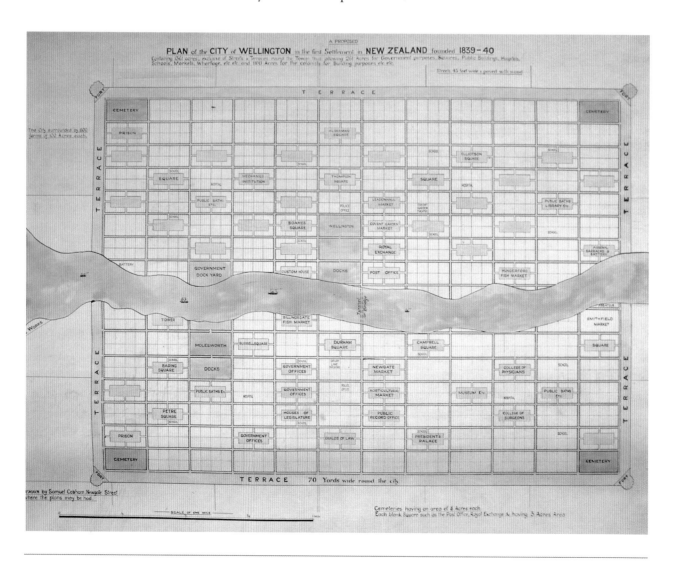

MASSIVE EARTHQUAKE HITS SOUTHERN NORTH ISLAND

23 January 1855

The magnitude 8.2 earthquake has had a profound impact on the development of Wellington city. Land raised from the harbour — along with additional reclamations — forms much of modern Wellington's central business district. The earthquake also drained notoriously swampy areas in the Hutt Valley and Wellington, including the site of the Basin Reserve cricket ground.

Movement on a fault in Palliser Bay caused the earthquake, which began at 9.11 p.m. and lasted for 50 seconds. It lifted the southern end of the Remutaka Range by a staggering 6 metres. About 10 minutes after the main shock, a 4-metre-high tsunami entered Wellington Harbour, sending water surging back and forth and flooding Lambton Quay.

Several buildings collapsed, including the two-storey council chambers and adjoining government offices. Most single-storey wooden buildings survived, despite damage caused by falling brick chimneys and shifting foundations.

Despite its strength, the quake killed only a few people — one in Wellington, two in Manawatū and up to six in Wairarapa.

Painting by Charles Gold of a landslip caused by the 1855 earthquake near Wellington.

SOVIET AMBASSADOR EXPELLED

The New Zealand government ordered the Soviet Union's ambassador, Vsevolod Sofinsky, to leave the country within 72 hours after he allegedly delivered money to the pro-Soviet Socialist Unity Party (SUP).

Sofinsky's expulsion resulted from an incident shortly before Christmas, when he met with SUP national secretary George Jackson at an Auckland motel. During the meeting, the Soviet ambassador supposedly handed over $10,000 (equivalent to $50,000 today). New Zealand's Security Intelligence Service, which had bugged the room, captured this transaction on tape.

Although there was some doubt about Sofinsky's precise role and both parties vehemently denied money had changed hands, Prime Minister Robert Muldoon felt there was sufficient evidence to expel the ambassador.

Despite fears that this move would derail New Zealand–USSR trade relations, the superpower retaliated merely by expelling New Zealand's ambassador to Moscow. The two countries re-established formal diplomatic relations in 1984.

The Soviet legation in Wellington, January 1951.

FIRST DAY OF COMPETITION AT CHRISTCHURCH COMMONWEALTH GAMES
25 January 1974

The opening ceremony of the 'Friendly Games' had featured performances by schoolchildren and a Māori concert party. Next day, Canterbury runner Dick Tayler ensured the success of the Games with a surprise victory for the host nation in the 10,000 metres track race. Tayler's effort was even more memorable because the field included English world record-holder David Bedford and three top-flight Kenyans, whose over-ambitious early pace played into Tayler's hands. The Kiwi's cat-and-mouse tactics against another Englishman, David Black, in the latter stages of the race before he pulled away on the final lap made it one of the Games' signature moments. His winning time of 27 minutes 46.4 seconds was then the sixth fastest 10,000 metres ever run. No New Zealander ran significantly faster until Zane Robertson recorded 27 minutes 33.67 seconds at the Rio Olympics in 2016. At 25, Tayler's best years should have been ahead of him. Instead, his career was ended within months by the onset of arthritis. Dick Tayler was made an inaugural member of the New Zealand Sports Hall of Fame in 1990.

Dick Tayler collapses after winning the 10,000 metres at the Christchurch Commonwealth Games, 1974.

FLOODS DEVASTATE SOUTHLAND

A record one-day total of up to 84.8 millimetres of rain caused extensive surface flooding in the streets of Invercargill, Riverton, Ōtautau, Tūātapere and Bluff.

Local waterways soon overflowed, and by 4 a.m., a state of emergency was declared. By morning, streets, houses, shops and factories were under water, and local streams sent torrents of water through Invercargill. Levels rose still further as high tide prevented floodwaters from draining into Invercargill Estuary. Invercargill Airport was flooded by water that was 3 metres deep inside the terminal.

By mid-morning of 27 January, the state of emergency included all of Southland. The rain stopped by noon, but the rivers continued to rise.

Floodwaters left around 1200 homes uninhabitable and forced the evacuation of more than 4000 people. No people died, but livestock losses were heavy — more than 12,000 sheep, 330 pigs, 100 cattle and 75 deer drowned. A relief appeal raised more than $3 million, and insurers paid out tens of millions of dollars in claims.

Minister of Internal Affairs Allan Highet with a display showing the effects of floods in Southland.

PETER SNELL BREAKS WORLD MILE RECORD
27 January 1962

The 23-year-old Olympic 800-metre champion (see 2 September) hoped to run the first four-minute mile on New Zealand soil. In fact, he broke Australian Herb Elliott's 3½-year-old world record by the smallest possible margin, one tenth of a second. This was an astonishing feat on a 353-metre grass track at Cooks Gardens, Whanganui, in a race that did not go to plan. When the starter's gun fired, the seven runners dawdled for several seconds before designated pacemaker Barry Cossar took off. He led through the half-mile in exactly two minutes. But no one else took up the running and Snell had to lead for the third quarter-mile. At the start of the last lap, Englishman Bruce Tulloh surged ahead. Snell burst past him and ran the last 440 yards in 54.6 seconds to stop the clock at 3 minutes 54.4 seconds. This was arguably a performance to equal John Walker's sub-3:50 mile in Gothenburg, Sweden in 1975. A week later, Snell smashed the world records for the 800 metres and 880 yards — again on a grass track (Lancaster Park, Christchurch) and again after the pacemaking went wrong.

Peter Snell sets a new world mile record at Cooks Gardens in Whanganui, 1962.

1827

D'URVILLE SAILS THROUGH 'FRENCH PASS'

In a feat of navigational daring — and after several attempts — the French explorer Jules Sébastien César Dumont d'Urville sailed the *Astrolabe* from Tasman Bay through the narrow 'French Pass' into Admiralty Bay in the Marlborough Sounds. His officers named the large island they passed in his honour.

D'Urville first visited New Zealand in 1824 as second-in-command to Louis Duperrey. At the Bay of Islands, he heard the Māori version of the 1772 death of Marion du Fresne and his crew (see 4 May).

On his second voyage of exploration and scientific investigation from 1826, d'Urville commanded the *Astrolabe*. He spent three months charting the northern coast of the South Island and the east coast of the North Island, also studying the local people and plant and animal life.

In the 1830s d'Urville published scholarly and popular accounts of the voyage of the *Astrolabe*. He made a third visit to New Zealand in 1840, arriving from the sub-Antarctic and sailing up the entire east coast of the country, with a stopover in Akaroa Harbour. By then New Zealand was in British hands.

Dumont d'Urville, commander of the *Astrolabe.*

AUCKLAND'S FIRST ANNIVERSARY DAY REGATTA

29 January 1842

Auckland's Anniversary Day commemorates the arrival of Lieutenant-Governor William Hobson in the Bay of Islands in 1840. Today it is best known for a regatta on Waitematā Harbour, possibly the largest in the world.

The first regatta on the harbour — an impromptu three-race affair — was held on 18 September 1840, the day an advance party arrived to found the colony's new capital.

The government chose 29 January as Auckland Province's official Anniversary Day in 1841, and the first regatta was held the following year. The regatta gave way to horse racing at Epsom for the next few years, but was revived in 1850. It became an annual event and has been cancelled only in 1900 during the South African War.

In the early years, races were between ship's gigs, dinghies, whaleboats and waka (canoes). Some of the most exciting racing was between working vessels — fishing boats, centreboard mullet boats and scows. Powerboats raced for the first time in 1903, and seaplanes in 1919. These days there are races for waka, tugboats, dragon boats and radio-controlled (as well as conventional) yachts.

Some of the most exciting racing was between working vessels — fishing boats, centreboard mullet boats and scows.

View of Auckland Harbour during the Anniversary Day regatta, 29 January 1862.

30 January 1911

BOOKIES TAKE LAST BETS ON NEW ZEALAND RACECOURSES

A 1910 amendment to the Gaming Act banned bookmakers from New Zealand racecourses, other public places and hotels. The bookies were farewelled after the last race at Takapuna, with a band playing appropriate tunes such as 'We Parted on the Shore'.

Bookies were private entrepreneurs who displayed the odds they were offering to the punters they hoped to outsmart. They came under increasing pressure from the late 19th century as mechanical totalisators began operating on New Zealand racecourses.

Totalisators computed the amounts bet on the horses in a race, deducted a fixed proportion, and distributed the balance among those who had selected the winners and placegetters. As betting continued, likely dividends were displayed in close to real time.

In reality, bookmakers did not disappear and many illegal operators continued to make a good living. Totalisator bets could not be placed by telephone or telegraph, technologies bookies embraced. In the 1940s it was estimated that the annual turnover from illegal bookmaking exceeded £24 million (equivalent to $1.8 billion in 2010, when actual TAB turnover was $1.6 billion).

Men queuing to place bets on the totalisator at Trentham Racecourse, 1912.

NEW ZEALAND'S FIRST REGULAR AIRMAIL SERVICE BEGINS

31 January 1921

Piloted by Captain Euan Dickson, the first flight of the Canterbury Aviation Company's new airmail service left Christchurch at 8 a.m., carrying several hundred letters to Ashburton and Timaru into the teeth of a south-westerly gale.

George Bolt had made the first official airmail flight in New Zealand in December 1919, from Auckland to Dargaville. The Canterbury Aviation Company hoped to go one better with a regular service using an Avro 504K biplane. This failed to gain the custom it needed to make a profit and closed in April. Bolt's attempt to establish a regular service between Auckland and Whāngārei using a seaplane also hit turbulence.

Sir Henry Wigram had established the Canterbury Aviation Company as a private flying school in 1916. As New Zealand had no air force, the company trained pilots for service in Britain during the First World War.

In 1923 the New Zealand government purchased the land and assets of the company for its newly formed air force. Renamed 'Wigram', the airfield was the RNZAF's main training base until 1995.

Canterbury Aviation Company's de Havilland DH9 aircraft about to leave for Wellington, 18 November 1921.

1981

TREVOR CHAPPELL BOWLS UNDERARM

Trans-Tasman sporting relations reached a new low at the Melbourne Cricket Ground when Australian captain Greg Chappell ordered his brother Trevor to bowl the final delivery of a 50-over cricket international against New Zealand underarm (along the ground).

The visitors needed a six just to tie the match — a tall order for no. 10 batsman Brian McKechnie at the world's biggest cricket ground. But the stakes were high: a tie would prolong the series. This possibility was removed by the underarm ball, a delivery then legal but contrary to the spirit of the game. McKechnie blocked it before throwing his bat away in disgust.

The real turning point of the match had also involved Greg Chappell. Having scored over 50, he was caught in the outfield by Martin Snedden. Chappell refused to take Snedden's word for it and the umpires disallowed the catch. Chappell went on to make 90 as the Australians compiled 235/4. To add to New Zealanders' chagrin, the underarm delivery should have been called a no-ball. In the excitement of the moment, the Australian field had been set incorrectly.

Trevor Chappell bowls underarm to Brian McKechnie.

'THE GREATEST MIDDLE-DISTANCE RACE OF ALL TIME'

The men's 1500 metres final was run on the last day of the 1974 Christchurch Commonwealth Games. Tanzanian Filbert Bayi ran the first 800 metres in 1 minute 52.2 seconds, conserved energy on the third lap, and held off 22-year-old New Zealander John Walker to set a new world record of 3:32.16. Walker also broke American Jim Ryun's world record.

Remarkably, the third, fourth and fifth placegetters ran the fourth, fifth and seventh fastest 1500 metres times to that date. Five national records were broken.

Bayi and Walker continued their rivalry in 1975. On 17 May, Bayi broke Ryun's eight-year-old record for the mile, clocking 3:51.0. This record was short-lived, as Walker became history's first sub-3:50 miler on 12 August, running 3:49.4 at Gothenburg, Sweden. The much-anticipated clash between the two runners at the 1976 Montreal Olympics failed to eventuate. Tanzania joined other African nations in boycotting the games in protest against the All Blacks' tour of South Africa. Bayi would probably not have run anyway, as he was stricken with malaria shortly before the Olympics began. Walker won gold.

Filbert Bayi holds off John Walker to win the 1500 metres at the Christchurch Commonwealth Games, 1974.

HAWKE'S BAY EARTHQUAKE STRIKES

When the deadly earthquake, measuring 7.8 on the Richter scale, struck at 10.47 a.m., many buildings in central Napier and Hastings collapsed immediately. In terms of loss of life, it remains the worst civil disaster to have occurred in New Zealand. Among the buildings destroyed were Napier's cathedral, public library and nurses' home, where clerical staff and off-duty nurses died. In Hastings, 17 people died when Roach's department store collapsed, and eight when the front of the Grand Hotel fell into the main street. Fifteen died at an old men's home near Taradale, where rescuers pulled a 91-year-old man alive from the rubble three days later. Nine students died in the wreckage of Napier Technical College and seven at the Marist Seminary in Greenmeadows.

Fire broke out in Napier's business district shortly after the earthquake, and once the reservoir emptied, firefighters were powerless. Flames gutted almost 11 blocks of central Napier, killing some people who were still trapped.

Rescue parties, boosted by sailors and soldiers, worked desperately to reach those trapped in wrecked buildings. Continuing aftershocks made such efforts dangerous and some rescuers were killed or injured as more buildings collapsed.

With Napier's hospitals badly damaged and unusable, medical authorities set up makeshift surgeries at the botanical gardens and at Hastings and Napier Park racecourses to treat the wounded. Two naval cruisers arrived from Auckland on the 4th with medical personnel and supplies. That day the army set up a tent camp for 2500 people. Refugee camps were created around the North Island for women and children, who were encouraged to leave the region. Able-bodied men were required to stay to help with searches, demolition and clean-up work.

The official death toll of the Hawke's Bay earthquake is 256 (161 in Napier, 93 in Hastings, 2 in Wairoa), although there are 258 names on the earthquake memorial in Napier. The earthquake ultimately had some positive outcomes: the 2.7-metre uplift drained much of Ahuriri Lagoon, making land available for farms, industry, housing and Napier Airport; and much of central Napier was rebuilt in an art deco style which would begin to attract tourists half a century later.

Rescue parties, boosted by sailors and soldiers, worked desperately to reach those trapped in wrecked buildings.

The ruins of the Napier nurses' home after the Hawke's Bay earthquake, 1931.

WOMAN SWIMS ACROSS COOK STRAIT

BORN ON THIS DAY
Arnold Downer,
1895–1984,
civil engineer

American Lynne Cox swam from the North Island to the South in 12 hours 7 minutes. The fourth person to do so, she battled heavy seas and strong winds. Twice the Cook Strait cargo ferry *Aratika* hove to alongside her to provide protection. Cox went on to swim in the sub-Arctic Bering Strait and in Antarctic waters.

The 22.5-kilometre Cook Strait crossing involves chilly water, treacherous tides and often-rough weather. R.G. Webster and Lily Copplestone made the first attempts in 1929. The first to succeed was Barrie Devenport on 20 November 1962. Philip Rush made the first non-stop double crossing on 13 March 1984.

Casey Glover swam the strait from north to south on 13 April 2008 in a record 4 hours 37 minutes. Eleven-year-old Aditya Raut became the youngest conqueror of Cook Strait on 20 February 2005. The oldest is Toshio Ogawa, who was 60 when he succeeded on 3 March 2015.

By February 2018, 100 people from 15 countries had made 112 successful crossings. Rush has swum the strait six times and Meda McKenzie four times.

Lynne Cox swimming Cook Strait, 1975.

FIRST BIG DAY OUT MUSIC FESTIVAL IN NEW ZEALAND

The Big Day Out, an Australian franchise based on the successful Lollapalooza model, brought alternative, hard rock, hip hop and, more recently, dance acts together in a one-day festival in Auckland.

Around 8000 punters turned up to the first 'BDO' at Auckland's Mt Smart Stadium to watch headliners Soundgarden, The Smashing Pumpkins, and The Breeders, who arrived to play on a massive pageant float. Sharing the stage with these international acts were local favourites like Shihad and Straitjacket Fits.

From there it only got bigger. Utilising the bulk of the Australian festivals' overseas line-up, backed by a strong local bill, it proved a popular formula, regularly attracting crowds between 30,000 and 40,000 during the 2000s. These were the festival's peak years.

Declining ticket sales saw New Zealand's leg of the Big Day Out tour close in 2012. The festival returned to Auckland in 2014, although this turned out to be a false dawn for BDO diehards, with promoters soon announcing that the 2015 event was off. There have been no subsequent BDOs.

The Big Day Out, Auckland, 2007.

TREATY OF WAITANGI SIGNED

More than 40 Māori chiefs signed a treaty with the British Crown in the Bay of Islands. This 'Treaty of Waitangi' remains controversial.

A week earlier, Captain William Hobson had landed at Kororāreka from HMS *Herald* and proclaimed himself lieutenant-governor of a colony that did not yet exist. His instructions from the Colonial Office in London were to seek Māori consent to British sovereignty. Officials drafted a document to present to a hui (meeting) of prominent chiefs, especially those who had signed the 1835 Declaration of Independence (see 28 October).

Missionary Henry Williams and his son Edward translated the English draft into Māori on the night of 4 February. Its three clauses transferred kawanatanga (governorship) from the Confederation and individual chiefs to Queen Victoria; guaranteed Māori continued possession of their taonga (property), with the right to sell land to the Crown should they wish; and granted Māori the 'rights and privileges' of British subjects. On the morning of 5 February, about 500 Māori, Hobson's retinue and local Pākehā gathered on the lawn in front of British Resident James Busby's house at Waitangi. After Hobson spoke in English, Henry Williams explained in Māori that the treaty was an act of love by the Queen and Busby emphasised that it protected land rights.

Many of the subsequent speeches — translated for Hobson by the missionaries — favoured the status quo, with missionaries rather than a governor as protectors of Māori. Some chiefs also foresaw the loss of their land. The tide was turned by two influential rangatira, with Tāmati Wāka Nene declaring it was too late to stop Pākehā arriving and Hōne Heke Pōkai advocating a covenant between Māori and the Queen.

Informal debate continued that evening. Hobson had announced that the hui would reconvene on the 7th, but many chiefs were eager to leave for home. When they assembled outside Busby's residence on the morning of the 6th, Hobson was summoned hastily from the *Herald* to accept signatures. By September 1840, another 500 Māori had signed one of the nine copies of the treaty and British sovereignty over the whole country had been declared.

On the morning of 5 February, about 500 Māori, Hobson's retinue and local Pākehā gathered on the lawn in front of British Resident James Busby's house at Waitangi.

A well-known — but historically questionable — painting of the treaty signing by Marcus King, 1938.

NEW ZEALAND'S WORST SHIPWRECK

For the British military it was the costliest day of the New Zealand Wars — but it occurred far from the battlefield. Bringing naval stores from Sydney, the modern 1706-ton steam corvette HMS *Orpheus* ran aground on the bar at the entrance to Auckland's Manukau Harbour. Of the 259 naval officers, seamen and Royal Marines aboard, 189 died. In terms of lives lost, it remains New Zealand's worst maritime disaster.

Minor errors and bad luck caused the tragedy. Instead of rounding North Cape to reach Waitematā Harbour, Commodore William Burnett decided to berth at Onehunga in Manukau Harbour to save time. Unfortunately, he carried outdated charts and the channel through the bar had moved. Although lookouts on shore signalled a warning when they realised the ship was off course, the *Orpheus* missed the message. After striking the bar, the vessel was pounded by waves and only one small boat got away. As the ship sank into the sand, the men climbed the rigging. The masts eventually collapsed, throwing the crew into the sea. Rescuers arrived too late to prevent a catastrophe.

The wreck of HMS *Orpheus* on the Manukau Bar,
Illustrated London News, 1863.

THE WRECK OF H.M.S. ORPHEUS ON MANUKAU BAR, NEW ZEALAND.

FIRST FATAL ACCIDENT ON A SCHEDULED AIR SERVICE IN NEW ZEALAND

All three people on board a Dominion Airlines Desoutter died after it crashed near Wairoa in Hawke's Bay. This was the first fatal accident involving a scheduled passenger air service in New Zealand.

New Zealand's first regular scheduled passenger service began in 1930, when Air Travel launched a tri-weekly service between Christchurch and Dunedin using a de Havilland DH50 borrowed from the government. Passenger numbers were low and, after nine months, Air Travel closed down.

Soon afterwards, Dominion Airlines Ltd began a daily service between Gisborne and Hastings. This proved invaluable in keeping the areas ravaged by the Hawke's Bay earthquake (see 3 February) in contact with the rest of New Zealand. Unfortunately, just five days after the earthquake, the company's Desoutter II monoplane crashed after dropping a bag of telegrams in a field near Wairoa. After making the drop, the aircraft's engine stalled and the Desoutter nosedived into nearby railway yards, killing pilot Ivan Kight and passengers Walter Findlay and W.C. Strand. The accident forced Dominion Airlines into liquidation.

The ill-fated Desoutter ZK-ACA.

1900

WANGANUI OPERA HOUSE OPENED

The large wooden building on St Hill Street has been a jewel in Whanganui's crown for more than a century. It is New Zealand's oldest municipal opera house. In 1897 Borough Councillor Frederick Spurdle suggested that the building of an opera house would be an appropriate way to mark Queen Victoria's then-record 60-year reign. The town lacked an appropriate theatrical venue, and his colleagues agreed. A public competition for a suitable design attracted nine entries and was won by Wellington architect George Stevenson. The foundation stone was laid by the Mayor of Wanganui, Alexander Hatrick, on 13 July 1899. By then Stevenson had died, and retired builder James Tawse supervised construction. The building was officially opened on 9 February 1900 by the premier, Richard Seddon. Unusually for the time, it was lit by gas and electricity. It has survived three fires.

The Opera House received a Category 1 listing from the Historic Places Trust in 1984 and was given a Royal Charter at the time of its centennial in 1999. In the early 21st century it was seismically strengthened and refurbished.

The Royal Wanganui Opera House after its refurbishing.

END OF FREE SCHOOL MILK
10 February 1967

New Zealand children received free milk at school from 1937 to 1967. The first Labour government initiated the scheme — a world first — to improve the health of young New Zealanders (and make use of surplus milk). Each day, milk monitors supplied a half-pint (284 millilitres) of milk to each pupil. By 1940 the milk was available to over 80 per cent of schoolchildren. For a few years during the Second World War, pupils also received an apple a day. The scheme lasted until 1967, when the government dropped it because of the cost — and because some were starting to question the health benefits of milk. In the 30 years of the scheme's existence, thousands of kids gulped down their daily ration of milk. In the 1950s school milk bottles had cardboard tops with a small hole for the straw. Not everyone enjoyed it. In the days before fridges and chillers, the warm milk nauseated many. Dairy giant Fonterra revived the scheme in 2013, supplying free long-life milk to schools throughout New Zealand following a successful pilot project in Northland.

Primary schoolboys drinking their school milk, Linwood, Christchurch, 1940s.

CHARLES HEAPHY EARNS VICTORIA CROSS

Recommended for a Victoria Cross after rescuing a soldier under fire at Waiari, near Pirongia, Charles Heaphy was given the decoration in 1867. His was the only VC awarded to a member of New Zealand's colonial forces, who in theory were not eligible for it.

Heaphy arrived in New Zealand in 1839 as a 19-year-old New Zealand Company draughtsman, and later became a surveyor and well-known artist. In 1846 he and Thomas Brunner made an epic trek from Nelson down the Buller River and the West Coast as far as Arahura — and back again.

As provincial surveyor, Heaphy helped survey the military road from Auckland to the Waikato River in the early 1860s. The volunteer officer was then appointed 'Military Surveyor and Guide to the Forces'. He was lucky to escape serious injury during the skirmish at Waiari while helping a wounded soldier.

As chief surveyor to the central government, Heaphy spent the next two years surveying confiscated land in Waikato. After an undistinguished term as MP for Parnell, he was appointed commissioner of native reserves.

Charles Heaphy, c. 1867.

BORN ON THIS DAY

Fred Evans,
1881–1912,
trade unionist,
Waihī striker

SS *PENGUIN* WRECKED IN COOK STRAIT

On the evening of 12 February 1909 the Union Steam Ship Company passenger steamer *Penguin* left Picton for Wellington in fine weather. Conditions quickly deteriorated as the *Penguin* reached Cook Strait. As the weather closed in, familiar landmarks disappeared. Unable to see Pencarrow light (see 1 January), Captain Francis Naylor set a course to steer clear of danger. Changing course again to ride out the storm, the ship struck rocks and began to sink in heavy seas.

The 'women and children first' custom proved disastrous as the lifeboats quickly capsized. No children and only one woman survived. Only 30 of the 102 people who set out from Picton made it ashore alive; contemporary accounts put the number of people on board at 105, with 75 dead.

Although some said the *Penguin* had struck a drifting wreck, it is widely believed that it hit Thoms Rock off Cape Terawhiti. A subsequent inquiry blamed Captain Naylor and suspended his certificate for 12 months, despite finding he 'did everything in his power to prevent loss of life' once disaster struck.

Men hauling wreckage and a body on the beach at Cape Terawhiti, Wellington, after the wreck of the *Penguin*.

LANCE CAIRNS HITS SIX SIXES AT MELBOURNE CRICKET GROUND

At 44/6 in reply to Australia's 302, New Zealand was heading for an embarrassing defeat in the second final of the Benson & Hedges World Series Cup when Lance Cairns took guard with the bat dubbed 'Excalibur'. Fast bowler Dennis Lillee welcomed him to the crease by hitting him on the head.

The burly swing bowler's response was to swipe two sixes off three balls from Ken MacLeay. Then he despatched two consecutive balls from Rodney Hogg over long on. When Lillee was brought back to deal with him, Cairns swatted the test record wicket-taker one-handed over the fine-leg boundary before flogging him over mid-off.

It was too good to last. Cairns carved a full ball from Geoff Lawson straight to cover and was dismissed for 52 from 25 balls. New Zealand lost the match by 149 runs, but those gigantic hits live on in memory.

Lance Cairns played 43 tests, taking 130 wickets at an average of 32.92. In 78 one-day internationals, he took 89 wickets at 30.52 and scored 987 runs off just 941 balls.

BORN ON THIS DAY

Godfrey Bowen,
1922–1994,
shearing champion

Lance Cairns in one-day action against England, 1978.

1998

TE PAPA MUSEUM OPENS

New Zealand's new national museum, the Museum of New Zealand Te Papa Tongarewa, officially opened on Wellington's waterfront after a decade of planning and construction.

The official opening ceremony began with the arrival of waka (canoes) at dawn, and culminated with the formal declaration of opening by two children, Tama Whiting and Grace Sweeney, accompanied by famous yachtsman Peter Blake.

Te Papa's new approaches and interactive techniques, which were audience rather than object-focused, proved very successful with a wide cross-section of New Zealanders, including many Māori visitors. It also introduced innovative bicultural practices, including its own functioning marae, a Māori director, or kaihautū, and the integration of Māori perspectives on collecting and display of taonga (treasures).

Despite its popularity, the museum was not without its critics. It was described by traditionalists as a 'theme park', and art lovers had misgivings about the integration of the former National Art Gallery collections into the new museum.

Crowds on Te Papa's
opening day.

FIRST FROZEN MEAT SHIPMENT LEAVES NEW ZEALAND

New Zealand's first successful shipment of frozen meat to Britain in 1882 had a huge impact on the colony, paving the way for trade in frozen meat and dairy products that became the cornerstone of New Zealand's 20th-century economy.

The voyage was organised by William Soltau Davidson, the British-based general manager of the New Zealand and Australian Land Company, whose landholdings in the two countries exceeded 1 million hectares. The entrepreneurial Davidson had taken a keen interest in experiments from 1876, which had proved the concept, if not yet the economic viability, of shipping frozen meat around the globe.

Davidson decided to fit out a passenger sailing ship, the Albion Line's *Dunedin*, with a coal-powered Bell Coleman freezing plant, which cooled the entire hold to 22 degrees Celsius below the outside temperature. Company employee Thomas Brydone was sent to Britain to study refrigeration technology and then handled the experiment in New Zealand. Most of the first cargo originated from Brydone's slaughterhouse at Totara Estate, near Oamaru. Sent by rail to Port Chalmers in iceboxes, the mutton and lamb carcasses were frozen aboard the *Dunedin*. Despite mechanical problems, the plant froze nearly 10,000 carcasses in two months.

About 5000 carcasses were on board the *Dunedin* when it sailed on 15 February. When the vessel became becalmed in the tropics, crew noticed that the cold air in the hold was not circulating properly. To save his historic cargo, Captain John Whitson crawled inside and sawed extra air holes, almost freezing to death in the process. Crew members managed to pull him out by a rope and resuscitated him. When the *Dunedin* arrived in London in late May, only one carcass had to be condemned and the cargo's superiority over Australian shipments was remarked on.

More than a single successful shipment was needed to create a new industry. Davidson set to work creating a marketing and insurance structure to underpin refrigerated shipping. The new technology ultimately enabled the owner-operated (family) farm to become the standard economic unit in rural New Zealand for the next century. The *Dunedin* made another nine successful voyages before disappearing in the Southern Ocean in 1890.

Meat labels produced by the Gear Meat Preserving and Freezing Company, 1890s–1920s.

16 February
1986

SINKING OF THE MIKHAIL LERMONTOV

With its hull sliced open in three places, the 155-metre vessel limped towards Port Gore, where it finally sank at 10.45 p.m.

At 5.37 p.m. on 16 February 1986 the Soviet cruise liner *Mikhail Lermontov* hit rocks off Cape Jackson in the Marlborough Sounds.

With its hull sliced open in three places, the 155-metre vessel limped towards Port Gore, where it finally sank at 10.45 p.m. A flotilla of small craft, the inter-island ferry *Arahura* and the LPG tanker *Tarihiko* rescued all but one of the 738 passengers and crew. Refrigeration engineer Pavel Zaglyadimov drowned.

In the aftermath of the sinking, allegations circulated that the crew had left passengers bewildered and without proper instructions during the initial evacuation. Most of the elderly passengers aboard the *Mikhail Lermontov* were Australians.

Soviet diplomats shielded the ship's captain, Vladislav Vorobyov, from the press; he later told Soviet television that Picton's harbourmaster, Don Jamison, who piloted the ship out of Picton, was responsible for the vessel's course. Jamison accepted his mistake, blaming it on mental and physical exhaustion.

Today, the wreck of the liner lies on its side 30 metres below the sea and is a popular dive site.

The liner *Mikhail Lermontov* sinking in the Marlborough Sounds.

'THE RUSSIANS ARE COMING!'
17 February 1873

Aucklanders reading their morning newspaper were shocked at a report that a Russian warship had entered Auckland Harbour undetected and landed troops ashore. For many readers, this seemed to confirm their worst fears about a Russian invasion. Anglo-Russian conflicts during the 19th century prompted many New Zealanders to view the Russians as potential aggressors. In the aftermath of the Crimean War of the 1850s, unannounced visits to the South Pacific by Russian warships created alarm in New Zealand.

David Luckie, editor of the *Daily Southern Cross*, exploited this fear to boost newspaper sales, publishing a hoax report of a Russian invasion of Auckland by the ironclad cruiser *Kaskowiski* — 'cask of whisky'. Despite an asterisk in the story's headline referring to a date almost three months in the future, gullible Aucklanders were alarmed to read that Russian marines from the *Kaskowiski* had seized gold and taken the mayor hostage. A full-blown Russian scare in 1885 grew out of Anglo–Russian rivalry in Afghanistan and led to the building of major fortifications to protect New Zealand's coastal cities.

David Mitchell Luckie, editor of the *Daily Southern Cross*.

NEW ZEALAND'S LAST EXECUTION

Walter Bolton, a 68-year-old Whanganui farmer, became the last person executed in New Zealand. Convicted for the murder of his wife, Beatrice, he was hanged at Mt Eden Prison following a controversial trial.

Beatrice's tea had contained traces of arsenic, and, over the best part of a year, she had consumed enough to kill her. Investigators found traces of arsenic in water on the Boltons' farm and in Walter and one of his daughters. The defence argued that sheep dip had accidentally contaminated the farm's water supply.

The idea that Beatrice's death was a result of accidental poisoning lost credibility after Bolton admitted to an affair with his wife's sister, Florence. The jury returned with a verdict of guilty.

A newspaper story later claimed that Bolton's execution had gone horribly wrong. Rather than having his neck broken instantly, he had allegedly suffocated slowly. The botched execution and lingering doubts over Bolton's guilt fuelled debate surrounding the use of capital punishment in New Zealand. Parliament eventually abolished the death penalty for murder in 1961.

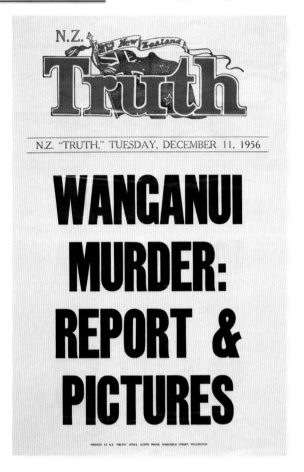

NZ Truth **headline about the murder of Beatrice Bolton, 11 December 1956.**

N.Z. "TRUTH," TUESDAY, DECEMBER 11, 1956

WANGANUI MURDER: REPORT & PICTURES

KŌPUAWHARA FLOOD KILLS 21
19 February 1938

Twenty men and one woman drowned when a sudden cloudburst sent a wall of water surging through a public works camp in the Kōpuawhara Valley, near Māhia. Located on the banks of the Kōpuawhara Stream, the no. 4 camp accommodated workers building the Wairoa–Gisborne railway. Houses for married men were on higher ground, with a cookhouse and huts for single men closer to the riverbank. Although the stream was in flood after heavy rain, the 5-metre-high wall of water that hit the camp sometime after 3 a.m. took everyone by surprise. Water began pouring across the campsite, sweeping away everything in its path. Some men took refuge on the roofs of huts, but most of these structures collapsed. Those who climbed onto the roof of the cookhouse managed to hang on until they were rescued at daybreak. The 11 men who took refuge in one of the work trucks were not so lucky. The force of the water tossed it onto its side and swept its occupants away; rescuers found remnants of the vehicle 12 kilometres downstream.

Flood debris from Kōpuawhara no. 4 public works camp, near Māhia.

SCOTLAND CROSSES SOUTHLAND IN PIONEERING FLIGHT

James Scotland flew a Caudron biplane from Invercargill to Gore, completing the first cross-country flight in New Zealand. From Gore, he made his way north, stopping at Dunedin, Timaru and Christchurch. His flight came to an uncomfortable end on 25 March when he crash-landed on Wellington's Newtown Park.

Kaipara-born Scotland was educated in England, where he gained his pilot's certificate — the second New Zealander to do so, after Aucklander J.J. Hammond. Returning to New Zealand, he joined New Zealand Aviation Ltd and gave aerial exhibitions in various centres. Early in 1914, in an attempt to popularise aviation and promote commercial opportunities, the company arranged for Scotland to make a series of cross-country flights from Invercargill northwards, putting on flying displays at stops along the way. On 7 March 4000 people watched his exhibition over Christchurch's Addington Showgrounds.

According to the Christchurch *Sun*, Scotland carried a small parcel and letter on the leg from Timaru to Christchurch. 'Passing over Temuka I dropped a parcel for a friend of mine, Mr Andrews,' the pilot recalled. 'There was nothing breakable in it.'

James Scotland's plane at Ōtaki before his visit to the South Island.

KAITANGATA MINING DISASTER
21 February 1879

On the morning of 21 February 1879, an explosion rocked the coalmine at Kaitangata, South Otago. On the day of the explosion, there were 47 men employed at the mine. At first, no one knew how many were underground. Debris from the explosion and the presence of firedamp — methane gas — thwarted initial rescue attempts. Rescue parties were unable to enter the mine until about midday. By early evening, it was clear that 34 men had been underground and that none had survived. The condition of their bodies showed that they had been suffocated by 'black damp' — a mixture of nitrogen and carbon dioxide. The coroner's report identified faults in the mine's safety practices and ventilation system. Apparently, the explosion was sparked when the mine manager's brother carried a candle into a disused part of the mine filled with firedamp. The accident led to the introduction of stricter controls on the mining industry — but it would not be New Zealand's last coalmine tragedy (see 26 March, 19 November).

Kaitangata Mine, 1900s.

CHRISTCHURCH EARTHQUAKE KILLS 185

On Tuesday, 22 February 2011, at 12.51 p.m., a magnitude 6.3 earthquake badly damaged Christchurch and Lyttelton, killing 185 people and injuring several thousand. The earthquake's epicentre was near Lyttelton, just 10 kilometres southeast of Christchurch's central business district. It occurred nearly six months after the magnitude 7.1 earthquake of 4 September 2010.

The earthquake struck at lunchtime, when many people were on the city streets. More than 130 people lost their lives in the collapse of the Canterbury Television and Pyne Gould Corporation buildings. Thirty-six others died in the central city, many of them crushed by falling bricks and masonry. Rock cliffs collapsed in the Sumner and Redcliffs area, and boulders tumbled down the Port Hills, with five people killed by falling rocks. Although not as powerful as the one in September 2010, this earthquake occurred on a shallow fault line that was close to the city, so the shaking was particularly destructive.

The earthquake brought down many buildings damaged the previous September, especially older brick and mortar buildings. Heritage buildings suffered heavy damage, including the Provincial Council Chambers, Lyttelton's Timeball Station, the Anglican Christchurch Cathedral and the Catholic Cathedral of the Blessed Sacrament. More than half of the buildings in the central business district have since been demolished, including the city's tallest building, the Hotel Grand Chancellor.

Liquefaction was much more extensive than in September 2010. Shaking turned water-saturated layers of sand and silt beneath the surface into sludge that squirted upwards through cracks. Thick layers of silt covered properties and streets, and water and sewage from broken pipes flooded streets. House foundations cracked and buckled, wrecking many homes. Irreparable damage led to the demolition of several thousand homes, and large tracts of suburban land were subsequently abandoned.

The government declared a national state of emergency the day after the quake. Authorities quickly cordoned off Christchurch's central business district. The cordon remained in place in some areas until June 2013. Power companies restored electricity to 75 per cent of the city within three days, but re-establishing water supplies and sewerage systems took much longer.

Although not as powerful as the one in September 2010, this earthquake occurred on a shallow fault line that was close to the city, so the shaking was particularly destructive.

Dust clouds caused by the 22 February earthquake.

100,000 WELCOME HOME HMS *ACHILLES* CREW

The Battle of the River Plate in December 1939 was the Allies' first naval victory of the Second World War (see 13 December). The involvement of the cruiser HMS *Achilles*, largely crewed by New Zealanders, was greeted with jubilation in New Zealand.

The German pocket battleship *Admiral Graf Spee* had been commerce raiding in the Atlantic and Indian Oceans since the beginning of the war in September. On 13 December, three Royal Navy cruisers, *Exeter*, *Ajax* and *Achilles*, intercepted the German warship off South America's River Plate estuary. While the *Exeter* sustained heavy damage in the brief encounter, the *Graf Spee* was also hit and forced to seek refuge in Montevideo, capital of neutral Uruguay.

The captain of the *Graf Spee*, Hans Langsdorff, believed the British were assembling an overwhelming force to prevent his escape. Rather than put his men at risk, he scuttled his ship on 17 December. Langsdorff committed suicide three days later. The crew of the *Achilles* received a hero's welcome when they returned to New Zealand in February 1940. Parades in Auckland and Wellington (on 2 April) drew huge crowds.

Crowds in Lambton Quay, Wellington, welcoming the crew of HMS *Achilles*.

TSS *EARNSLAW* LAUNCHED ON LAKE WAKATIPU

For more than 50 years after it was launched, the twin-screw steamship *Earnslaw* carried freight and people to and from remote lakeside settlements. Affectionately known as the 'Lady of the Lake', and named after Mt Earnslaw to the north of the lake, the ship has also been used for scenic cruises since the 1970s.

During the 1900s the government decided to invest in a new lake steamer to cater for increasing tourist numbers on Central Otago's Lake Wakatipu. Their preference was for New Zealand shipbuilders. The Dunedin naval architect Hugh McRae provided the design and the tender was given to John McGregor and Co., who had built Otago Harbour ferries.

McGregor's completed the keel in July 1911. Once the framing was completed, shipbuilders dismantled the ship plate by plate. Each part was meticulously numbered and transported by rail to Kingston, at the southern end of Lake Wakatipu, for reassembly.

Three months after building began, the *Earnslaw* was launched in front of a large crowd. The minister of marine captained the steamer on its maiden journey to Queenstown.

The first scheduled voyage took place in October that year. Queenstown marked this event with a holiday.

BORN ON THIS DAY

Ettie Rout,
1877–1936,
social reformer,
safe sex campaigner

Workers reassembling the *Earnslaw* at Kingston on Lake Wakatipu.

49 KILLED IN FEATHERSTON POW INCIDENT

BORN ON THIS DAY

Hester Maclean,
1859–1932,
nurse, hospital administrator

Just outside the Wairarapa town of Featherston, a memorial garden marks the site of a Second World War riot that resulted in the deaths of 48 Japanese prisoners of war (POWs) and one guard.

The camp opened in 1942 to hold 800 Japanese POWs captured in the South Pacific. In early 1943, a group of recently arrived prisoners staged a sit-down strike, refusing to work. Guards fired a warning shot, which may have wounded Lieutenant Toshio Adachi. The prisoners then rose and the guards opened fire. Wartime censors kept details of the tragedy quiet amid fears of Japanese reprisals against Allied POWs.

A military Court of Inquiry absolved the guards of blame, but acknowledged the fundamental cultural differences between captors and captives. The Japanese government did not accept the court's decision.

After the war, the first POW to return to Featherston burned incense at the site in 1974 and a joint New Zealand–Japanese project established a memorial ground. Today, a plaque commemorates the site with a 17th-century haiku:

Behold the summer grass
All that remains
Of the dreams of warriors.

Fatigue squad on the way to work at the Japanese prisoner of war camp near Featherston, 1943.

'PISTOLS AT DAWN': DEADLY DUEL IN WELLINGTON

William Brewer died of wounds received during a pistol duel with another Wellington lawyer, H. Ross, on 26 February 1844. The duel followed a quarrel over a case in the Wellington County Court.

When the two men faced off in Sydney Street, Thorndon, Brewer fired into the air but 'received Mr. Ross' ball in the groin'. He died four days later.

Although several people witnessed the duel, the coroner's inquest concluded that there was no proof as to who had inflicted the wound. The fact that the survivor of a duel could be charged with murder may explain the witnesses' reticence. On the other hand, perhaps it was a case of 'what happens on the duelling field stays on the duelling field'.

Brewer was no stranger to duelling. In 1840 he had 'threatened to call out the next man' who associated him with a certain young woman. Surveyor John Kelly called Brewer's bluff and was lucky to survive the resulting duel on Oneroa Beach at Kororāreka (now Russell) — part of his wig was shot away.

BORN ON THIS DAY

Helen Clark,
1950–,
Labour prime minister,
UN administrator

Duel with pistols, 1830.

1951

TROOPS DEPLOYED IN WATERFRONT DISPUTE

The waterfront dispute of 1951 was the biggest industrial confrontation in New Zealand's history. Although it was not as violent as the Great Strike of 1913, it lasted longer — for five months, from February to July — and involved more workers. At its peak, 22,000 waterside workers ('wharfies') and other unionists were off the job.

Sid Holland's National government declared a state of emergency on 21 February, warning the following day that New Zealand was 'at war'. On the 27th, troops were sent onto the Auckland and Wellington wharves to load and unload ships. Emergency regulations imposed strict censorship, gave police sweeping powers of search and arrest, and made it an offence for citizens to assist strikers — even giving food to their children was outlawed. As the dispute dragged on through autumn and winter, there were sporadic outbursts of violence. By the end of May, with new unions of strike-breakers (denounced by unionists as 'scabs') registered in the main ports, the wharfies' position was becoming increasingly hopeless. They conceded defeat on 15 July.

Watersiders' loyalty card, 1951.

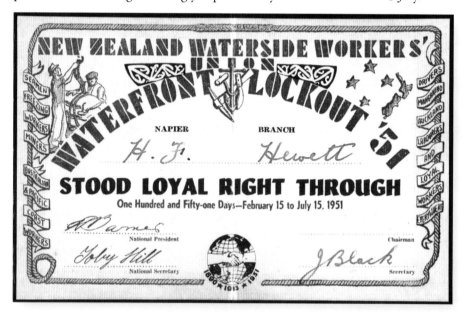

KIWI SOLDIER FACES FIRING SQUAD
28 February 1945

After more than a year on the run in northern Italy, New Zealand prisoner of war David Russell was recaptured and executed. His courage in the face of death earned him the first George Cross awarded to a member of New Zealand's military forces. Captured by German forces in July 1942 at Ruweisat Ridge in Egypt, Russell spent over a year in an Italian work camp before making his escape after Italy's surrender in 1943. He joined a local partisan group and began moving around northern Italy. Despite having chances to escape to safety, Russell chose to remain in Italy to find and assist other escaped Allied prisoners. After a series of narrow escapes, Fascist troops caught up with him in February 1945. Despite brutal interrogation, Russell refused to reveal the whereabouts of other escaped prisoners and partisans. He was executed at Ponte di Piave on 28 February. For his heroism Russell received a posthumous George Cross in 1948. The following year Napier Hospital opened the David Russell Memorial Ward in his honour.

David Russell.

THE RETURN OF THE KING WINS 11 OSCARS

Peter Jackson's last film in the colossal *Lord of the Rings* trilogy, *The Return of the King*, won all 11 Oscars it was nominated for at the 76th Academy Awards in Los Angeles. This set a record for the largest clean sweep in one night and equalled the highest number of wins achieved by *Ben-Hur* (1959) and *Titanic* (1997).

It was the first time the Academy Awards had recognised a fantasy film as Best Picture. Jackson remarked, 'I'm so honoured, touched, and relieved that the Academy . . . has seen past the trolls, the wizards and the hobbits, recognising fantasy this year.'

Many excited New Zealanders gathered around their screens to watch the award ceremony, and in Wellington a special live telecast was held at the Embassy theatre, where families of the film-makers joined politicians and costumed *Rings* fans to watch the show.

Peter Jackson's mammoth *The Lord of the Rings* trilogy began in 2001 with the release of *The Fellowship of the Ring*. A year later, the highly anticipated *The Two Towers* came out, increasing the fan base in New Zealand and around the world. On 1 December 2003, *The Return of the King* staged its world premiere in 'Middle-earth', Wellington.

The award winners for *The Return of the King* were:

Best Picture:
Barrie M. Osborne, Peter Jackson and Fran Walsh (Producers)

Best Director:
Peter Jackson

Best Art Direction:
Grant Major (Art Direction), Dan Hennah and Alan Lee (Set Direction)

Best Sound Mixing:
Christopher Boyes, Michael Semanick, Michael Hedges and Hammond Peek

Best Music (Original Score):
Howard Shore

Best Music (Original Song):
'Into the West', music and lyrics by Fran Walsh, Howard Shore and Annie Lennox

Best Film Editing:
Jamie Selkirk

Best Visual Effects:
Jim Rygiel, Joe Letteri, Randall William Cook and Alex Funke

Best Costume Design:
Ngila Dickson and Richard Taylor

Best Makeup:
Richard Taylor and Peter King

Best Writing (Adapted Screenplay):
Screenplay by Fran Walsh, Philippa Boyens and Peter Jackson

Caricature of Peter Jackson with the 11 Oscars won by his film *The Return of the King*, 2004.

NEW ZEALAND DIVISION FORMED

After the evacuation from Gallipoli in December 1915, New Zealand forces returned to Egypt to recover. In February 1916, it was determined that Australian and New Zealand infantry divisions would be sent to the Western Front. On 1 March, the New Zealand Division was formed.

Commanded by Major-General Andrew Hamilton Russell, the Division consisted of three brigades of four battalions each, with supporting artillery and other units.

In April 1916 the Division crossed the Mediterranean to France. In mid-September it joined the Battle of the Somme as part of a renewed offensive to break the German lines around Flers. In June 1917 the New Zealanders helped capture the Messines Ridge in Flanders. On each occasion the Division achieved its objectives, but suffered heavy casualties. In October the New Zealanders experienced devastating losses at Passchendaele, with an attack on Bellevue Spur on the 12th costing the lives of more than 840 soldiers.

The Division's last major action was liberating the French town of Le Quesnoy on 4 November 1918 — just a week before the end of the war.

Soldiers of the NZ Division during the Battle of Flers-Courcelette on the Somme, September 1916.

MISSIONARY CARL VÖLKNER KILLED AT ŌPŌTIKI

Local Māori adherents of a new religion, Pai Mārire, which incorporated biblical and Māori spiritual elements, hanged the Church Missionary Society (Anglican) missionary Carl Völkner from a willow tree near his church at Ōpōtiki.

Many among Te Whakatōhea felt Völkner had betrayed them during the Waikato War (1863–64) by acting as an informant to Governor George Grey and accusing a popular Catholic missionary of aiding the Kīngitanga. Völkner's return to Ōpōtiki on 1 March — despite warnings to stay away — unfortunately coincided with a visit from Pai Mārire emissaries. Völkner's body was later taken down and beheaded. Many of those present tasted his blood or smeared it on their faces. In a final insult, Pai Mārire firebrand Kereopa Te Rau swallowed Völkner's eyes, dubbing one 'Parliament' and the other the 'Queen and English law'.

The government responded swiftly to Völkner's killing. Troops hunted down those responsible and took reprisals against local Māori. Much of the best land in eastern Bay of Plenty was confiscated and occupied by military settlers. Völkner was buried at his church, which was later dedicated to St Stephen the Martyr.

Völkner's death as depicted in the *Illustrated London News*, 1865.

BARRY CRUMP PUBLISHES *A GOOD KEEN MAN*
3 March 1960

One of the most-read books in New Zealand publishing history, *A Good Keen Man* established Barry Crump's reputation as an iconic 'Kiwi bloke'. Crump's 20-odd books capturing the humour and personalities of rural New Zealand had sold more than a million copies by the time he died in 1996 at the age of 61. He appealed to many Kiwis as a 'man's man' who could tell a great yarn. Toyota utilised Crump's down-to-earth style in a series of 1980s TV advertisements promoting four-wheel-drive utility vehicles. Crump, with his rugged 'she'll be right' attitude, had a foil in city slicker Lloyd Scott as he pulled off implausible feats of driving. While he inspired many, others criticised Crump for what they saw as less endearing aspects of a 'good keen man'. He married five times, but had little to do with most of the nine children he fathered with four different women. He converted to the Baha'i faith some years after the death by drowning of five boys at a camp he had organised.

Cover of *A Good Keen Man*.

1855

LEGENDARY SHEEP RUSTLER JAMES MACKENZIE CAUGHT

In March 1855 shepherds searching for 1000 missing sheep in the upper reaches of the Waitaki River apprehended suspected rustler James (sometimes John) Mackenzie (also McKenzie), one of New Zealand's first and most enduring folk heroes.

Caught red-handed, Mackenzie denied the theft, claiming he had been hired to drive the sheep to Otago. After escaping his captors, he walked 160 kilometres to Lyttelton, where he was recaptured on 15 March. A Supreme Court found Mackenzie guilty, sentencing him to five years' hard labour.

Mackenzie escaped from his road gang twice, remaining at large for a few days each time. In September 1855 a new magistrate reinvestigated his case and found flaws in the police inquiry and trial. Pardoned in January 1856, Mackenzie probably returned to Australia, but details of his later life are scarce.

The exploits of Mackenzie and his loyal dog 'Friday' left an indelible mark on the South Island high country. Canny pastoralists quickly realised the significance of the pass where he was found with the stolen sheep, and the open country beyond. This region was subsequently dubbed the Mackenzie Country.

Memorial to James Mackenzie, Fairlie.

The exploits of Mackenzie and his loyal dog 'Friday' left an indelible mark on the South Island high country.

CENSUS HELD AFTER TWO-YEAR DELAY
5 March 2013

New Zealand's five-yearly census had been scheduled for 8 March 2011. But after Canterbury's devastating February earthquake (see 22 February), Government Statistician Geoff Bascand and Statistics Minister Maurice Williamson announced that it would not go ahead. Statistics New Zealand's Christchurch operations had been significantly disrupted, and the exodus of people from the city would have skewed the results. Cancelling the census so close to the due date cost around $65 million. All the forms had been printed and contractors had delivered them to half a million houses. Statistics New Zealand recognised there would be longer-term costs too, as government agencies would have to rely on outdated data from 2006. The census has only been cancelled on two other occasions — in 1931 as an economy measure during the Depression, and in 1941 because of the Second World War. Neither of these was rescheduled, leading to two decade-long gaps between censuses. The census planned for 1946 was, however, brought forward six months to September 1945 so electorate boundaries could be redrawn in time for the first post-war election.

Census notice at the Lyttelton Information Centre, Oxford Street.

NEW ZEALAND SYMPHONY ORCHESTRA DEBUTS

Classical music lovers packed Wellington's Town Hall for the debut performance of New Zealand's first national orchestra. After opening with an obligatory rendition of 'God Save the King', the orchestra performed works by Dvořák, Brahms, Butterworth, Enesco, Wagner and Richard Strauss.

Attempts to form a permanent national orchestra in New Zealand began in the late 1930s. The success of the Centennial Festival Orchestra in 1940 encouraged the government to form a permanent orchestra within the National Broadcasting Service. The Second World War delayed plans until 1946, when some of New Zealand's best classical musicians gathered in Wellington for the first rehearsals.

Andersen Tyrer was appointed principal conductor and Vincent Aspey orchestra leader. Various radio orchestras provided a core of players who, at the end of several weeks' rehearsal, returned to their home cities, reassembling in Wellington a month before the inaugural concert in Wellington.

The National Orchestra became the NZBC Symphony Orchestra in 1963 and the New Zealand Symphony Orchestra in 1988.

BORN ON THIS DAY

Kiri Te Kanawa,
1944–,
opera singer

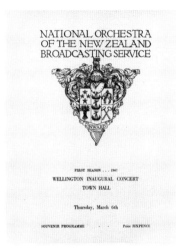

NATIONAL ORCHESTRA
OF THE NEW ZEALAND
BROADCASTING SERVICE

FIRST SEASON . . . 1947
WELLINGTON INAUGURAL CONCERT
TOWN HALL

Thursday, March 6th

SOUVENIR PROGRAMME   -   Price SIXPENCE

Cover of the programme for the debut performance of the National Orchestra, 1947.

CYCLONE BOLA STRIKES
7 March 1988

Cyclone Bola, one of the most damaging storms to hit New Zealand, struck Hawke's Bay and Gisborne–East Cape in March 1988. The weather system slowed as it moved over the area, bringing torrential rain for more than three days. Worst affected was the hill country behind Gisborne, where warm, moist air increased rainfall. In places, more than 900 millimetres of rain fell in 72 hours, and one area had 514 millimetres in a single day — more rain than parts of Central Otago get in an average year. Ensuing floods overwhelmed river stopbanks, damaged houses, swept away bridges and sections of roads and railway lines, and destroyed parts of Gisborne's main water pipeline. Three people died in a car swept away by floodwaters, and thousands were evacuated from their homes. Horticulture and farming losses amounted to $90 million (equivalent to $170 million today). Farmers lost large tracts of grazing area, and thick sediment from the ebbing floods smothered pastures, orchards and crops. The government repair bill for the cyclone was more than $111 million ($210 million).

Bridge washout at Wairoa after Cyclone Bola.

FIRST 'TALKIE' DRAWS CROWDS IN WELLINGTON

Moviegoers flocked to see Frank Borzage's *Street Angel*, an American silent picture with a recorded musical soundtrack, at Wellington's Paramount Theatre. There were also five 'talkie shorts', including an interview with the King of Spain. Live music usually accompanied silent movies, so a recorded soundtrack was a real novelty.

Street Angel told the story of a spirited young woman, Angela (Janet Gaynor). Down on her luck and living on the streets, she joined a travelling carnival and met a 'vagabond' painter, Gino (Charles Farrell). Gaynor won the Best Actress Oscar for this and two other performances.

The first feature-length movie with synchronised dialogue was *The Jazz Singer*, released in the United States in October 1927. The new technology did not convince everyone: United Artists president Joseph Schenck asserted in 1928 that the talkies were just a passing fad. But by the following year virtually every American film had a recorded soundtrack. The first New Zealand-made talkie screened in early 1930 (see 3 January) and within a few years they were a global phenomenon.

Exterior of the Paramount Theatre building, Wellington.

DEATH OF OPO 'THE FRIENDLY DOLPHIN'
9 March 1956

'Opononi George' or 'Opo' was a young female bottlenose dolphin who warmed the hearts of thousands of people at Opononi in Hokianga Harbour between June 1955 and March 1956. That spring and summer, the dolphin regularly approached the beach near Opononi wharf to play with locals. Opo's antics included juggling beach balls and beer bottles on her snout. Newspaper articles and photos attracted thousands of holidaymakers. Concerns for her welfare led to the formation of the Opononi Gay Dolphin Protection Committee. The government responded with an order in council on 8 March 1956 that made it an offence to 'take or molest any dolphin in Hokianga Harbour'. The measure did not save Opo. She was found dead the next day, jammed in a crevice between rocks. Some people suggested she had become stranded while fishing, others that she had been killed by fishermen using gelignite. Her death devastated the people of Opononi, who buried her above the beach where she had entertained so many. Messages of sympathy poured in from around the country, including from the governor-general.

Opo the dolphin and admirers, Opononi, 1956.

AUCKLAND WARRIORS DEBUT

The Auckland Warriors played their first match in the New South Wales Rugby League's expanded Winfield Cup competition. Thirty thousand fans at Mt Smart Stadium — and hundreds of thousands watching television — saw New Zealand's first fully professional rugby league team run out alongside the Brisbane Broncos. A mock battle and an excited ground announcer heralded them. The Warriors led 22–10 before the Broncos rallied to win 25–22.

Coached by John Monie and captained by Dean Bell, the Warriors had their first win in their third match, only to be stripped of two points for inadvertently fielding too many replacement players. As a result, they missed the end-of-season playoffs.

After a year in the breakaway Super League Telstra Cup competition in 1997, the rebranded New Zealand Warriors made the National Rugby League playoffs for the first time in 2001.

The Warriors' best year so far has been 2002, when they were minor premiers (topped the regular season table) and reached the grand final. They have made the playoffs six more times since, reaching the grand final again in 2011.

Thirty thousand fans . . . saw New Zealand's first fully professional rugby league team run out . . .

Auckland Warriors' captain Dean Bell leads the team out for their debut game in the Winfield Cup.

11 March
1884

NEW ZEALAND FREETHOUGHT ASSOCIATION FOUNDED

Forty delegates from six regional associations met in Dunedin to adopt a constitution and elect the first officeholders in the new organisation.

'Freethinker' was the 19th-century term for people (mostly middle-class men) who viewed the world through the lenses of reason and logic. Freethinkers were as diverse as the religious believers they condemned; freethought organisations were often riven by feuds and disappeared as quickly as they had sprung up. Dunedin's, for example, built an impressive public hall in 1882 but by 1885 had torn itself apart over the validity of spiritualism (the belief that human spirits can be communicated with after death). Though always a tiny minority and often mocked, freethinkers were not fringe-dwellers. The president and vice-president of the new association, Robert Stout and John Ballance respectively, would both serve terms as premier (prime minister) within the next decade.

The new body passed motions protesting against the recent criminalisation of blasphemous libel and supporting Charles Bradlaugh, who had refused to take the religious oath of allegiance when elected to the British House of Commons.

The Lyceum public hall built by the Freethought Association in Dunedin, 1882.

NEW ZEALAND RED CROSS WORKER KILLED IN VIETNAM

12 March 1975

Returning from leave in Laos, 30-year-old Malcolm 'Mac' Riding was aboard an Air Vietnam DC-4 when it crashed 25 kilometres from his Red Cross team's compound near Pleiku, South Vietnam.

The plane crashed into territory controlled by the North Vietnamese Army (NVA), which made it difficult for investigators to get to the crash site and determine the cause. Eyewitness accounts saw the plane trailing smoke and attempting to land at an airstrip before pulling up and then crashing. Subsequent reports indicated that it had fallen victim to a heat-seeking missile. Riding's body has never been found. Seven weeks later Saigon fell to the NVA, bringing an end to the decades-long war.

British-born but New Zealand-educated, Riding was an optical engineer and former relieving lighthouse keeper who had spent time in the Peruvian Andes and Antarctica. He arrived in Vietnam with the Red Cross in 1973 and became leader of the organisation's sixth welfare team in September 1974. In 2003 Riding was awarded the New Zealand Operational Service Medal for his services to the Red Cross.

Mac Riding, 1975.

BORN ON THIS DAY

Rita Angus,
1908–1970,
artist

NEW ZEALAND'S FIRST TEST CRICKET VICTORY

New Zealand was already 3–0 down in the series going into the fourth and final test at Eden Park in Auckland. Their West Indies opponents included household names such as Gary Sobers and Everton Weekes, who broke batting records for a New Zealand season. New captain John Reid won the toss and decided to bat first. His aggressive innings of 84 underpinned a New Zealand total of 255. Then Tony MacGibbon and Harry Cave each took four wickets as the West Indies was dismissed for 145.

New Zealand declared its second innings closed at 157/9, with wicketkeeper Sam Guillen top-scoring with 41. West Indian-born Guillen had played on the Caribbean side's tour of Australia in 1951–52 before settling in Christchurch.

The West Indies needed 268 for victory in two sessions, but another four-wicket haul by Cave saw them skittled for just 77 as rain threatened. In the last act of the match, Guillen stumped Alf Valentine. After 22 losses and 22 draws in 26 years of test cricket, New Zealand had at last tasted victory.

New Zealand players celebrate their first test victory, 1956.

SPLIT ENZ HIT NO. 1
14 March 1980

The Kiwi group's first New Zealand no. 1 hit, from their album *True Colours*, also topped the charts in Australia and Canada. It reached no. 12 in Britain and no. 53 in the United States. 'I Got You' was written and sung by Neil Finn and featured a chorus reminiscent of the Beatles. *True Colours* launched Split Enz onto the international stage after years spent struggling for commercial success. Originally called Split Ends, the Auckland art-rock band burst onto the music scene in the early 1970s. They generally avoided the pub scene, instead performing in theatres and halls. Initially known more for their idiosyncratic, theatrical style, they achieved wider popularity thanks to a string of radio-friendly songs written by brothers Tim and Neil Finn. Between them, the Finns created a substantial catalogue of songs that resonated for decades: 'I Got You', 'I Hope I Never', 'I See Red', 'History Never Repeats', 'Six Months in a Leaky Boat', 'Message to My Girl' and many others. Split Enz disbanded in 1984.

Split Enz publicity shot.

51 KILLED IN MOSQUE SHOOTINGS

15 March 2019

New Zealand's Muslim community suffered an horrific attack when a self-proclaimed 'white nationalist' opened fire on worshippers at mosques on Deans Avenue and in Linwood in Christchurch. Fifty were killed and another 50 wounded, one of whom died six weeks later. The gunman used five weapons, including two semi-automatic assault rifles, in the attack, which was livestreamed on some websites. The death toll would have been higher but for the heroism displayed by unarmed men at both mosques, and by the police officers who forced the assailant's car off the road. Prime Minister Jacinda Ardern described it as one of New Zealand's darkest days.

In the following weeks, memorial events around the country were attended by thousands of people. Mosques welcomed visitors as the Muslim community displayed a remarkable capacity for forgiveness. Millions of dollars were raised to support the victims and their families. Military-style semi-automatic weapons of the type used in the attack were soon outlawed. The government introduced a buy-back scheme for registered owners of these weapons and announced that firearms as well as their owners would be licensed. A Royal Commission of Inquiry into what state sector agencies knew or should have known about the accused attacker was established in April 2019.

The alleged gunman was charged with 51 counts of murder, 40 of attempted murder, and one of engaging in a terrorist act. The latter charge was the first laid under the Terrorism Suppression Act 2002. Ardern has played a leading role in an international movement to persuade major technology companies to stop the dissemination online of terrorist and violent extremist content.

Prime Minister Jacinda Ardern visits the Wellington Islamic Centre and Masjid in Kilbirnie on 16 March 2019.

JOCKEY Y-FRONTS HIT NEW ZEALAND SHOPS

'If old-fashioned underwear makes you squirm, switch to Jockey.' That was the message from clothing manufacturer Lane Walker Rudkin when it began marketing the Jockey Y-front to New Zealand men on 16 March 1940. The Canterbury firm had successfully bid to manufacture Jockey's new range of underwear, making New Zealand one of the first four countries in the world to make the iconic American brand.

Before the Second World War, men's underwear was 'all-wool and all-enveloping', extending to the ankles and elbows. Given the obvious disadvantages of the traditional undergarment, especially in summer, the Y-front quickly established itself as a market leader. Newspaper advertisements praised Jockey's 'sleek and fitting scientific designs' and 'real masculine comfort'. Jockey soon had the market covered.

Despite increasing competition from other brands and styles, Jockey products continued to sell well in New Zealand. By the 21st century, Kiwis were buying around one million pairs of Jockey men's underwear a year. On a per capita basis, New Zealanders purchased more Jockey products than the men of any other country.

BORN ON THIS DAY

James Hector,
1834–1907,
geologist, explorer

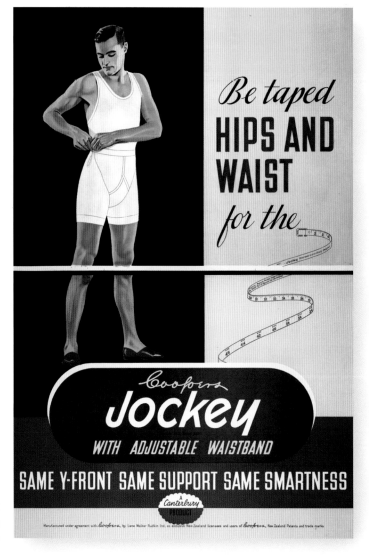

Advertisement for Jockey underwear, 1940.

FIRST TARANAKI WAR ERUPTS AT WAITARA

1860

The opening shots of the first Taranaki War were fired when British troops attacked a pā built by Te Āti Awa chief Te Rangitāke at Te Kōhia, Waitara.

A minor chief, Te Teira Mānuka, had offered to sell Governor Thomas Gore Browne land in 1859. Te Rangitāke (also known as Wiremu Kīngi) denied the validity of the sale and his supporters erected a flagstaff to mark their boundary.

Browne went against official policy by pursuing a contested land sale. He hoped to win support from New Plymouth settlers desperate for land. When Browne ordered surveyors onto the Pekapeka block, Māori pulled up their pegs. The governor declared martial law and sent in British troops.

Te Rangitāke's L-shaped pā incorporated anti-artillery bunkers. Built overnight just inside the disputed land, it withstood close-range fire from 500 troops and 200 artillery rounds. No Māori were killed before Te Rangitāke and his 70 men abandoned the pā that night.

L-shaped pā were quick to build, effective and expendable. New Plymouth District Council purchased the Te Kōhia site in 2016.

Built overnight just inside the disputed land, it withstood close-range fire from 500 troops and 200 artillery rounds.

Charles Gold's painting of the 65th Regiment encamped at Waitara, 1860.

WAITANGI TRIBUNAL RULES ON MOTUNUI CLAIM

MOTUNUI—WAITARA REPORT

WAITANGI TRIBUNAL 1983

In a landmark ruling, the Waitangi Tribunal (see 10 October) found that the Crown's obligations under the Treaty of Waitangi included a duty to protect Māori fishing grounds.

One of the first claims to the tribunal (number Wai 6) was made by Te Āti Awa of Taranaki, who opposed the construction of an outfall to discharge waste from the Motunui synthetic fuels plant, 6 kilometres east of Waitara, into the Tasman Sea.

The tribunal found that industrial waste from Motunui — one of the National government's flagship 'Think Big' energy projects — had already polluted Taranaki fishing grounds. The proposed outfall should not be built and a regional task force should be set up to find an alternative way to treat the waste.

On 28 March, Prime Minister Robert Muldoon announced his government's rejection of the tribunal's recommendations. After much public debate, the government introduced legislation designed to placate Te Āti Awa while still allowing eventual construction of the outfall. In the wake of further uproar, all provision for an outfall was removed from this bill in September 1983.

Cover of the first Waitangi Tribunal report.

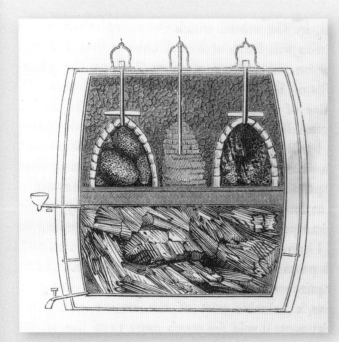

Sketch of a wine barrel converted into a storage chamber for transporting bees from England to New Zealand.

HONEY BEES BROUGHT TO NEW ZEALAND
19 March 1839

Mary Bumby, the sister of a Methodist missionary, was probably the first to introduce honey bees to New Zealand from England. She brought two hives ashore when she landed at the Mangungu Mission Station at Hokianga in March 1839. While New Zealand has at least 20 native bee species, none is known to be suitable for producing honey. The Reverend Richard Taylor, Lady Hobson, James Busby and William Cotton brought more bees in 1843. In 1848 Cotton wrote a manual for New Zealand beekeepers, describing the basics of bee husbandry and production of honey. The New Zealand bush proved a hospitable place for bees, and the number of wild colonies multiplied rapidly, especially in the Bay of Islands. Isaac Hopkins, regarded as the father of beekeeping in New Zealand, observed that by the 1860s bee nests in the bush were plentiful, and considerable quantities of honey were being sold by Māori. The commercial production of honey in New Zealand began during the late 1870s following the introduction of the Langstroth hive, the boxed-framed beehive model still used today.

NEW ZEALAND'S FIRST RECOGNISED FLAG CHOSEN

ANew Zealand flag was first suggested in 1830 after Sydney customs officials seized a Hokianga-built ship. Australia was subject to British navigation laws under which ships had to carry official certificates. As New Zealand was not then a British colony, New Zealand-built ships could not sail under a British flag or register. Without this, they and their cargoes would continue to be seized.

In 1833 British Resident James Busby suggested the adoption of a New Zealand flag. This would both solve the trade problem and encourage Māori chiefs to work together as an embryonic collective government. Church Missionary Society (CMS) missionary Henry Williams arranged for three alternative designs to be made up in Sydney. On 20 March 1834, 25 northern chiefs met at Waitangi to view the three flags. Many Pākehā also attended. Following an address by Busby, each chief was called forward to vote.

The preferred design — that of the CMS flag — incorporated the flag of the Anglican diocese of New South Wales into the Royal Navy's white ensign. Busby declared it the national flag of New Zealand.

The ensign of the United Tribes, as depicted in an 1845 book of flags.

KIWIS WIN OSCARS FOR *THE PIANO*
21 March 1994

Eleven-year-old Anna Paquin became the first New Zealander to win an Academy Award for acting when she picked up the best supporting actress award for her role as Flora McGrath in the acclaimed historical drama *The Piano*. She was the second youngest recipient of this award in Oscar history. New Zealander Jane Campion, the film's writer and director, chose the then nine-year-old Paquin from 5000 hopefuls who attended an open audition in New Zealand. Despite having no acting experience, Paquin impressed Campion with a monologue about Flora's father. The film reached the pinnacle of success for cinema worldwide, winning the coveted Palme d'Or at Cannes and three Oscars at the 1994 awards. Along with Paquin's statuette, Campion picked up the award for best original screenplay, while American actor Holly Hunter won the best actress Oscar for her portrayal of Ada McGrath, Flora's mother. In 2013 Campion revealed that she had originally intended Hunter's character to die at the end of the film, but changed her mind during shooting.

Three Oscar winners for *The Piano*: from left, Holly Hunter, Anna Paquin and Jane Campion, 1993.

GEORGE VON ZEDLITZ ARRIVES IN WELLINGTON

Victoria College's first professor of modern languages joined the fledgling institution's four foundation professors. Despite a less than ringing endorsement from New Zealand's London-based Agent-General William Pember Reeves — 'You are the best of a poor lot' — the urbane intellectual was an immediate success as a lecturer and enriched Wellington's cultural life.

Just before Britain entered the First World War, von Zedlitz compounded his misfortune in having a German father by offering his services to Germany in a non-combatant capacity. He was an easy target as anti-German sentiment grew. In October 1915 Parliament passed an Alien Enemy Teachers Act to force Victoria to sack him. The government stymied attempts to reappoint him to his chair after the war.

To make ends meet, he founded the University Tutorial School. He was also active in the egalitarian Workers' Educational Association. Victoria made him professor emeritus when he turned 65, and he also served for five years on the Senate of the University of New Zealand. In the 1970s Victoria University's new von Zedlitz building was named in his honour.

Painting of George von Zedlitz by Christopher Perkins, 1933.

SCOTTISH SETTLERS ARRIVE IN OTAGO

Otago celebrates the arrival of the immigrant ship *John Wickliffe* as the founding day of the province. The ship and its 97 passengers sailed from Gravesend, England on 24 November 1847. Three days later, the *Philip Laing* left Greenock, Scotland, with a further 247 people. Both ships were carrying Scottish settlers bound for New Zealand.

Plans for a Scottish settlement in New Zealand had begun in 1842. Scottish architect and politician George Rennie, concerned at English dominance over the first New Zealand Company settlements, hoped to establish 'a new Edinburgh' in the southern hemisphere. Dunedin — the Gaelic form of Edinburgh — became feasible once the New Zealand Company purchased the large Otago block from Ngāi Tahu in 1844.

Divisions within the Church of Scotland transformed Rennie's original plan. Unhappy with patronage and state control, 400 clergy and about one-third of laypeople quit the established church. Some of these dissenters, including Thomas Burns, William Cargill and John McGlashan, saw Otago as a home for a new 'Free Church'. Two-thirds of the original Otago settlers were Free Church Presbyterians.

BORN ON THIS DAY

Michael Joseph Savage,
1872–1940,
First Labour prime minister

Painting depicting the arrival of the *Philip Laing* at Port Chalmers on 15 April 1848, with the *John Wickliffe* at anchor.

1770

MĀORI KIDNAP VICTIM DIES ON FRENCH SHIP

Ranginui was a Ngāti Kahu chief from Doubtless Bay who was kidnapped by the French explorer Jean François Marie de Surville. De Surville's ship, the *St Jean Baptiste*, had arrived off northern New Zealand in December 1769. The expedition spent two weeks in Doubtless Bay.

De Surville respected Māori etiquette and relations were mostly friendly. Māori supplied the French with much-needed greens in return for European foodstuffs and cloth. The ship's officers recorded valuable impressions of Māori customs and artefacts in their journals. The ship's chaplain probably presided over New Zealand's first Christmas Day service.

Later the atmosphere soured. When Māori took a small boat that had drifted ashore, de Surville 'arrested' Ranginui, who had been hospitable towards the visitors, and ordered the destruction of houses and other property.

Ranginui was taken aboard the *St Jean Baptiste*. Strong winds then forced the ship to set sail and it headed east across the Pacific. Ranginui was treated well by his captors. But no land was encountered, the crew became ill and Ranginui died of scurvy on 24 March 1770.

When Māori took a small boat that had drifted ashore, de Surville 'arrested' Ranginui ...

Ranginui, captive chief of Doubtless Bay, 1769, by R.R.D. Milligan.

JOHN A. LEE EXPELLED FROM LABOUR PARTY
25 March 1940

A charismatic ex-soldier, orator and writer, John A. Lee had been active in the New Zealand Labour Party since shortly after the First World War. Following Labour's landslide victory in 1935, Lee expected to be appointed to Cabinet, but Prime Minister Michael Joseph Savage thought him too wild and unconventional. Instead, Lee was made a parliamentary under-secretary with responsibility for Labour's state housing scheme. The success of this landmark programme owed much to his enthusiasm and organisational ability. Overlooked for Cabinet again after the 1938 election, Lee intensified his attacks on Labour's leadership. The prime minister was dying of cancer and the party quickly turned this into an issue of loyalty. Preparations were begun to have Lee expelled at the 1940 conference. Before the conference in March, Savage penned an addition to his annual report. He accused Lee of having made his life 'a living hell' for the past two years. Although his supporters maintained that the real issue was party democracy, Lee was expelled by 546 votes to 344. Savage died two days later (see 30 March).

John A. Lee, who lost his left forearm in the First World War, 1936.

BRUNNER MINE DISASTER KILLS 65

At 9.30 a.m. an explosion tore through the Brunner Mine in Westland's Grey Valley. Two men sent underground to investigate were later found unconscious from black damp, a suffocating mixture of nitrogen and carbon dioxide.

Rescuers began bringing out bodies around 11 a.m. The noxious gases took their toll on those in the rescue parties, many of whom collapsed and had to be carried out. The final death toll was 65 — almost half of Brunner's underground workforce. This remains New Zealand's deadliest industrial accident.

Fifty-three of the victims were buried in Stillwater Cemetery, 33 of them in a single grave. The funeral procession stretched 800 metres.

The official inquiry determined that the cause was the detonating of a charge in a part of the mine where no one should have been working. However, some experienced miners claimed that firedamp — methane gas produced by coal — had accumulated and not been cleared by an ineffectual ventilation system.

BORN ON THIS DAY

Matiu Rata,
1934–1997,
Māori politician

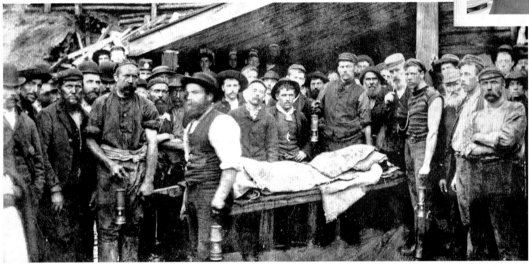

The first bodies recovered from the Brunner Mine, 1896.

TRADES' HALL BOMBING
27 March 1984

Caretaker and unionist Ernie Abbott was killed by a bomb at Trades' Hall in Wellington's Vivian Street. Trades' Hall was the headquarters for many trade unions and police suspected that they were the targets. Designed to go off when moved, the bomb was hidden in a suitcase and left in the foyer of the building. The device contained the equivalent of at least 1 kilogram of gelignite, although the actual explosive is still unidentified. The lack of a clear motive hampered police investigations. An initial theory centred on a bus strike the previous day, but police concluded that it would have been difficult to assemble the bomb and put it in place so quickly. Some suggested that the culprit was a suspected killer on the run from the Irish Republican Army. Although the crime remains unsolved, it appears to have been the action of an isolated individual with a hatred of unions. The attack came during a period of heightened industrial tensions, when Prime Minister Robert Muldoon made frequent verbal attacks on the union movement.

Police poster about the Trades' Hall bombing.

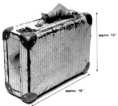

MĀORI TELEVISION LAUNCHED

A dawn pōwhiri (welcoming ceremony) at Māori Television's new offices in Newmarket, Auckland, was covered in the first transmission next day.

The birth of a separate Māori channel followed a prolonged and difficult gestation. In 1985 the New Zealand Māori Council had proposed to run the planned third television channel through the Aotearoa Broadcasting System. This application failed and the legislation creating TVNZ Ltd as a state-owned enterprise in 1988 did not address the portrayal of Māori language and culture on television.

Aotearoa Television began broadcasting in 1996 with public funding, but it folded the following year amid allegations of undue haste and mismanagement. Māori Television's first two chief executives resigned under clouds and the channel's launch was delayed.

Māori Television's founding legislation requires it to inform and educate, and broadcast 'mainly' in the Māori language. Largely taxpayer-funded, it has become New Zealand's de facto public TV channel, especially on national occasions such as Anzac and Waitangi Days. More than half its audience is non-Māori. A second channel, Te Reo, which broadcasts entirely in Māori, began in 2008.

Māori Television logo.

. . . it has become New Zealand's de facto public TV channel, especially on national occasions such as Anzac and Waitangi Days.

Newspaper report on the Ross hoax.

NAZI SABOTAGE HOAX
29 March 1942

During the Second World War convicted conman Sydney Gordon Ross duped New Zealand's intelligence service into believing that Nazi agents were planning to carry out sabotage in New Zealand. The day after his release from prison in March 1942, Ross contacted government minister Robert Semple, claiming he had been approached by a German agent to join a sabotage cell active in Ngongotahā, near Rotorua. Prime Minister Peter Fraser referred Ross to Major Kenneth Folkes, a British officer in charge of the newly established Security Intelligence Bureau (SIB). Folkes believed Ross's story. He approached the government for more troops and greater powers to arrest and detain suspects. Fraser asked the police to investigate the 'Nazi headquarters' in Ngongotahā, which turned out to be occupied by an elderly Native Department clerk, a dry-cleaner and three nurses. Ross's story quickly unravelled. The hoax was a huge embarrassment for New Zealand's fledgling intelligence service. Folkes returned to Britain and the police took over the SIB. Ross, who was not charged in relation to the hoax, died of tuberculosis in August 1946.

FUNERAL PROCESSION FOR PRIME MINISTER SAVAGE

New Zealand's first Labour prime minister, Michael Joseph Savage, died in office on 27 March 1940. His body lay in state at Parliament for two days before his funeral cortège, which was more than 1.6 kilometres long, set off for the railway station at 9 a.m. on 30 March. It was to be the longest funeral procession, and perhaps the most striking outpouring of public grief, in New Zealand's history.

The special funeral train took 28 hours to transport the casket and official mourners to Auckland. At 20 stops along the route, crowds of up to 12,000 people filed past the casket and laid wreaths. Regular updates on the train's progress were broadcast on radio, allowing people elsewhere in the country to feel part of the events.

An estimated 200,000 people lined the route of Savage's cortège from central Auckland to his burial site at Bastion Point (Takaparawhā), above Waitematā Harbour. Savage's body was finally entombed there two years later, below an elaborate memorial dedicated to his memory.

Michael Joseph Savage's funeral procession, Lambton Quay, Wellington.

REWI'S LAST STAND?

The last battle of the Waikato War began when the spearhead of a strong British force charged an apparently weak Māori position at Ōrākau, south-east of Te Awamutu. After two frontal assaults failed, the British besieged the pā.

The battle immortalised as 'Rewi's last stand' was not of Rewi Maniapoto's choosing. The Ngāti Maniapoto leader did not want to fight in territory that was effectively already occupied by the British. Forced to do so by Tūhoe and Ngāti Raukawa, he advocated fortifying a nearby position that had a water supply and a line of retreat — and lost that argument too.

By 2 April attackers outnumbered defenders six to one. The latter had no water and artillery had breached their defences. Death or surrender seemed their only options.

That afternoon the defenders — men and women — left the pā in a disciplined body, broke through the British cordon and made for the Pūniu River, pursued by mounted units. Up to 160 Māori were killed, most during the retreat, against 17 British. But the Kīngitanga (King Movement) retained the capacity to fight.

Rewi defying the British troops at Ōrākau; illustration that appeared in a supplement to the *Auckland Weekly News*, 16 December 1893.

TEAL BECOMES AIR NEW ZEALAND

1 April
1965

New Zealand's international airline, Tasman Empire Airways Limited (TEAL), was renamed Air New Zealand Limited. The New Zealand, United Kingdom and Australian governments had established TEAL in 1939 to provide a trans-Tasman air link. TEAL's Auckland–Sydney flights began in April 1940, using Short S30 Empire flying boats. For 20 years TEAL's flying boats provided a memorable spectacle for thousands of people. The renowned 1950s Coral Route from Auckland to Fiji, Samoa, the Cook Islands and Tahiti contributed its own distinctive legends to the era of flying boats. Conversion to land-based planes began in 1954, when the popular Auckland–Sydney service switched to Douglas DC-6 aircraft. In 1960 land planes took over the Coral Route. New Zealand assumed full ownership of TEAL in April 1961.

In 1947 the New Zealand government had established the New Zealand National Airways Corporation (NAC), which became the country's primary domestic carrier. In April 1978 NAC merged with Air New Zealand. The enlarged Air New Zealand was the first local carrier to offer both international and domestic services.

BORN ON THIS DAY

Frederic Truby King,
1858–1938,
child health reformer

Air New Zealand DC-8 aircraft at Christchurch International Airport, 1960s.

ACC COMES INTO OPERATION

1 April
1974

In 1972 government legislation established the Accident Compensation Commission (ACC) to provide insurance for all personal injury.

The 'no-fault' principle was first introduced in the Workers' Compensation for Accidents Act 1900. The act provided injured workers with weekly benefits, and compensated the families of those killed at work. However, the benefits paid were small and lasted for a maximum of six years.

This system became outdated over the next 60 years. It did not cover non-work accidents or motor vehicle injuries, and employers and insurers often used legal arguments to dispute their obligation to pay compensation. A Royal Commission on Compensation for Injury set up in 1966 recommended that the state provide 24-hour, no-fault insurance for all personal injury. In return, New Zealanders would give up the right to sue for damages arising from personal injury.

These recommendations were adopted in the Accident Compensation Act 1972. This required all taxpayers, employers, self-employed people and motor vehicle owners to pay a levy to a new state agency, the Accident Compensation Commission (later renamed the Accident Compensation Corporation).

ARREST OF RUA KĒNANA

On Sunday, 2 April 1916, 57 police raided the Ngāi Tūhoe settlement of Maungapōhatu in the Urewera region.

By 1907 prophet and community leader Rua Kēnana had attracted a following of 600 people. Many Pākehā saw the avowedly autonomous kāinga (village) as subversive. Māori politicians like Māui Pōmare and Āpirana Ngata believed that traditional tohunga (spiritual leaders) such as Rua inhibited Māori progress.

In 1915 Rua was charged with illicitly selling alcohol. Concerned about his opposition to Tūhoe men enlisting for military service, the government seized this opportunity to punish him.

After Rua failed to appear before a magistrate when summonsed in January 1916, Police Commissioner John Cullen instigated an armed police expedition to Maungapōhatu. In an exchange of gunfire probably begun by the police, two Māori were killed, including Rua's son Toko.

Rua and others were arrested on charges ranging from resisting arrest to treason, and taken to Auckland for trial. Rua was sentenced to 12 months' hard labour followed by 18 months' imprisonment. He was released from jail in April 1918, but the Maungapōhatu community never recovered.

Rua Kēnana and his son Whatu, handcuffed.

BATTLE OF MANNERS STREET

Hundreds of soldiers and civilians slugged it out on the streets of Wellington during the 'Battle of Manners Street', the most infamous clash between New Zealanders and American servicemen during the Second World War.

Allies fighting each other was not good publicity, and news of the three-hour brawl outside the Allied Services Club was hushed up at the time. The incident may have begun after white soldiers from the southern United States objected to Māori using the club. American sailors and New Zealand merchant seamen also became involved.

At any one time during the two years after June 1942, between 15,000 and 45,000 American soldiers and sailors were based in New Zealand (see 12 June), either before or immediately after experiencing the horrors of war in the Pacific.

The 'American invasion' led to a clash of cultures. Romantic liaisons developed between American troops and New Zealand women, and about 1500 New Zealand women married Americans during the war.

Many New Zealand men, especially soldiers serving overseas, resented the popularity of these American 'bedroom commandos'. Tensions erupted into large-scale fights in Auckland and Wellington.

US troops resting near Oriental Bay in Wellington during a route march, c. 1942.

2001

SILVIA CARTWRIGHT BECOMES GOVERNOR-GENERAL

The swearing in of Dame Silvia Cartwright as New Zealand's eighteenth governor-general completed a female clean sweep of the country's most powerful political and legal positions. Four other prominent women attended the ceremony: Prime Minister Helen Clark, opposition leader Jenny Shipley, Chief Justice Sian Elias and Attorney-General Margaret Wilson. Dame Silvia was the second female governor-general of New Zealand. Dame Catherine Tizard, former Mayor of Auckland, held the post between 1990 and 1996. Cartwright came to prominence when she headed an inquiry into the treatment of women with cervical cancer at National Women's Hospital, Auckland. In 1993 she became New Zealand's first female High Court judge.

As governor-general, Dame Silvia broke with convention by publicly offering views on issues such as the use of 'reasonable force' by parents against their children and the length of prison sentences. After finishing her term as governor-general in 2006, Dame Silvia was appointed to a panel of judges trying former Khmer Rouge leaders in Cambodia. In 2014 she took part in a United Nations investigation of alleged war crimes and human rights abuses in Sri Lanka.

Silvia Cartwright sworn in as governor-general, 2001.

DEATH OF PHAR LAP
5 April 1932

The champion racehorse Phar Lap was New Zealand born and bred, but never raced in this country. He won 37 of his 51 races and 32 of his last 35, including the 1930 Melbourne Cup. In the gloom of the Great Depression, Phar Lap's exploits thrilled two countries. Phar Lap arrived in Australia as a two-year-old. His name meant 'lightning' in the Thai language, and he lived up to it with his ability to finish races with a surge of speed. He was no looker, though, with warts all over his head. Having conquered Australia, Phar Lap was sent to North America. On 24 March 1932, he won the rich Agua Caliente Handicap in Mexico in record time. Invitations to race at major meetings flooded in, but the horse died 12 days later. Suspicions he had been poisoned were never confirmed. The champion's remains were keenly sought after. His 6.3-kilogram heart (the equine average is 3.6 kilograms) went to Canberra, while the Museum of Victoria in Melbourne obtained his hide. Phar Lap's skeleton is on display at Te Papa in Wellington.

Phar Lap at Flemington Racecourse, Melbourne, c. 1930.

MĀORI PIONEER BATTALION RETURNS FROM WAR

The all-Māori Pioneer Battalion was one of only two New Zealand Expeditionary Force formations — and the only battalion — to return from the First World War as a complete unit. This, and the opportunity for a proper welcome, saw both Pākehā and Māori communities make a special effort to mark their return.

More than 1000 men of the battalion arrived in Auckland on the *Westmoreland* on the evening of 5 April 1919. As the ship came in to the wharf the next morning, guns fired a salute, steamers sounded their sirens and bands played patriotic music. Dignitaries, including Acting Prime Minister James Allen, greeted the men with brief speeches. The battalion then marched to a pōwhiri (welcoming ceremony) at Auckland Domain, where representatives of iwi (tribes) from throughout the country greeted them. After this initial event, the various units returned to their home regions. Parades and receptions involving Pākehā dignitaries were held, but the most important events for the soldiers were the traditional welcomes at their home marae by their own people.

Men of the Māori Pioneer Battalion marching up Queen Street, Auckland, April 1919.

FIRST STATE SECONDARY SCHOOL OPENS
7 April 1856

The first state secondary school in New Zealand, Nelson College, opened in temporary premises in Trafalgar Street with a roll of just eight boys. It eventually attracted boys from around the country as well as the local area. It remains a boys-only school, with a current roll of over 1000, and continues to take both boarders and day pupils. The original wooden school burnt down in 1904. A new brick building, opened in 1907, suffered considerable damage during the 1929 Murchison earthquake. The school's clock tower collapsed during the severe shaking, showering the main entrance with rubble. Remarkably, only two boys suffered injuries. Notable old boys include Nobel Prize winner Ernest Rutherford, Victoria Cross recipient Leonard Trent, Commonwealth Secretary-General and Deputy Prime Minister Don McKinnon, and two Labour prime ministers: Wallace ('Bill') Rowling and Geoffrey Palmer. Perhaps the school's biggest claim to fame is its association with the game of rugby. A Nelson College team played Nelson Town at Nelson Botanical Reserve in what is believed to have been the first game played in New Zealand, in May 1870.

Nelson College, with Principal's residence at left, 1861.

JULIUS VOGEL BECOMES PREMIER

Julius Vogel was the dominant political figure of the 1870s, serving as colonial treasurer and premier on several occasions, and launching a massive programme of immigration and public works.

Born in London of Jewish–Dutch parentage, Vogel worked as a journalist and editor in Australia before settling in Dunedin in 1861. Elected to Parliament in 1863, he became Colonial Treasurer in William Fox's government in 1869.

To revive the faltering economy, Vogel initiated a bold 10-year programme of public works and large-scale assisted immigration, funded by extensive borrowing on the London money market. The success of this policy depended on the rapid and cheap acquisition of Māori land by the Crown. Vogel and his supporters were certain that Māori and settlers would be reconciled after the recent New Zealand Wars once Māori — and their land — were fully integrated into the European economy.

Vogel served as premier until July 1875 and for another seven-month period in 1876. His ambitious and revolutionary programme had transformed the colony, the non-Māori population of which nearly doubled between 1871 and 1881.

Julius Vogel, 1860s.

SISTERS OF MERCY ARRIVE IN NEW ZEALAND
9 April 1850

Nine Sisters of Mercy led by Mother Cecilia Maher arrived in Auckland on the *Océanie* with Bishop Pompallier (who had taught them Māori on the voyage) and a number of priests. The Irish nuns of the order were the first canonically consecrated religious women to become established in New Zealand. The Institute of Our Lady of Mercy had been founded in Dublin in 1831 to educate working-class children, protect and train young women, and care for the sick. It grew into the largest religious society founded by an English-speaking Catholic. In Auckland the Sisters immediately took in orphans and took over St Patrick's Girls' School in Wyndham Street. Fees paid by well-off families of pupils at the Select School established in 1851 helped fund the education of the poor. In 1855 they took charge of St Anne's, a school for Māori girls on 'Mount St Mary' in Ponsonby. The sisters also visited the sick at home and in hospital, and prisoners in the city's jail. A convent was built in New Street, Ponsonby, in 1862. Its kauri Gothic Revival chapel still stands, the oldest of its kind in the country.

St Mary's Old Convent Chapel, Ponsonby.

NEW ZEALAND ALMOST VOTES FOR PROHIBITION

Aspecial liquor referendum initially gave prohibition a majority of 13,000 over continuance (the status quo), raising the hopes of those who had for decades campaigned against the manufacture and sale of alcohol.

However, special votes of nearly 40,000 troops still overseas, aboard ships, or in camps or hospitals in New Zealand were still to be counted. Fighting for King and country was clearly thirsty work, as 32,000 of these men voted to retain the right to drink. When all votes were counted, continuance won by 264,189 votes to 253,827.

This was the first — and last — time that the question would be decided by a simple majority in a nationwide poll. A second referendum held alongside the December 1919 general election included a third option: state purchase and control of the sale of alcohol. This time prohibition came within 1600 votes of victory. Although the prohibitionist cause remained strong until the 1930s, New Zealand would never again come as near to banning the bottle as it did in the twin referendums of 1919.

THE TANTALISING TENTH
SOLDIERS HOLD THE SITUATION—SAINTS AND SINNERS IN SUSPENSE.

Special votes cast by soldiers serving overseas tipped the balance against prohibition in a referendum, April 1919.

WAHINE WRECKED

The sinking of the Lyttelton–Wellington ferry *Wahine* is New Zealand's worst modern maritime disaster. Fifty-one people lost their lives that day, another died several weeks later and a fifty-third victim died in 1990 from injuries sustained in the wreck. Would-be rescuers stood helplessly on beaches as the *Wahine* succumbed to one of the worst storms recorded in New Zealand history. Driven onto Barrett Reef, at the entrance to Wellington Harbour, the ship lost its starboard propeller and power to its port engine. The 8948-ton vessel drifted further into the harbour before leaning to starboard. Because of the heavy list, crew could only launch four of the eight lifeboats, and most of the inflatable life rafts capsized in the savage seas.

The *Wahine* finally capsized at 2.30 p.m. Most deaths occurred on the Eastbourne side of the harbour, where people were driven against sharp rocks by waves.

Although the main cause of the accident was the atrocious weather conditions, the subsequent inquest also acknowledged that those on board the ferry and on shore had made errors of judgement.

The *Wahine* founders in Wellington Harbour.

1869

NEW ZEALAND'S FIRST ROYAL VISIT

The Duke of Edinburgh, Prince Alfred Ernest Albert, arrived in Wellington as captain of the frigate HMS *Galatea*. The first member of the British royal family to visit New Zealand, he was greeted with haka, speeches and bunting.

Prince Alfred, the second son of Queen Victoria and Prince Albert, made three visits to New Zealand in 1869 and 1870. A planned visit in 1868 had been cancelled after a gunman shot and wounded the prince in Sydney.

During his 1869 visit, the prince spent nearly a week in the capital, attending official functions and enjoying a pig hunt before sailing to Nelson. He subsequently visited Christchurch, Dunedin and Auckland, where he received 150 Māori chiefs and shot pūkeko and pigeons. The prince's vessel returned briefly to Wellington in late August 1870 and made a final visit in December.

To commemorate the royal tour, Galatea district in Bay of Plenty was named after the prince's vessel. The name was originally applied to an Armed Constabulary redoubt built during the hunt for Māori resistance leader Te Kooti.

An engraving depicting the visit of the Duke of Edinburgh, Auckland, 1869.

RECEPTION OF THE DUKE OF EDINBURGH AT AUCKLAND, NEW ZEALAND.

HMS *NEW ZEALAND* BEGINS TOUR OF NATION'S PORTS

The Royal Navy battlecruiser HMS *New Zealand* arrived in Wellington as part of a 10-week tour during which an estimated 500,000 New Zealanders inspected the vessel. Ten sailors deserted in Auckland, while boats ferried Dunedin sightseers to the ship because it was too large to enter Otago Harbour.

The ship was a gift from New Zealand, which funded its construction for the Royal Navy. Commissioned in November 1912, it cost the country £1.7 million (equivalent to $270 million today).

Māori presented the ship's captain, Lionel Halsey, with a piupiu (flax kilt) and a greenstone hei tiki (pendant) to ward off evil. He wore them during the early part of the First World War, and they were on board the ship during the Battle of Jutland in May 1916 (see 31 May). Some attributed *New Zealand*'s reputation as a lucky ship to the presence of these items. The ageing battlecruiser returned to New Zealand in 1919 during a tour of the Dominions. New Zealand finally finished paying for the ship in 1944, 22 years after it was sold for scrap.

Māori presented the ship's captain, Lionel Halsey, with a piupiu (flax kilt) and a greenstone hei tiki (pendant) to ward off evil.

The battlecruiser HMS *New Zealand* **in Wellington Harbour, 1913.**

13 April 1896

NATIONAL COUNCIL OF WOMEN FORMED

Three years after New Zealand became the first self-governing country in which all women could vote, representatives of 11 women's groups met in Christchurch's Provincial Council Buildings to form the National Council of Women (NCW). The NCW aimed to:

unite all organised societies of women for mutual counsel and co-operation in the attainment of justice and freedom for women, and for all that made for the good of humanity; to encourage the formation of societies of women engaged in trades, professions, and in social and political work; and to affiliate with other national councils of women for the purpose of facilitating international Conferences and co-operation.

The NCW's first office holders were heavyweights of the suffrage movement: Kate Sheppard was the president, Marion Hatton, Annie Schnackenberg, Margaret Sievwright and Anna Stout were vice-presidents, Ada Wells was the secretary, and Wilhelmina Sherriff Bain was the treasurer.

In the 21st century, the NCW still works in the interests of women, specifically for gender equality, and represents over 100,000 women in its member organisations.

The first meeting of the National Council of Women, Christchurch, 1896.

UNEMPLOYED RIOT ROCKS QUEEN STREET

Auckland's Queen Street riot was by far the most destructive of the disturbances that rocked the four main centres in the 'angry autumn' of 1932.

Trouble first flared in Dunedin in January and again in April. Worse soon followed in Auckland on 14 April when a large crowd of unemployed relief workers joined Post and Telegraph Association members marching to a Town Hall meeting, swelling their numbers to around 15,000. Angry at being turned away from the overflowing hall, some demonstrators scuffled with the police barring the entrance. When a leader of the unemployed, Jim Edwards, rose to speak — apparently to urge calm — a policeman struck him down. The crowd erupted and surged down Queen Street. Armed with fence palings and stones taken from a mini-golf course in Civic Square, they smashed hundreds of shop windows and looted jewellery, liquor, clothing and tobacco.

One chemist shop was cleaned out of contraceptives; a man was seen staggering off with a grandfather clock on his back, and the department store Milne & Choyce 'grieved over the spoliation of their very costly wax "dummies"'.

Reinforced by armed navy sailors and volunteers, the police regained control of the central city several hours later. Hundreds of people were injured, including several policemen, and 35 people were arrested for looting. Ninety-eight Waikato Territorial Army troops and 1000 volunteer ('special') police constables bolstered government forces the next day, but violence flared again that night. As crowds massed in Karangahape Road, scuffles broke out and more windows were smashed. By the end of the night, there had been another 50 injuries and 35 arrests.

Auckland's riots were followed by further disturbances in Christchurch and Wellington in early May 1932. A state of siege settled on the main centres, with 'specials' patrolling the street, all outdoor meetings banned and shop windows boarded up for weeks, but there was no more major trouble.

BORN ON THIS DAY

Alan MacDiarmid,
1927–2007,
scientist

Street scene during the Queen Street disturbances, 1932.

15 April
1868

FIRST MĀORI MPS ELECTED TO PARLIAMENT

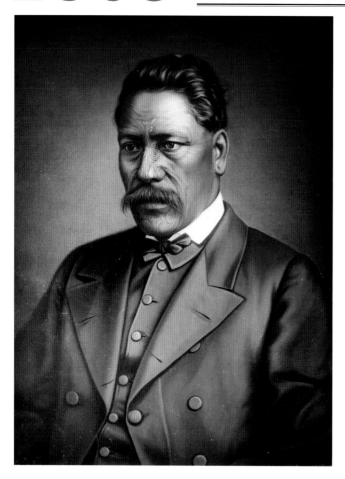

The Maori Representation Act 1867 established four Māori seats in the House of Representatives, initially for a period of five years. The act gave the vote to all Māori males aged 21 and over.

This innovation was intended to bring Māori into mainstream political life, albeit in a limited way. It was also, initially at least, seen as a way of rewarding those iwi who had supported the Crown during the New Zealand Wars.

The first elections were held in 1868, with nomination day in all four Māori seats set for 15 April. Frederick Nene Russell (Northern Maori) and Mete Kīngi Te Rangi Paetahi (Western Maori) were elected unopposed. In Eastern Maori, there were two candidates and Tāreha Te Moananui was elected after a show of hands. In Southern Maori, there were three candidates and a poll was demanded. This was won in June by John Patterson (also known as Hōne Paratene Tamanui a Rangi).

The experiment was extended in 1872 and, four years later, the Māori seats were established on a permanent basis.

Tāreha Te Moananui became the first MP for Eastern Maori in 1868.

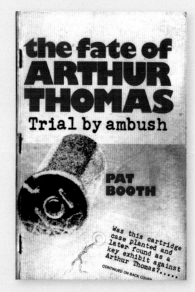

The cover of journalist Pat Booth's book, *The Fate of Arthur Thomas: trial by ambush*.

ARTHUR ALLAN THOMAS CONVICTED OF CREWE MURDERS – AGAIN
16 April 1973

Waikato farmer Arthur Allan Thomas was found guilty — for the second time — of the 1970 murder of his neighbours Harvey and Jeanette Crewe at Pukekawa. Searchers discovered the Crewes' bullet-ridden bodies in the Waikato River three months after their disappearance in June 1970. The killer spared their two-year-old daughter, discovered in her cot by her grandfather five days after her parents went missing. Originally convicted of double murder in 1971, Thomas protested his innocence and appealed. A protracted legal struggle ensued, culminating in a retrial in March 1973. Despite doubts over police evidence, especially a cartridge case found in the Crewes' garden, Thomas was convicted for a second time. Influential books by journalists Pat Booth and David Yallop contributed to the public perception that Thomas's conviction was unjust. In December 1979 he received an official pardon after nine years in jail. In 1980 a Royal Commission concluded that police had committed 'an unspeakable outrage' by planting the cartridge case that had been key to the original conviction. Thomas received $950,000 (equivalent to $4.5 million today) in compensation.

GENERAL GATES SENT TO SYDNEY UNDER GUARD

The American sealer *General Gates* — named for a War of Independence general and commanded by Captain Abimelech Riggs — had sailed from Boston in October 1818. In July 1819 the *General Gates* brought the missionaries Samuel Marsden and John Butler from Sydney to the Bay of Islands after Riggs induced 11 convicts to sign on as crew. Riggs dropped off two of these men with a sealing gang on an isolated island in the Southern Ocean, but the other nine were still on board when HMS *Dromedary* visited the Bay of Islands in April 1820 during a voyage to investigate the suitability of New Zealand timber for Royal Navy spars. Riggs had treated the men badly and his cover story soon unravelled. In the first official coercive operation undertaken in New Zealand, he and the *General Gates* were seized and returned to Sydney, where Riggs was fined heavily and the vessel detained for nine months.

Painting of the missionary establishment at Kerikeri, New Zealand, by French artist Antoine Chazal, c. 1824–26.

SAMUEL REVANS PRINTS FIRST NEWSPAPER
18 April 1840

The first newspapers published in New Zealand rolled off Samuel Revans' printing press a month after his arrival at Port Nicholson (Wellington). Revans had published the first issue of the *New Zealand Gazette* in London in August 1839, just before the New Zealand Company's emigrant ships departed. He was also secretary to the colonists' council, and the news in the first New Zealand issue was semi-official. Advertisements touted useful items such as 'Manning's portable colonial cottages' and 'pumps suitable for emigrants and foreigners, made in the simplest manner'. Lists of consignments also featured prominently, with spirits clearly in high demand. 'All persons taking up their residence on the Beach' — or leaving it — were asked to notify the Land Office. The settlement founded less than three months before was in the process of shifting to Wellington because of recurrent flooding at Petone ('the Beach'). The entrepreneurial Revans also ran a timber yard, a stationery business and later a farm. The *Gazette* went through several changes of name, each title less profitable than the last, before closing in 1844.

BORN ON THIS DAY

Mabel Howard,
1894–1972,
first woman Cabinet minister

1893

STATE BUYS CHEVIOT ESTATE

In the 1890s the Liberal government, especially Minister of Lands John McKenzie, were determined to 'burst up' large estates for settlement by prospective small farmers, who were among its key supporters. The first property purchased under this policy was the 34,300-hectare Cheviot Estate in North Canterbury. The night after it came into government ownership, the stables, granary and store were destroyed by fire.

The Liberal Party had won power following the 1890 general election on a platform which included promoting closer settlement by selling Crown land only to genuine farmers, extending state leasehold rather than offering land freehold, purchasing large estates for subdivision, introducing a graduated land tax, and providing cheap finance for farm development.

In general, the policy was a success. Between 1892 and 1911, the Crown offered 3.4 million hectares of land for settlement, subdivided into 33,000 holdings. This included 209 estates totalling 486,000 hectares bought for a total of £6 million (about $1 billion today) and subdivided into 4800 holdings. The prices offered were mostly generous, and provisions for compulsory purchase were used just 13 times.

Painting of Cheviot Hills homestead by Charles Barraud, 1870s.

ALLISON ROE WINS BOSTON MARATHON
20 April 1981

1981 was a memorable year for Allison Roe. In April she became the first New Zealand woman to win the prestigious Boston race, burning off American star Patti Catalano and taking nearly eight minutes off the course record for the 42.2-kilometre course, running 2 hours 26 minutes 46 seconds. Six months later, she overtook Grete Waitz to win the New York City Marathon. Her time of 2:25.29 was thought to be a world's best for the marathon, but the course proved to be 150 metres short. Legendary coach Arthur Lydiard had dismissed Roe's prospects as a marathoner, feeling that at 1.73 metres she was too tall. Her victory in two of the five 'majors' in one year showed that on this rare occasion Lydiard's judgement was faulty. The marathon for women was included at the summer Olympics for the first time in Los Angeles in 1984. By then injury had unfortunately curtailed Roe's career. Her 1981 New York time remained an unofficial New Zealand best until 2010, when Kimberley Smith ran eight seconds faster in the London Marathon.

Allison Roe on her way to victory in the Boston Marathon, 1981.

COURT THEATRE STAGES FIRST PLAY

It was opening night for *The Prime of Miss Jean Brodie* in Christchurch's Provincial Council buildings. Based on Muriel Spark's novel, the play was produced and directed by Yvette Bromley. She and Mervyn Thompson co-founded The Court, Christchurch's first professional company, following the lead of Wellington's Downstage and Auckland's Mercury. After performing in temporary venues, from 1972 until 1976 The Court was based in four separate locations, including the Orange Hall in Worcester Street. For the next 35 years, its home was in the former Canterbury University engineering school buildings, which became part of the Christchurch Arts Centre. For much of this era Elric Hooper was artistic director, a role Ross Gumbley assumed in 2006. The February 2011 earthquake made the Arts Centre unusable. The players once again trod temporary stages until The Court reopened in a former grain silo in Addington that December. 'The Shed' houses all departments of the company, and the auditorium seats 300.

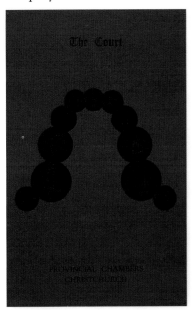

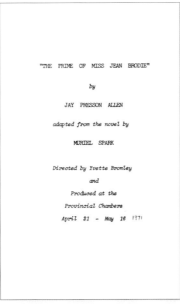

"THE PRIME OF MISS JEAN BRODIE"

by

JAY PRESSON ALLEN

adapted from the novel by

MURIEL SPARK

Directed by Yvette Bromley

and

Produced at the

Provincial Chambers

April 21 – May 16 1971

Programme for *The Prime of Miss Jean Brodie*, Court Theatre, 1971.

RĀTANA AND LABOUR SEAL ALLIANCE
22 April 1936

The alliance between the Rātana Church and the Labour Party was cemented at an historic meeting between Tahupōtiki Wiremu Rātana and Prime Minister Michael Joseph Savage. In 1928, 10 years after his first religious visions, T.W. Rātana announced his intention to enter politics, referring to the four Māori seats as the 'four quarters' of his body. He aimed to win these seats by harnessing the voting power of his followers, who by 1934 were said to number 40,000. In 1932, Eruera Tirikātene became the first Rātana MP when he won a by-election for Southern Maori. He was instructed to support the Labour opposition. Rātana favoured the Labour Party because it had consulted his supporters when devising its Māori policy. When Labour won a landslide election victory in 1935, the Rātana movement took a second seat, Western Maori. In 1943, the Rātana–Labour alliance succeeded in capturing all 'four quarters' when Tiaki Omana defeated Sir Āpirana Ngata for the Eastern Maori seat. Labour was to hold all the Māori seats for the next 50 years.

Tahupōtiki Wiremu Rātana, c. 1935.

23 April 1979

BLAIR PEACH KILLED IN LONDON

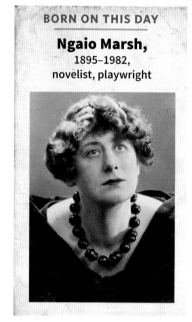

New Zealander Blair Peach died during a clash between police and protesters at a 1979 anti-fascism rally in Southall, London. The 33-year-old special-needs teacher and member of the Anti-Nazi League suffered head injuries during the protest and died later in hospital. Peach's death transformed him into a political martyr in Britain. Just days after the Southall rally, 10,000 people marched past the place where his body had been found, and a similar number attended Peach's funeral in June 1979. In 1986 the Borough of Ealing named a Southall primary school in his honour. London's Metropolitan Police Service finally released its report into Peach's death in 2010. Police investigators concluded that Peach had had his skull crushed by an 'unauthorised weapon', possibly a lead cosh or police radio. The blow

was 'almost certainly' delivered by an officer of its elite riot squad, the Special Patrol Group (SPG), but the individual's identity could not be determined with certainty because of collusion among SPG members.

Blair Peach.

23 April 1983

PRINCE WILLIAM MEETS BUZZY BEE

Among the highlights of the April 1983 royal tour were photographs of the Prince and Princess of Wales' infant son, Prince William, playing with New Zealand's iconic Buzzy Bee toy. These family snapshots, taken on the lawn at Government House in Auckland, made front pages around the world.

Prince Charles and Princess Diana's visit to Australia and New Zealand attracted considerable public attention. The princess was the focus of much of it, with Charles detecting disappointment among the crowd on his side of the street during walkabouts. The presence of nine-month-old William was another highlight, as it was the first time a royal prince had accompanied his parents to this country.

Over 40,000 screaming children welcomed the royals at Auckland's Eden Park on 18 April, where Charles happily announced an extra holiday for New Zealand schools. Over the next 12 days, the royal couple moved up and down the country, attending ballets, state banquets and Anzac Day ceremonies, visiting marae, paddling in waka (canoes), and planting numerous trees.

Prince Charles, Princess Diana and Prince William, Auckland.

PRINCE OF WALES ARRIVES FOR NEW ZEALAND TOUR

King George V's son, Edward, Prince of Wales (who later reigned briefly as Edward VIII), visited New Zealand partly to thank the Dominion for its contribution to the Empire's war effort. Arriving in Auckland on the battlecruiser HMS *Renown* on 24 April, he spent four weeks travelling the country aboard a lavishly appointed Royal Train and by motor coach, visiting 50 towns between Auckland and Invercargill.

The dashing young 'playboy' prince was mobbed by adoring crowds everywhere he went, and was said to have shaken more than 20,000 hands during his visit. But he was less impressed by his hosts, complaining in a letter to his mistress: 'We managed to keep fairly cheery despite never 1 hr free from returned soldiers & schoolchildren! Christ their cheers & "God saves" and "God blesses" get on my nerves.'

The prince saved his worst insults for the 'pricelessly pompous' and 'grossly fat' governor-general, Lord Liverpool: 'It makes me so angry to have my job bitched by other people, darling, especially by hopeless _____s like "Liver"!!'

Edward, Prince of Wales meeting returned soldiers, Ashburton, 1920.

1915

GALLIPOLI LANDINGS

Each year on Anzac Day, New Zealanders (and Australians) mark the anniversary of the Gallipoli landings of 25 April 1915. On that day, thousands of young men, far from their homes, landed on the beaches of the Gallipoli Peninsula, in what is now Turkey. British and French forces made the main landing at Cape Helles on the tip of the peninsula, while General William Birdwood's Australian and New Zealand Army Corps, commonly known as Anzacs, landed 20 kilometres north. New Zealand troops, who were part of the New Zealand and Australian Division under Major-General Alexander Godley, followed the Australians ashore on the first morning of the assault.

In the face of vigorous Ottoman Turkish defence, no significant Allied advance proved possible. The fighting quickly degenerated into trench warfare, with the Anzacs holding a tenuous perimeter. The troops endured heat, flies, the stench of rotting corpses, lack of water, dysentery and other illnesses, and a sense of hopelessness.

An attempt to break the stalemate in August failed, though not without a stirring New Zealand effort in briefly capturing part of the high ground at Chunuk Bair (see 8 August). In this assault, men of the Māori Contingent, recently arrived from garrison duty in Malta, took part in the first attack by Māori soldiers outside New Zealand. With the failure of the August offensive, the stalemate resumed.

Ultimately, the Allies cut their losses, evacuating all troops from Gallipoli by early January 1916. By the time the campaign ended, more than 130,000 men had died: at least 87,000 Ottoman soldiers and 44,000 Allied soldiers, including more than 8700 Australians. Among the dead were 2779 New Zealanders, about a sixth of all those who had landed on the peninsula.

In the wider story of the First World War, the Gallipoli campaign made no large mark. The number of dead, although horrific, pales in comparison with the death toll in France and Belgium during the war. Yet the campaign remains significant in New Zealand, Australia and Turkey, where it is commonly viewed as a formative moment in each country's national history.

BORN ON THIS DAY

Keith Elliott,
1916–1989,
VC winner, clergyman

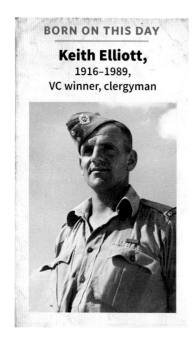

The Landing at Anzac,
Charles Dixon, 1915.

FIRST ANZAC DAY

Communities across New Zealand and overseas gathered to commemorate the first anniversary of the Gallipoli landings. New Zealand observed a half-day holiday from 1 p.m., with ceremonies held throughout the country. The mood was solemn; race meetings were deferred and cinemas stayed shut until late afternoon.

The first Anzac Day provided an opportunity for the country's political leaders to remind young men of their duty to volunteer for war service. Prime Minister William Massey concluded a speech at Wellington's Town Hall by calling for more young men to come forward for King and country.

Large crowds attended local ceremonies; there were 2000 at a religious service in Ashburton and around 8000 at the dedication of a memorial flagpole at Petone railway station. At Tīnui in Wairarapa, locals erected a large cross on top of a hill overlooking the village. New Zealanders took part in commemorative activities in Malta, Egypt and London, where crowds lined the streets to watch 2000 New Zealand and Australian soldiers march to Westminster Abbey for a solemn service.

The mood was solemn; race meetings were deferred and cinemas stayed shut until late afternoon.

Anzac Day commemoration at Petone, 1916.

26 April 1943

NEW ZEALAND SHIP TORPEDOED IN TASMAN SEA

Like many New Zealand merchant ships, the Union Steam Ship Company freighter *Limerick* undertook military missions during the Second World War, carrying munitions, food and equipment between New Zealand, Australia, North America and the Middle East.

On the night of 25/26 April 1943, the *Limerick* was sailing from Sydney to Brisbane. Around 1 a.m., it was torpedoed by the Japanese submarine *I-177* off Cape Byron. Two of the crew — a New Zealand engineer and an Australian officer — went down with the ship. The other 70 on board were rescued after spending 10 hours in lifeboats or on rafts. Although the Tasman Sea was not a major hunting ground for enemy submarines, in 1942 and 1943 up to 10 long-range Japanese 'I-boats' operated off Australia's east coast, sinking 18 Allied merchant ships. As well as the *Limerick*, New Zealand's Union Steam Ship Company lost the small freighter *Kalingo*, which was torpedoed by *I-21* 110 kilometres east of Sydney on 18 January 1943. Again, two crew members were lost; the remainder were rescued after three days adrift in a lifeboat.

Crewman Allan Wyllie on the *Limerick*.

MOEHANGA BECOMES FIRST MĀORI TO VISIT ENGLAND

Moehanga of Ngāpuhi became the first recorded Māori visitor to England when the whaler *Ferret* berthed in London. Moehanga (or Te Mahanga) had boarded the *Ferret* when it visited the Bay of Islands late in 1805.

While Māori had travelled as far as Tahiti and Australia in the late 18th century, Moehanga was the first to reach the northern hemisphere. He took a keen interest in the sights and people of the great city, which had a population of more than a million. He met Earl Fitzwilliam and also (he claimed subsequently) King George III and Queen Charlotte, who apparently gave him tools and money.

Moehanga sailed on the *Ferret* when it left for Port Jackson (Sydney) in June. After spending the summer in Sydney, he returned to his home in the Bay of Islands in March 1807.

Moehanga was still living in the Bay of Islands in 1827, when he was described as the uncle of Te Whareumu, the Ngāti Manu leader at Kororāreka (now Russell).

Ngāpuhi chiefs Waikato (at left) and Hongi Hika visited London with the missionary Thomas Kendall in 1820.

FIRST BRITISH RUGBY TOURISTS TAKE THE FIELD

The first British rugby team to tour New Zealand played its first match, against Otago, at Dunedin's Caledonian Ground in front of 10,000 spectators. Behind at halftime, the visitors were expected to tire. Instead they played 'harder and rougher', scoring two dropped goals and a try to win 8–3. They won a return fixture four days later 4–3.

Unlike later British Lions teams, this was not a full-strength side: only three of the 21 players had represented one of the four home unions. The (English) Rugby Football Union refused to sanction the privately organised tour, ruling it a commercial enterprise that rendered the players professionals — a cardinal sin in the eyes of upper-class administrators. Rugby unions in Australasia, however, welcomed any sportsmen from 'Home'.

The British team travelled north, losing only two of their seven matches before sailing to Australia. After playing 35 matches across the ditch, they returned to New Zealand in September for another 10 matches. The British did not meet a representative New Zealand team, but defeated an under-strength South Island XV twice.

The (English) Rugby Football Union refused to sanction the privately organised tour, ruling it a commercial enterprise that rendered the players professionals — a cardinal sin in the eyes of upper-class administrators.

The British rugby team that toured New Zealand, 1888.

ASSAULT ON GATE PĀ REPULSED

29 April
1864

The British attacked the Ngāi Te Rangi stronghold of Pukehinahina (Gate Pā), defended by just 230 warriors, after a heavy artillery bombardment. When Gate Pā was built within 5 kilometres of Tauranga to provoke a British response, Lieutenant-General Duncan Cameron duly arrived from Auckland with reinforcements. On 28 April, 1700 troops marched towards the pā, which was shelled from daybreak next day.

The artillery bombardment was the heaviest of the New Zealand Wars, with huge Armstrong guns supported by howitzers. But Gate Pā withstood the barrage. Firing few shots, the defenders created the impression that the shelling had largely wiped them out.

In fact, 15 Māori at most were killed by the bombardment. When a British raiding party assaulted the pā, it became disoriented in a maze of trenches and was routed by warriors firing from concealed positions. Within 10 minutes, the storming party suffered 100 casualties and fled.

The disaster required scapegoats. The assault party were branded as cowards, the army blamed naval troops, and Cameron was accused of being either too rash or too timid.

Horatio Robley's watercolour depicts the attack on Gate Pā by imperial forces.

1917

WILLIAM SANDERS WINS NEW ZEALAND'S ONLY NAVAL VICTORIA CROSS

William Sanders received the Victoria Cross (VC) for bravery during a German U-boat (submarine) attack on his ship. He became the first — and only — New Zealander to win the British Empire's highest military decoration in a naval action.

Sanders, a Royal Naval Reserve officer, assumed command of the schooner HMS *Prize* in February 1917. *Prize* was a Q-ship, an armed merchant vessel designed to deceive and destroy enemy submarines. *Prize* was attacked by German submarine *U-93* during a patrol south-west of Ireland. The U-boat shelled the schooner for nearly half an hour, hitting it several times, before approaching. As the shells rained down, Sanders crawled along the deck, organising his crew. When *U-93* was just 70 yards (64 metres) away, *Prize* hoisted its naval ensign, dropped screens hiding its guns, and returned fire, destroying the submarine's forward gun and conning tower.

Q-ship secrecy meant military authorities did not reveal the details of Sanders' VC award until after the war. Sanders was not around to receive the accolades. He and his crew perished in another U-boat attack on the night of 13/14 August 1917.

The U-boat shelled the schooner for nearly half an hour, hitting it several times, before approaching.

Cigarette-card portrait of William Sanders.

'KING DICK' SEDDON BECOMES PREMIER

English-born Richard Seddon became premier following the death of John Ballance. Immortalised as 'King Dick' (in part for his autocratic style), Seddon dominated the New Zealand political landscape for the next 13 years. He remains this country's longest-serving prime minister. Seddon was first elected to Parliament in 1879 for Hokitika, and later represented the Westland seat. In the House, he was notoriously long-winded and ridiculed as boorish. But the astute politician turned his apparent lack of sophistication to his advantage, presenting himself as a man of the people.

After winning the 1893 election, Seddon entrenched the major Liberal reforms to land, labour and taxation previously thwarted by the upper house. He even took credit for enfranchising women, a reform he had opposed.

Seddon's five consecutive election victories have never been matched. At his peak, he exercised almost one-man rule, but the quality of his ministry declined as he monopolised important portfolios and meddled in the rest. New Zealanders were shocked when he died while returning from Australia in 1906; famously, his last shipboard telegram read: 'Just leaving for God's own country.'

New Zealanders were shocked when he died while returning from Australia in 1906; famously, his last shipboard telegram read: 'Just leaving for God's own country.'

Caricature of Richard Seddon, 1900.

NEW ZEALAND'S LAST ELECTRIC TRAM TRIP

Tram no. 252, displaying the message 'End of the line' and driven by Wellington Mayor Frank Kitts, travelled from Thorndon to Newtown zoo. Large crowds lined the streets to witness the end of electric trams in New Zealand.

In 1878, Wellington had been the first city in the southern hemisphere to operate a steam tram service (see 24 August), but this proved unpopular and by 1892 the city had reverted to horse-drawn trams.

Facing financial problems, the Wellington City Tramways Company was purchased by the Wellington City Corporation (WCC) in 1900. Two years later the WCC decided to introduce electric trams. On 30 June 1904, the first electric tram ran from a new depot in Newtown to the northern side of the Basin Reserve. The system was later extended to the new Lambton railway station at the junction of Thorndon Quay and Featherston Street. In its heyday, Wellington's tramway network covered more than 52 kilometres. The increasing number of private cars and buses eventually forced the closure of New Zealand's last electric tramway system in 1964.

The second-to-last tram at the railway station stop on its way to Newtown, 2 May 1964.

NEW ZEALAND'S FIRST WOMAN DOCTOR REGISTERED
3 May 1897

Margaret Cruickshank, the first female doctor registered in New Zealand, practised in Waimate, South Canterbury, until her death from influenza in 1918. Cruickshank studied medicine at the University of Otago Medical School, where she became the second woman in New Zealand to complete a medical course in 1897, a year after Emily Siedeberg. Following graduation, she accepted a position in Dr H.C. Barclay's medical practice in Waimate, where she worked for the rest of her life. She visited backblocks patients by horse and gig, and cycled or walked shorter distances. Attending to accident victims and assisting during childbirth were among her most frequent duties. Under the auspices of charitable organisation St John, she offered first-aid classes to 'ladies'. She worked tirelessly during the influenza pandemic that began in October 1918 before falling victim to the disease herself on 28 November. In 1923, residents of Waimate erected a memorial statue in honour of Cruickshank on which was inscribed, 'The Beloved Physician / Faithful unto Death'. It is one of New Zealand's few memorials to a woman other than Queen Victoria.

Margaret Cruickshank's graduation photo.

MARION DU FRESNE ARRIVES IN BAY OF ISLANDS

Du Fresne's was the second French expedition to visit New Zealand, following that of de Surville in 1769 (see 24 March). Du Fresne's acceptance of the philosopher Jean-Jacques Rousseau's beliefs about 'noble savages' was to have unfortunate consequences.

The crews of the *Mascarin* and *Marquis de Castries* spent five weeks exploring the Bay of Islands and repairing their ships. Their many interactions with Māori gave them ample opportunity to unwittingly give offence.

They violated tapu by fishing in a bay where bones were scraped before being laid to rest, and they unknowingly allowed themselves to be used by one iwi to diminish the status of another. Their lengthy sojourn placed strains on the local economy. Māori may have feared the establishment of a permanent French settlement.

In mid-June, local Māori killed du Fresne and 24 of his crew. In reprisal, the French killed up to 250 Māori, burned several settlements and destroyed canoes and other resources. The French survivors were able to provide many insights into Māori society. Some communication had been possible, as they had brought a Tahitian vocabulary with them.

Painting by Charles Meryon showing the death of Marion du Fresne.

DOG TAX WAR NARROWLY AVERTED
5 May 1898

War threatened sleepy Hokianga as government troops marched towards armed Māori 'rebels'. This was the climax of widespread Māori opposition to dog registration. Most Māori had little involvement with the cash economy and owned many dogs, especially for hunting. They saw the annual 'dog tax' of 2s 6d per dog as discrimination. In April 1898 a relative of Hōne Tōia of Te Mahurehure told officials that his people would not pay land, dog or other taxes — and would continue to shoot pigeons out of season. After armed Māori visited Rāwene, Richard Seddon's government rushed troops and a gunboat from Auckland. As Lieutenant-Colonel Stewart Newall's force trudged towards Waimā, Hōne Heke Ngāpua MP urged Hōne Tōia to surrender. In the nick of time, Tōia sent a messenger to call off a planned ambush. Next day the Waimā leaders laid down their arms. Sixteen men, including Tōia, were arrested and pleaded guilty to illegal assembly; the 'ringleaders' were jailed for 18 months. The fines and taxes were paid after the authorities prudently awarded Te Mahurehure a contract to produce railway sleepers.

Police with Māori arrested for taking part in the 'Dog Tax Rebellion'.

COLONIAL TROOPS INVADE THE UREWERA

The invasion was intended to punish Tūhoe for supporting Te Kooti Arikirangi Te Tūruki, whose 'rebel' force it had sheltered after their defeat at Ngātapa, inland from Poverty Bay, in January. The expedition was also intended to send a signal that there was no sanctuary — however remote from Pākehā settlement — for disaffected Māori.

Three columns of Armed Constabulary and allied Māori were to converge on Ruatāhuna, deep in the interior. The 1300 men outnumbered the entire population of the Urewera. Two columns started in Bay of Plenty, while a third on the east coast got no further than Waikaremoana.

The Rangitāiki column first saw action on 6 May near today's village of Te Whāiti, killing five Tūhoe. After the two columns met at Ruatāhuna on 9 May, the troops spent several days destroying settlements, crops and food supplies.

This invasion of the Urewera was followed by another three-pronged attack in 1870 and several subsequent Māori incursions in search of Te Kooti, who hid in Tūhoe territory with his dwindling force even after he was renounced by the iwi.

Captain Thomas Porter with his Māori auxiliaries outside a stockade and blockhouse near Rotorua.

The 1300 men outnumbered the entire population of the Urewera.

DEVASTATING LANDSLIDE AT LAKE TAUPŌ

A devastating landslide obliterated the Ngāti Tūwharetoa village of Te Rapa on the south-west shore of Lake Taupō. Sixty people were killed, including the paramount chief Mananui Te Heuheu Tūkino II. This remains New Zealand's highest death toll from a landslide.

Te Rapa sat below the volcanic springs of Mt Kākaramea. The missionary Richard Taylor recorded that an 'unusually rainy season occasioned a large landslip' on the mountain. The slip dammed a stream which, three days later, 'burst its barriers, and, with irresistible force, swept rocks, trees and earth with it into the lake'. The avalanche of debris buried Te Rapa and only a few people managed to escape.

In 1910, another landslide killed one person in a new village near the old site of Te Rapa. After this second event, the village was abandoned. The source of the landslides was an unstable geothermal area known as the Hipaua Steaming Cliffs. This still causes problems for road engineers working on State Highway 41, which passes between the cliffs and Lake Taupō.

The site of the 1846 landslide in the 1990s.

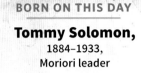

BORN ON THIS DAY

Tommy Solomon,
1884–1933,
Moriori leader

'CHERYL MOANA MARIE' HITS NO. 1

Pop singer John Rowles established himself as an international star in the late 1960s. His hit single 'Cheryl Moana Marie' sold a million copies worldwide. After starting out in an Auckland club band, Rowles 'crossed the ditch' to perform in Melbourne and Sydney. In 1966 he began working with Kiwi promoter Graham Dent. A new hairstyle and mod clothes saw the good-looking boy from Kawerau make a successful appearance on Australian television.

His big break came after he moved to England in late 1967. His hit songs 'If I Only Had Time' and 'Hush, Not a Word to Mary' featured prominently in the British top-20 singles charts.

Now a star, Rowles returned to New Zealand, performing to sell-out crowds. In late 1969 he released the album *Cheryl Moana Marie*, with 'Cheryl Moana Marie'/'I Was a Boy' reaching no. 1 in New Zealand.

During the 1970s and early 1980s, he regularly performed in Australia, the United States and New Zealand. His last top-10 chart success in New Zealand came in 1981, with his version of 'Island in the Sun'.

Poster advertising a John Rowles concert at Wellington Town Hall, March 1970.

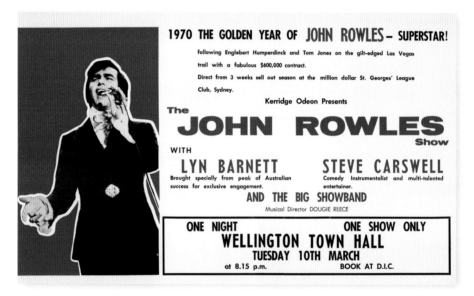

FIRST SCHOOL JOURNAL PUBLISHED
9 May 1907

New Zealand pupils were for the first time able to read a schoolbook published in their own country. Inspector-General of Schools George Hogben initiated the quarterly *School Journal* as a free publication containing information on history, geography and civics. This was a cheaper option than publishing several separate textbooks. Until 1939, when a School Publications Branch was formed, the *School Journal* was the Department of Education's sole publication for children. Learning Media published the *School Journal* for the Ministry of Education from 1993 until 2013, when it moved to a private publisher, Lift Education. Believed to be the longest-running serial publication for children in the world, the *School Journal* continues to provide seven- to 13-year-olds with reading material that is relevant to their lives. Around 750,000 copies are published annually in four parts. Many of New Zealand's foremost authors and illustrators have had their work published in the *School Journal*, including Rita Angus, James K. Baxter, Alistair Campbell, Russell Clark, Jack Lasenby, Margaret Mahy and E. Mervyn Taylor.

School Journal cover, 1916.

ALL-WHITE ALL BLACKS LEAVE FOR SOUTH AFRICA

Despite protests, the controversial rugby tour went ahead. The issue of sporting ties with South Africa would eventually split the country in 1981 (see 12 September). The All Blacks first toured South Africa, with its entrenched racial segregation, in 1928. Although Māori had always been eligible to represent New Zealand, the New Zealand Rugby Football Union chose not to select them to play in South Africa. In 1928 this meant leaving behind players like the legendary George Nēpia. No players identifiable as Māori would tour South Africa until 1970 and, even then, they did so as 'honorary whites'.

In 1960 nearly 160,000 people signed a petition opposing that year's tour by an 'all-white All Blacks' team. Groups like the Citizens' All Black Tour Association campaigned with the slogan, 'No Maoris — No Tour'. Others argued that politics had no place in sport. In the end, Wilson Whineray's team left as planned, their aircraft narrowly missing demonstrators who were sprinting across the runway at Whenuapai airport.

The All Blacks lost the test series 2–1, with one test drawn.

ALL BLACK–MAORI ISSUE

SIGN THE

PROTEST PETITION

AGAINST RACIAL DISCRIMINATION

Poster, New Zealand Citizens' All Black Tour Association, 1959.

. . . nearly 160,000 people signed a petition opposing that year's tour by an 'all-white All Blacks' team.

CHARLES UPHAM PRESENTED WITH HIS FIRST VICTORIA CROSS
11 May 1945

New Zealand's most-decorated soldier, Charles Upham, received the first of his two VCs — won for outstanding gallantry and leadership during the Battle of Crete in 1941 — from King George VI at Buckingham Palace. Later that year Upham would earn a Bar to his VC for his actions at Ruweisat Ridge, Egypt, in July 1942. Captured during this action, he had spent the intervening years as a prisoner of war. In 1944 an audacious solo effort to scale his camp's barbed-wire fences in broad daylight saw Upham transferred to the infamous Colditz camp for 'incorrigible' Allied officers. The intensely private Upham did not enjoy the attention that came with the awards. When informed of his first VC he was genuinely upset, believing others more deserving. Only by seeing it as recognition of his unit was Upham able to accept the medal. Upham's second VC was approved on 26 September 1945. He remains the only combat soldier to have twice been awarded the honour — the highest decoration for valour for which members of the New Zealand armed forces are eligible.

Charles Hazlitt Upham VC (centre right) congratulated by members of his platoon.

12 May
1971

ANTI-VIETNAM WAR PROTESTS IN AUCKLAND

Anti-war protesters disrupted a civic reception in Auckland for New Zealand soldiers returning from the Vietnam War.

The civic parade was led by the Band of the Royal New Zealand Artillery, followed by Land Rovers carrying the gunners of 161 Battery and troopers from New Zealand's Special Air Service. The march was relatively uneventful until the column reached the reviewing platform outside Auckland Town Hall.

As the parade approached the platform, red paint bombs and firecrackers were thrown on the road. Demonstrators used red paint to symbolise bloodshed in Vietnam. Several paint-covered protesters broke from the crowd and sat on the road. Despite forcing the band to alter course, they caused only a momentary disruption before police removed them.

New Zealand's involvement in the Vietnam War aroused considerable public debate. By 1971 up to 35,000 people were protesting on the streets. Many argued that the conflict was a civil war in which New Zealand should play no part. They wanted this country to follow an independent path in foreign policy, not take its cue from the United States.

Police lead away an anti-Vietnam War protester during the parade for 161 Battery, Auckland, 1971.

NATIONAL PARTY FOUNDED

Following their crushing defeat by the Labour Party in the 1935 general election, the remnants of the United–Reform coalition government met in Wellington on 13–14 May 1936 to establish a new 'anti-socialist' party.

The conference in the Dominion Farmers' Institute Building was attended by 11 members of the Dominion Executive of the National Political Federation (the body that had run United–Reform's 1935 campaign), 232 delegates from around the country, representatives of women's and youth organisations, and most of the re-elected anti-Labour MPs.

The party was named the New Zealand National Party to signal a clean break with United and Reform, which had been discredited by their handling of the Depression. Adam Hamilton was elected as its first leader in October 1936.

The National Party grew quickly and by the time of its third annual conference in August 1938 it boasted more than 100,000 members. Even so, it would take a further 11 years for the party to win office for the first time.

National Party members of Parliament, c. 1937.

NEW ZEALAND WINS SAILING'S AMERICA'S CUP

Few New Zealanders in 1995 could have avoided television commentator Peter Montgomery's line, 'the America's Cup is now New Zealand's cup!' The phrase was repeated endlessly as New Zealanders enjoyed a famous victory.

The 5–0 sweep achieved by *Black Magic* (*NZL 32*) over *Stars & Stripes* in San Diego was impressive. Their opponent, the controversial American helmsman Dennis Conner, was a four-time winner known as 'Mr America's Cup'.

Team New Zealand had made the finals of the Louis Vuitton challenger series in 1987 and 1992. In 1995 syndicate head Peter Blake assembled a dream team of New Zealand sailors. An extremely fast boat was superbly sailed by 1984 Olympic gold-medallist Russell Coutts, ably backed up by the astute tactician Brad Butterworth and navigator Tom Schnackenberg.

Five years later, in Auckland in 2000, Team New Zealand became the first team from a country outside the United States to successfully defend the America's Cup. A depleted Team New Zealand was well beaten by the Swiss syndicate Alinghi in 2003 and mounted unsuccessful challenges in 2007 and 2013. Emirates Team New Zealand won the trophy from Oracle Team USA in 2017.

America's Cup parade, Wellington, 26 May 1995.

PLUNKET SOCIETY FORMED

Dr Frederic Truby King helped form the Society for the Promotion of the Health of Women and Children at a meeting in Dunedin Town Hall. The society, later known as the Plunket Society after Lady Victoria Plunket, the wife of the governor and an ardent supporter, spread rapidly. Later that year, Plunket opened the first Karitane Home for Babies, in Dunedin. A further six Karitane hospitals were established to supplement home and clinic visits. These operated both as training bases for nurses and as care units for babies. By 1909 there were Plunket Society branches in all four main centres. Sixty more branches opened following a lecture tour by King in 1912.

Mothers were educated in 'domestic hygiene' and 'mothercraft' practices based on King's ideology of regular feeding, sleeping and bowel habits. The Plunket philosophy became parenting lore in New Zealand, and within three decades it was credited with giving this country the lowest infant mortality rate in the world.

Following his death in 1938, King became New Zealand's first private citizen to be honoured with a state funeral.

Dr Frederic Truby King with 'Madelaine' at the Karitane Hospital, Wellington, 1932.

WHANGANUI MAYOR SHOOTS POET
15 May 1920

The victim of the shooting, poet Walter D'Arcy Cresswell, alleged that Mayor Charles Mackay had made sexual advances towards him in the mayoral office and panicked when faced with the prospect of public exposure. The incident ended Mackay's 11-year career as mayor of Whanganui. D'Arcy Cresswell was only slightly injured. Later known to be gay himself, he may not have been an entirely innocent party. There were unsubstantiated rumours that he had tried to blackmail the mayor into resigning. Mackay was sentenced to 15 years' hard labour for attempted murder. His wife divorced him, the street named after him had its name changed, his portrait was removed from the council chambers and destroyed, and he was not mentioned in local histories for 50 years. Released from prison in 1926, Mackay travelled to England. In 1928 he moved to Berlin, where he worked as a reporter and English language teacher. He was accidentally shot and killed by a police officer while covering May Day riots in 1929.

Walter Cresswell, 1948.

EIGHT SOLDIERS KILLED IN ATTACK ON BOULCOTT FARM

D isagreements over the validity of land purchases by the New Zealand Company led to a series of skirmishes between local Māori and government forces in the Wellington region in 1846.

The prominent Ngāti Toa chief Te Rangihaeata backed local Māori who opposed European settlement in Hutt Valley. However, Te Mamaku of Ngāti Haua-te-rangi of Whanganui led the attack on the British outpost at Boulcott Farm (now within the suburb of Epuni). He had come to Hutt Valley with 200 warriors to support both Te Rangihaeata and kin in the area.

The taua (war party) crossed the Heretaunga (Hutt) River at dawn and surprised the garrison. Six soldiers were killed and two more Europeans were mortally wounded in the attack, a demoralising blow to the settler community. An armed patrol was ambushed by Māori near Taitā a month later, with four further fatalities. In July Governor George Grey responded by arresting Ngāti Toa's paramount chief, Te Rauparaha. Te Rangihaeata withdrew from Battle Hill above the Horokiri Valley in mid-August, effectively ending Ngāti Toa resistance in the Wellington region.

Six soldiers were killed and two more Europeans were mortally wounded in the attack, a demoralising blow to the settler community.

George Page painting of Boulcott's Stockade, 1846.

CATHOLIC BISHOP FOUND NOT GUILTY OF SEDITION

James Liston, the assistant bishop of Auckland, was found not guilty of sedition following a high-profile court case. He found himself in the dock after a St Patrick's Day address in which he questioned the Anglo-Irish treaty and described the Irish rebels of 1916 as having been 'murdered' by 'foreign' (meaning British) troops.

Many New Zealanders staunchly loyal to Britain took offence at these comments. The New Zealand Welfare League believed that the speech had engendered 'bitterness and strife amongst our people' and encouraged 'those whose efforts are directed to the destruction of the Empire'. New Zealand's Irish Catholic community rallied to the bishop's defence. In the end, an all-Protestant jury found Liston not guilty of sedition, with the rider that he had committed a 'grave indiscretion'.

Following Liston's acquittal, much of the bitterness surrounding the 'Irish issue' in New Zealand gradually dissipated. In 1929 Liston became bishop of Auckland, a role he held for over 40 years.

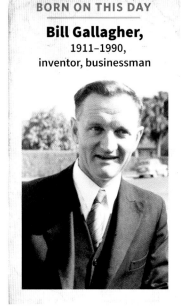

BORN ON THIS DAY

Bill Gallagher,
1911–1990,
inventor, businessman

. . . he questioned the Anglo-Irish treaty and described the Irish rebels of 1916 as having been 'murdered' by 'foreign' (meaning British) troops.

Cartoon about the Liston sedition trial.

GEORGE WILDER ESCAPES FROM PRISON

Geroge Wilder was a burglar who left apology and thank-you notes for his victims. He was at large for 65 days, becoming a renegade folk hero in the process.

Wilder was serving time for burglary and theft when he scaled one of New Plymouth Prison's highest walls in May 1962. His ability to stay one step ahead of the police while on the run caught the public imagination. The Howard Morrison Quartet later celebrated his exploits with their song 'George, the Wild(er) N.Z. Boy'. Recaptured in July 1962, he escaped on two further occasions, before breaking out of Mt Eden Prison with three others in January 1963. This time he managed to elude police for 172 days. Newspapers provided regular updates on his escapades before police finally caught him near Taupō.

Wilder escaped from Mt Eden again in February 1964. Unlike previous breakouts, this one was short-lived. Wilder and two fellow escapees took refuge in a house in Mt Eden, only 1.5 kilometres from the prison. After a tense three-hour standoff with police, the fugitives surrendered when threatened with tear gas.

George Wilder (left) handcuffed to a police officer following his capture.

NEW ZEALAND NURSES DETAINED ON WAY TO SPANISH CIVIL WAR

The only organised New Zealand contingent to serve in the Spanish Civil War were New Zealand Spanish Medical Aid Committee (SMAC) nurses René Shadbolt, Isobel Dodds and Millicent Sharples. On the day they were to leave Auckland, police interrogated them about their reasons for going.

Though the nurses were released in time to board the *Awatea* for Sydney, SMAC wrote to the government demanding an explanation and inquiry. Neither was forthcoming, although Police Minister Peter Fraser eventually admitted that the government had overreacted to a fear that 'three dedicated revolutionaries [would be] flying New Zealand's flag in Spain'.

The nurses arrived in Spain on 15 July 1937. Posted to a makeshift hospital in Huete, south-east of Madrid, Shadbolt and Dodds remained there until mid-1938, when the hospital moved to Barcelona. By this time, Sharples had returned to New Zealand. Dodds and Shadbolt arrived back in New Zealand in January 1939. In February they embarked on a speaking tour to raise awareness of, and money for, the hundreds of thousands of Republican refugees in France.

The New Zealand nurses who served in Spain during the Spanish Civil War, 1936–39.

New Zealand's
NURSES

✝

New Zealand's
Responsibility

Nurse Dodds.   Sister Shadbolt.   Nurse Sharples.

ATTEMPTED HIJACKING IN FIJI FOILED
19 May 1987

Cabin crew foiled the attempted hijacking of an Air New Zealand Boeing 747 at Nadi airport, Fiji, by striking the hijacker on the head with a whisky bottle. Flight TE24 was en route to Auckland from Tokyo when it made a scheduled refuelling stop in Nadi. Ahmjed Ali, a Fiji Indian who worked for Air Terminal Services, walked onto the flight deck and revealed to the captain that he was carrying dynamite. Ali wanted to escape from Fiji, where the elected government of Prime Minister Timoci Bavadra had been overthrown by a military coup five days earlier. All 105 passengers and 21 cabin crew disembarked while the drama unfolded in the cockpit. For six hours, Ali talked to relatives in the Nadi tower and Air New Zealand negotiators in Auckland. At around 1 p.m., while Ali was distracted by the radio, flight engineer Graeme Walsh hit him with a bottle of duty-free whisky. The crew overpowered Ali and handed him over to local police. He received a suspended sentence for taking explosives onto a plane.

Nevile Lodge cartoon about the attempting hijacking in Fiji.

1773

NEW ZEALAND'S FIRST SHEEP RELEASED

During his second voyage to New Zealand, in 1773, James Cook released a ewe and a ram in Queen Charlotte Sound. They survived only a few days — an inauspicious start to this country's long association with sheep.

Sheep farming was established by the 1850s, and has played an important role in New Zealand's economic history ever since. For several decades wool accounted for more than a third of New Zealand's exports by value. Following the first export shipment of frozen meat in 1882 (see 15 February), sheep meat became a significant source of revenue as New Zealand forged a role as Britain's farmyard.

For many, sheep symbolise New Zealand as a nation. The sheep population peaked at just over 70 million in 1982. By 2018 numbers had dropped to 27 million, after profits declined compared to other types of farming, notably dairying.

More than half of New Zealand's sheep are Romney, an English breed capable of producing both wool and meat of good quality. Romneys are also able to tolerate New Zealand's varied weather.

Sheep in the fields around Waimate Mission Station; reproduction of a painting by Cyprian Bridge, 1845.

HOBSON PROCLAIMS BRITISH SOVEREIGNTY OVER NEW ZEALAND
21 May 1840

Lieutenant-Governor William Hobson proclaimed British sovereignty over all of New Zealand — the North Island on the basis of cession through the Treaty of Waitangi, and South and Stewart Islands by right of discovery. When sovereignty was proclaimed, Māori signatories to the treaty were still being actively sought — the last were not acquired until 3 September. Hobson's decision to declare the Crown's authority over the whole country may have been motivated by rumours that the New Zealand Company was intending to set up its own administration in the Cook Strait region. Hobson's deputy, Major Thomas Bunbury, also proclaimed sovereignty over Stewart Island by right of discovery on 5 June, as no Māori could be found there to sign the treaty. In late May, Hobson sent Colonial Secretary and Police Magistrate Willoughby Shortland to Port Nicholson (Wellington) to read the proclamation and demand allegiance to the Crown. The settlers grudgingly assented. New Zealand was a dependency of New South Wales until May 1841, when it became a separate British colony with Hobson as its governor.

Portrait of William Hobson, 1913.

WAIKATO-TAINUI SIGNS TREATY SETTLEMENT

Waikato–Tainui was the first iwi to reach an historical Treaty of Waitangi settlement with the Crown for injustices that went back to the wars and land confiscations (raupatu) of the 1860s. The Deed of Settlement included cash and land valued at a total of $170 million. The agreement was a major landmark in New Zealand's developing treaty settlements process. As historian Richard Hill later explained in his book *Maori and the State* (2009):

> *The settlement was for some $150 million more than the government had been prepared to offer less than five years before. A mere six years before the signing, in fact, there were no state plans to supersede the 1946 agreement. Matters had, certainly in international terms, moved fast.*

The agreement also included a formal apology from the Crown. Queen Elizabeth II signed the act that made the agreement law during her state visit later in 1995. Tainui established a commercial framework to manage its tribal assets and, by 2016, Tainui Group Holdings and Waikato–Tainui Fisheries had assets of over $1.2 billion.

The agreement also included a formal apology from the Crown.

Queen Elizabeth II and Te Arikinui Dame Te Atairangikaahu with Prime Minister Jim Bolger (left) and Treaty Negotiations Minister Douglas Graham, 1995.

1861

FIRST MAJOR GOLD RUSH IN OTAGO

Gabriel Read gained fame and provincial government bonuses when he found gold near the Tuapeka River, a tributary of the Clutha River in Otago.

The Otago provincial government had offered a £1000 reward for the discovery of 'payable quantities' of gold. Read, a prospector from Tasmania, claimed the reward (equivalent to more than $110,000 today) after finding gold 'shining like the stars in Orion'. His discovery sparked the country's first major gold rush.

Thousands of diggers rushed to 'Gabriel's Gully' hoping to strike it rich. A slice of the goldfields population of Victoria moved across the Tasman — not only miners, but also businesspeople and entertainers. The discovery was a major economic boost to both Otago province and the wider New Zealand economy. But there were fears that criminal elements seeking potentially rich pickings would also flock to the goldfields.

The Otago gold rush peaked in the mid-1860s, after which miners left in large numbers for the new West Coast goldfields. Read returned to Tasmania in 1864 and spent his final years in a mental hospital.

Gabriel's Gully, 1862.

PARLIAMENT'S FIRST SITTING IN AUCKLAND

It started with a bang — 21 in fact, fired from the guns at Auckland's Fort Britomart. Once the smoke cleared, New Zealand's first Parliament was in business.

It was noon on Wednesday, 24 May 1854, and Auckland was to be the colony's capital city (and home to Parliament) for the next 10 years. Though the day was auspicious — it was Queen Victoria's birthday — the weather was wet and miserable and the parliamentary building was not yet completed. Still, there was excitement in the air as New Zealand took an important step in its history.

The colony's first elected parliamentarians, all 37 of them, were sworn in, making their oaths of allegiance to the Crown in the person of the acting governor, Colonel R.H. Wynyard. A formal reception in the afternoon was followed by a ball that evening. Three days later came the state opening of the General Assembly with all the pomp and ceremony that could be mustered — a treat for the locals who turned out to watch.

It started with a bang — 21 in fact, fired from the guns at Auckland's Fort Britomart. Once the smoke cleared, New Zealand's first Parliament was in business.

Watercolour showing the first Parliament building — the plain three-gabled structure at far left, 1859.

SCOTT DIXON WINS INDIANAPOLIS 500

Starting from pole position, Dixon was in or near the lead throughout the race and won by nearly two seconds. The Indianapolis ('Indy') 500 is traditionally one of the world's three most important motorsport races, alongside the 24 Hours of Le Mans and the Monaco Grand Prix. First contested in 1911, the Indy 500 has in recent years been part of the lucrative Indy Racing League, which Scott Dixon won in his debut season of 2003 with Chip Ganassi Racing.

His 2008 victory was the first at the 'Brickyard' by a New Zealander and helped secure his second championship. He was recognised as New Zealand's 2008 Sportsman of the Year, an honour repeated in 2013 after he won his third IndyCar title. By the time he won his fourth title in 2015, Dixon had won 38 of his 215 IndyCar races. By mid-2019 Dixon had 45 wins and was third on the all-time IndyCar list. In 2012, Scott Dixon was appointed a Member of the New Zealand Order of Merit. In 2013, *Autosport* magazine named him as one of the 50 best drivers who had never raced in Formula One. A documentary film, *Born Racer: The Scott Dixon Story*, was released in 2018.

Scott Dixon after winning the Indy 500, 2008.

ANNA PAVLOVA DANCES IN NEW ZEALAND FOR THE FIRST TIME
26 May 1926

The world's best-known ballerina performed her famed 'Dying Swan' and 'Fairy Doll' to a full house in His Majesty's Theatre, Auckland. Reporters were enraptured: 'Pavlova ... is superb. An artist to the tips of her twinkling toes, every fibre of her lithe body seems to respond to the music.' Her 66-strong company (counting the orchestra) included former Wellingtonian Thurza Rogers. It spent six weeks in New Zealand, playing three different programmes in each of the four main centres. Other highlights included adaptations of *The Magic Flute* and Tchaikovsky's *Nutcracker*. The petite 'Madame' Pavlova took time out to dispense health advice — eat plenty of green vegetables and fruit, avoid red meat and potatoes, walk whenever you can — and even to assist the victim of a motorcycle accident in Christchurch. Back in Australia, she praised New Zealanders' hospitality while hinting that they had not fully understood her artistry — and their houses were too cold. The first known recipe for the pavlova dessert, in the form we now enjoy, was published in New Zealand in 1929.

Anna Pavlova, 1926.

AMY BOCK SENTENCED IN DUNEDIN SUPREME COURT

The Tasmanian-born confidence trickster had topped off a long career impersonating well-off men for financial gain by posing as a sheep farmer and bishop's nephew. 'Percy Redwood' had married the daughter of 'his' South Otago landlady on 21 April 1909. Bock had managed to keep up appearances while wooing Agnes Ottaway, but was arrested within four days of the glittering Port Molyneux nuptials. Amid speculation as to the consummation of the union, postcards depicting a dapper pipe-smoking Redwood sold by the dozen.

In court, Bock pleaded guilty to charges of false pretences, forgery and making a false statement under the Marriage Act. With a string of mostly minor fraud convictions dating back 23 years — a flair for amateur dramatics had allowed her to evade many more — she was now the first New Zealand woman declared to be a 'habitual criminal' and therefore liable to indefinite detention.

The sham marriage was annulled on 17 June 1909. Released on probation after two years in jail, Amy Bock had her final day in court — inevitably, charged with false pretences — in 1931, aged 72.

BORN ON THIS DAY

Neil Finn,
1958–,
musician

Amy Bock.

FINGERPRINTS HELP CONVICT MURDERER
28 May 1920

In what may have been a world first for a capital crime, the conviction of Dennis Gunn was based almost entirely on fingerprint evidence. Postmaster Augustus Braithwaite was murdered on 13 March 1920. The murderer took his keys and ransacked the Ponsonby Post Office. Police found fingerprints on three cash boxes and sent them to the Criminal Registration Branch (CRB) for analysis. Dennis Gunn came to the police's attention after he was seen hanging around the Post Office. They sent his name to the CRB, who held his fingerprints on file from a previous conviction. The fingerprints on the cash boxes matched Gunn's fingerprint form. Following his arrest, police found property stolen during the robbery and a recently fired gun near Gunn's house. Grooves on the weapon corresponded with marks on the bullets found in Braithwaite's body. One of Gunn's fingerprints was found on the weapon. While admitting to the robbery, Gunn claimed Braithwaite had been killed by an accomplice. The jury was not convinced and Gunn was sentenced to death. He was hanged in Auckland on 22 June.

The fingerprint evidence that convicted Dennis Gunn.

1953

HILLARY AND TENZING REACH SUMMIT OF EVEREST

From the moment Hillary told Lowe that they had 'knocked the bastard off', his life changed forever.

A beekeeper from New Zealand, Edmund Hillary, and the Nepalese Sherpa Tenzing Norgay became the first people to stand on the summit of the world's highest peak. After climbing with British teams in the Himalayas in 1951 and 1952, Hillary and another New Zealander, George Lowe, were invited to join John Hunt's 1953 British Everest Expedition. On 29 May — four days before the coronation of Queen Elizabeth II — the chosen pair, Hillary and the experienced Tenzing, reached the 8848-metre summit of Mt Everest via the south-east ridge.

From the moment Hillary told Lowe that they had 'knocked the bastard off', his life changed forever. Before the expedition had even emerged from the mountains, Queen Elizabeth bestowed a knighthood on the surprised New Zealander. In Britain, he and Tenzing became the subject of media frenzy. They attended formal events and lectured to packed halls. In 1957–58 Hillary led the New Zealand section of a British trans-Antarctic expedition, and, although merely tasked with setting up supply depots, he beat expedition leader Vivian Fuchs to the South Pole (see 4 January).

In the 1960s Hillary returned to the Himalayas to help build schools and health facilities for the sherpas of Nepal. In 1978 he led an expedition up the Ganges River and six years later he became New Zealand's High Commissioner to India.

The ascent of Everest enhanced interest in mountaineering throughout the world. In New Zealand, Hillary and Everest helped turn mountaineering from a somewhat fringe activity into something that had new-found respect.

Hillary accepted with unfailing grace the responsibilities that his fame brought, including countless media appearances, book signings and requests to write forewords. Aside from his humanitarian work, he also helped mentor a new generation of climbers.

Despite a multitude of honours and accolades, including membership of the Order of New Zealand, honorary citizenship of Nepal, and a portrait on New Zealand's five-dollar note, Hillary remained humble about his achievements until his death in January 2008, aged 88. He remains one of New Zealand's most loved national figures.

Edmund Hillary and Tenzing Norgay on the slopes of Mt Everest, 1953.

NEW ZEALAND SAYS NO TO FEDERATION WITH AUSTRALIA

30 May 1901

A 10-man Royal Commission reported unanimously that New Zealand should not become a state of the new Commonwealth of Australia. Although New Zealand had participated in Australian colonial conferences since the 1860s, federation only became a serious prospect following the decision to unite Australia's six colonies in 1899. Premier Richard Seddon preferred to be the leader of an independent country rather than an Australian state. He set up the Royal Commission in 1900 to buy time and get a sense of public opinion. While most submissions opposed union with Australia, many farmers were in favour, fearing new trade barriers to their produce. The prevailing view was that New Zealanders were of superior stock to their counterparts across the Tasman. New Zealand's trade was mostly with the United Kingdom; Australians were economic rivals rather than partners. Although New Zealand and Australia eventually signed a Free Trade Agreement in 1965, and the two economies have become closely integrated, political union is no closer today than it was in 1901.

Cartoon about New Zealand joining the Australian federation, *New Zealand Graphic and Ladies' Journal*, 1900.

AUCKLAND HARBOUR BRIDGE OPENS

30 May 1959

New Zealand's best-known bridge opened after four years of construction. The need for better transport links between Auckland city and the North Shore had long been the subject of inquiry and agitation. The Auckland Harbour Bridge Authority was set up in 1950 to raise funds and organise construction. The bridge's 'coat hanger' design, with lattice girders on the 243-metre span, allowed ships to pass beneath.

Building the bridge involved clever cantilevering of the steel girders, and staff worked 33 metres below sea level preparing the foundations of the reinforced concrete piers. The bridge is 1017 metres long, and used 5670 tonnes of steel, 17,160 cubic metres of concrete and 6800 litres of paint.

Originally, the bridge had only four lanes, but this quickly proved inadequate. In September 1969 the 'Nippon clip ons' — two lanes on each side, prefabricated in Japan — were added. At the time, this was pioneering technology, but 15 years later fatigue was discovered in the splice joints and several thousand had to be replaced. Tolls were charged on the bridge until 1984.

In September 1969 the 'Nippon clip-ons' — two lanes on each side, prefabricated in Japan — were added.

Traffic on the Auckland Harbour Bridge, 1959.

1916

HMS *NEW ZEALAND* FIGHTS AT JUTLAND

In the misty North Sea on the last day of May 1916, 250 warships from Britain's Royal Navy and Germany's High Seas Fleet clashed in the First World War's greatest and bloodiest sea battle. Among them was HMS *New Zealand*, the battlecruiser the Dominion had gifted to the Royal Navy.

Outgunned and outnumbered, the Germans inflicted more damage on their opponents but returned to port, leaving Britain in command of the high seas. Britain lost three battlecruisers and Germany one; both fleets lost smaller cruisers and destroyers. Six thousand British and 2500 German sailors died.

Among them was one of the few New Zealanders serving with the fleet — 21-year-old Leslie Follett of Marton, a stoker on the battlecruiser HMS *Queen Mary*. Follett died when the *Queen Mary* exploded after German shells struck it.

HMS *New Zealand* survived with only light damage. The ship's good fortune was attributed to the presence on board of a lucky piupiu (flax kilt) and greenstone hei tiki (pendant), which had been bestowed during the battlecruiser's visit to New Zealand in 1913 (see 12 April).

HMS *New Zealand*, Gerald Maurice Burn, 1915.

NEW ZEALAND'S FIRST OFFICIAL TV BROADCAST

Broadcast from Shortland Street in central Auckland, New Zealand's first official television transmission began at 7.30 p.m. The first night's broadcast lasted just three hours and was only available to viewers in Auckland. It included an episode of *The Adventures of Robin Hood*, a live interview with a visiting British ballerina and a performance by the Howard Morrison Quartet.

The television age was slow to arrive in New Zealand. Britain's BBC led the way when it started the world's first public service in 1936. The NBC began broadcasting in the United States in 1939. Australia had its first stations operating by 1956.

In New Zealand, a government committee began studying the new medium in 1949. Experimental broadcasts began in 1951 — with the proviso that they should not include anything that could be classified as 'entertainment'. Prime Minister Walter Nash made the decision to proceed with public broadcasts in 1959.

Initially television broadcasts had limited coverage. Transmission did not begin in Christchurch until June 1961; Wellington followed four weeks later. Dunedin had to wait until 31 July 1962. By 1965 the four stations were broadcasting seven nights a week for a total of 50 hours. There was no national network and each centre saw local programmes. Overseas programmes were flown from centre to centre and played in different cities in successive weeks. By 1969 the four television stations were broadcasting for 65 hours each week, between 2 p.m. and 11 p.m. from Sunday to Thursday, and 2 p.m. and midnight on Friday and Saturday. Television licences, which cost £4 each year (equivalent to around $170 today), were introduced in August 1960. By 1965 more than 300,000 licences had been issued. Operating costs were also partly offset by the introduction in 1961 of what many see as the scourge of modern TV — advertising. Initially advertisements were allowed only on Tuesday, Wednesday, Thursday and Saturday. More revenue was raised from television licences than from advertising. In February 1966 the average price of a 23-inch black and white television 'consolette' was £131, equivalent to nearly $5000 today.

Cartoon about New Zealand's first live television broadcast, 1960.

DEATH OF MOTOR-RACING DRIVER BRUCE MCLAREN

Bruce McLaren, 1970.

In 1958 Bruce McLaren was the first recipient of the Driver to Europe award, which enabled promising Kiwis to race against the world's best (see 22 October). The following year, aged just 22, he became the then youngest Formula One race winner in the United States Grand Prix.

McLaren won three more races and achieved 23 other podium finishes in 100 starts in F1. He was runner-up in the 1960 World Championship and third in 1962 and 1969. He won the 24 Hours of Le Mans race in 1966.

In 1963 he established Bruce McLaren Motor Racing. His abilities as an analyst, engineer and manager contributed much to the success of the cars that bore his name. McLarens dominated the Can-Am series from 1967 until 1971 and had success in Formula One in the 1970s.

Aged 32, Bruce McLaren died when he crashed while testing a Can-Am car on the Goodwood circuit in England. McLaren Racing was taken over by Ron Dennis in the 1980s and became the most successful F1 team in the late 20th century.

FIRST WOMEN ENTER POLICE TRAINING
3 June 1941

Calls for policewomen had been expressed since the 1930s when the National Council of Women started lobbying for women officers. Their efforts were rewarded when 10 women from various parts of New Zealand were recruited in June 1941 — a time of workforce pressures due to the Second World War. Trainees were required to be well educated, aged between 25 and 40, unmarried or widowed, have shorthand and typing skills, and pass a strict medical test. The 10 women selected, all aged between 30 and 35, trained at the Police Training school on Rintoul Street in the Wellington suburb of Newtown for three months. Upon completion of their training in October, the policewomen were sent to Auckland, Wellington, Christchurch and Dunedin to work as temporary constables in detective branches. Most dealt with cases involving women and delinquent children. Although they were not uniformed until 1952, they had full authority to arrest lawbreakers.

This photograph of the first uniformed policewomen in 1952 includes members of the 1941 intake.

RAIL TRAGEDY AT HYDE

The Cromwell–Dunedin express, travelling at speed, derailed while rounding a curve near Hyde in Central Otago. Twenty-one of the 113 passengers on board were killed and 47 injured in what was then New Zealand's worst rail accident.

When locomotive A^B 782 left the rails at 1.45 p.m. all seven carriages followed. Four were telescoped together and several were smashed to pieces. The survivors did what they could for each other until help arrived 90 minutes later. Rescue work continued through the night.

A board of inquiry found the locomotive had entered the bend at perhaps 112 kilometres per hour, more than twice the speed limit for that section of track. Engine driver John Corcoran was subsequently found guilty of manslaughter and sentenced to three years in prison. Some have argued that Corcoran, fatigued after working long hours, was a scapegoat for a Railways Department happy to absolve itself of any blame.

The Hyde derailment remains the second-worst rail disaster in New Zealand's history — surpassed only by the 1953 Tangiwai tragedy (see 24 December).

Onlookers view the crumpled carriages after the Cromwell–Dunedin express came off the rails near Hyde.

AUCKLAND SAVINGS BANK OPENS FOR BUSINESS

The New Zealand Banking Company, Auckland's first bank, had been wound up two years earlier. The new bank was launched at a meeting of prominent gentlemen. Its formation was encouraged by Governor George Grey, who hoped it would attract business from working men of both races and become 'an immediate and active agent in civilization'. Māori in particular were, it was claimed, 'becoming awake to the pleasure of simple accumulation, to the advantage of putting their money out of their own power', at least temporarily.

The bank opened to receive deposits for an hour each Saturday evening in the new brick store on Queen Street of John Montefiore, one of its 17 founding trustees. When Matthew Fleming made the first deposit of £10 two weeks later, it was secured in Montefiore's fireproof safe. By the end of the year, 14 Pākehā and seven Māori had opened accounts with a total balance of £166 4s. From May 1848, they received 5 per cent interest. ASB Bank has been fully owned by the Commonwealth Bank of Australia since 2000.

View of Queen Street, with the Auckland Savings Bank at centre, c. 1910.

The bank opened to receive deposits for an hour each Saturday evening in the new brick store on Queen Street of John Montefiore . . .

NEW ZEALAND'S FIRST WIND FARM BECOMES OPERATIONAL

Commissioned by Wairarapa Electricity, New Zealand's first commercial wind farm opened in the windy hills of Wairarapa. Named Hau Nui Farm, meaning Big Wind, this location was wisely chosen due to the ideal wind currents that are funnelled and accelerated from nearby Cook Strait and the Rimutaka Range.

Stage one of the project was constructed at the northern end of Range Road and saw the installation of seven E-40 wind turbines, a third-generation wind-energy technology. Each turbine has three 20-metre blades, making the overall height of each turbine an impressive 46 metres. This allows each turbine to generate electricity in wind speeds anywhere between 10 and 120 kilometres per hour. When the wind exceeds 120 kilometres per hour, the turbines automatically shut down to avoid damage. Eight more turbines were installed in stage two of the project, which was completed in December 2004. With 15 turbines, the farm produces enough energy to power 4200 homes. Genesis Energy took over operation of the wind farm in 1999.

Turbine under construction at Wairarapa Electricity's wind farm, May 1996.

MCDONALD'S ARRIVES IN NEW ZEALAND
7 June 1976

The golden arches appeared for the first time in New Zealand at Cobham Court, Porirua. Big Macs were priced at 75 cents (equivalent to about $6 today), cheeseburgers 40 cents and hamburgers 30 cents. More than 100 eager customers were queuing outside when the doors opened at 10 a.m. Twenty years later the American fast-food giant opened its 100th outlet in the country. Rivals Kentucky Fried Chicken (now KFC) had arrived in New Zealand in August 1971. Both organisations faced challenges here. A licensing system restricted the importing of products that could be made in New Zealand. The McDonald's kitchen was supposed to be sent back to the USA once local companies were able to reproduce it. The resulting trade negotiations were a windfall for the New Zealand Dairy Board (the predecessor of Fonterra), which was able to offload some of its cheese surplus in exchange for more imported kitchens for McDonald's. New Zealand's second McDonald's restaurant opened in Queen Street, Auckland in July 1977. The first drive-throughs opened the following year, in New Lynn (Auckland) and Lower Hutt.

McDonald's opens its first outlet in New Zealand, 1976.

NEW ZEALAND GOES NUCLEAR-FREE

The New Zealand Nuclear Free Zone, Disarmament, and Arms Control Act was passed into law, establishing this country as a nuclear and biological weapons-free zone. The act was passed in the aftermath of the mid-1980s nuclear ships stand-off between New Zealand and the United States. The nuclear-free movement, however, had its roots in ideas that emerged in the 1960s: a push for an independent, ethical foreign policy, which had grown out of opposition to the Vietnam War; and environmentalism, which sought to preserve New Zealand as a green, unspoilt land.

In a largely symbolic action, the US Congress retaliated with the Broomfield Act, downgrading New Zealand's status from ally to friend. Labour Prime Minister David Lange's response was that if the cost of New Zealand's nuclear-free status was the end of the ANZUS security alliance, this was a 'price we are prepared to pay'.

In 1989, 52 per cent of New Zealanders indicated that they would rather break defence ties than admit nuclear-armed ships to their harbours. By 1990, even the National opposition had signed up to anti-nuclearism.

Nuclear-free New Zealand badge.

Colonial forces come under attack at Te Ngutu-o-te-Manu, South Taranaki in this romanticised image from the *Illustrated New Zealand Herald*, 1868.

BEGINNING OF TĪTOKOWARU'S WAR
9 June 1868

Ngā Ruahine warriors led by Riwha Tītokowaru killed three settlers near Ketemarae, north of Hāwera, provoking a resumption of fighting in South Taranaki. Tītokowaru was both a tohunga (spiritual leader) and a Wesleyan lay preacher. In the 1860s his opposition to land-selling led him to support the King Movement (Kīngitanga). He lost an eye in the Pai Mārire attack on Sentry Hill in April 1864. In 1867 Tītokowaru called for peaceful resistance to Pākehā encroachment, but the confiscation of Ngā Ruahine land continued. After fighting began in July, he won a series of victories over much larger colonial and allied Māori forces, who were simultaneously fighting Te Kooti on the east coast (see 4 July and 10 November). In February 1869 the Armed Constabulary faced further humiliation at Taurangaika, near Whanganui. But Tītokowaru's fighters abandoned him, possibly because of a sexual indiscretion, and his campaign collapsed. He retreated into the interior. Tītokowaru eventually returned to South Taranaki and became a successful businessman. Such was his military reputation that land confiscation in the area did not resume until the late 1870s.

ERUPTION OF MT TARAWERA

The eruption lasted six hours and caused massive destruction. It destroyed several villages and buried the famous silica hot springs known as the Pink and White Terraces. Approximately 120 people, nearly all Māori, lost their lives.

Locals awoke in the early hours of 10 June to earthquakes, lightning, fountains of molten rock, and columns of smoke and ash up to 10 kilometres high. People as far away as Blenheim heard the eruption. Some thought it was an attack by a Russian warship.

A 17-kilometre-long rift split Mt Tarawera and extended as far south as Waimangu. The eruption covered land with millions of tonnes of ash and debris, transformed lakes, and flattened bush. It was over by dawn, though ash made day as dark as night. Men from Rotorua and Ōhinemutu formed rescue parties and began digging out survivors and casualties. Settlements at Te Tapahoro, Moura, Te Ariki, Totorariki, Waingongongo and Te Wairoa were destroyed or buried. Te Wairoa, known as 'The Buried Village', later became a tourist attraction.

Locals awoke in the early hours of 10 June to earthquakes, lightning, fountains of molten rock, and columns of smoke and ash up to 10 kilometres high.

Painting of Mt Tarawera erupting by Charles Blomfield.

1901

CORNWALL PARK GIFTED TO AUCKLAND

At a civic reception for the Duke and Duchess of Cornwall and York, John Logan Campbell handed over the deed to land around One Tree Hill/Maungakiekie. The new park was named in honour of the royal couple.

The Duke and Duchess, later King George V and Queen Mary, were touring the Empire to express gratitude for the support given to Britain during the South African War. During their visit to New Zealand, Campbell, a prominent Auckland merchant, was asked to be the city's honorary mayor. In response, he donated his country estate to the people of Auckland, and asked that it be named Cornwall Park.

In the centre of the park is a volcanic cone, which Māori called Maungakiekie — mountain of the kiekie (a climbing plant). The site of a pre-European pā, it was dubbed One Tree Hill by Pākehā after a solitary tree that grew on the summit when Europeans first settled Auckland. An obelisk built during the 1940 Centennial as a memorial to Māori still stands at the summit. Campbell is buried beside it.

John Logan Campbell in The Avenue, Cornwall Park, Auckland, c. 1900.

Dean Cornwell, *Have a "Coke" = Kia Ora*, c. 1943–45.

FIRST US TROOPS ARRIVE IN AUCKLAND
12 June 1942

Over the following two years, about 100,000 American servicemen would spend time in New Zealand, which became a rear base for the Allies' counter-offensive against Japan. This American 'invasion' led to a considerable clash of cultures (see 3 April). At any one time during the period from June 1942 to mid-1944, between 15,000 and 45,000 Americans were stationed in New Zealand; most were in camps around Auckland and Wellington. As well as soldiers and Marines, many US naval and merchant marine personnel spent time in this country. For both visitor and host it was an intriguing experience with much of the quality of a Hollywood fantasy. The American soldier found himself 'deep in the heart of the South Seas' — a land of tree-ferns and semi-tropical 'jungle' — in the words of his army-issue pocket guide. Little wonder that marine Leon Uris would later write a novel about the experience (*Battle Cry*) and that Hollywood itself would make a film (*Until They Sail*) based on a James Michener story, with Paul Newman as the troubled heart-throb.

MURDER ON THE MAUNGATAPU TRACK

The murder of five men on the Maungatapu track, south-east of Nelson, in June 1866 shocked the colony. These killings by the so-called 'Burgess gang' resembled something from the American Wild West.

Richard Burgess, Thomas Kelly, Philip Levy and Joseph Sullivan had come to New Zealand via the goldfields of Victoria, Australia. Three of them had been transported to Australia for crimes committed in England. They were just the sort of 'career criminals' that authorities had feared would arrive following the discovery of gold in the South Island in the 1860s.

After killing a prospector on 12 June, the gang ambushed and murdered a party of four on their way to the West Coast the following day. They were arrested in Nelson within a week, having aroused suspicion by spending money freely. The public followed their trial with great interest, eagerly snapping up sketches and accounts of the case. It became more intriguing when Sullivan turned on his co-accused and provided the evidence that convicted them. He escaped the gallows; the other three men were not so lucky.

The Maungatapu murderers: clockwise from top, Joseph Sullivan, Thomas Kelly, Philip Levy and Richard Burgess, 1866.

MULDOON CALLS SNAP ELECTION
14 June 1984

Prime Minister Robert Muldoon surprised many by announcing a 'snap' election to be held in exactly one month's time. He hoped to catch the opposition Labour Party under-prepared, but the gamble backfired and National suffered a heavy defeat. The dominant politician of his era, Muldoon had held power since 1975. He now found himself increasingly under pressure, grappling with economic uncertainty, backbench criticism and a resurgent opposition led by the charismatic David Lange. Labour would sweep to victory with 43 per cent of the vote to National's 36 per cent, and 56 parliamentary seats to their opponents' 37. Social Credit held the other two seats. Labour's winning margin was inflated by the performance of the newly formed right-wing (but anti-Muldoon) New Zealand Party, which won 12 per cent of the vote but no seats. The 1984 election is often regarded as the most significant in New Zealand's modern history. Labour's victory was followed by some of the most far-reaching economic and state sector reforms ever seen in this country, as well as new directions in foreign policy.

Robert Muldoon and his wife, Thea, at Wellington Town Hall, June 1984.

LOVELOCK WINS 'MILE OF THE CENTURY'

The Ivy League Princeton University hosted an annual elite mile race during the 1930s. New Zealand medical student Jack Lovelock, who had set a world record there in 1933, was invited to return in 1935 to run in what became known as the 'Mile of the Century'. It was a match race between Lovelock and the top Americans: world record holder Glenn Cunningham, Glen Dawson (who had beaten Cunningham a few weeks earlier), Bill Bonthron (the world record holder for the 1500 metres), Gene Venzke and Joe Mangan. On a warm and windy evening no world record would be set, so it became a tactical affair.

Dawson led for most of the race, followed by Cunningham and Lovelock. The New Zealander made his move just before the final straight and finished comfortably ahead of Cunningham, who was also overtaken by the fast-finishing Bonthron.

Lovelock's time of 4 minutes 11.5 seconds was his second-fastest mile but well outside the world record. As hundreds crowded around him, someone stole his trademark panama hat, but later returned it.

BORN ON THIS DAY

Keith Park,
1892–1975,
military aviator and leader

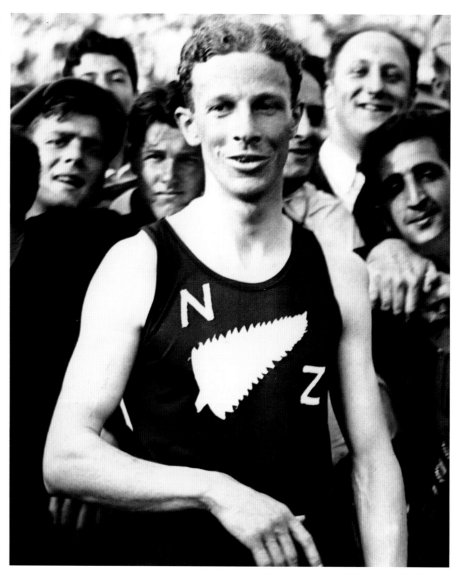

Jack Lovelock after his victory in the 'Mile of the Century'.

'BABY-FARMER' DANIEL COOPER HANGED

A generation after the hanging of the infamous Minnie Dean (see 12 August), the murder trial of Daniel and Martha Cooper revealed that 'baby farming' and illegal abortion were still regarded as solutions to the problem of unwanted children in New Zealand. After watching the Coopers for some time, police arrested Daniel in December 1922 for performing an abortion. The discovery of a baby's body days later at their Newlands property, near Wellington, saw the couple charged with illegally detaining children and murder. By the time their trial began on 14 May, two more babies' bodies had been unearthed.

Martha's lawyer portrayed her as a victim of mistreatment, describing her as 'a soulless household drudge without a mind of her own'. This was in sharp contrast to a reporter's depiction of Daniel's 'dark piercing eyes set far back in his head and a mouth like the seam in a saddle bag'.

While the jury cleared Martha of all charges, Daniel was found guilty and sentenced to death. He was hanged at the Terrace Gaol, Wellington, on 16 June 1923.

Newspaper caricature of Daniel Cooper.

THE WAIRAU INCIDENT
17 June 1843

Four Māori and 22 Europeans were killed in the first violent clash between Māori and Pākehā since the signing of the Treaty of Waitangi. Nelson colonists were keen to occupy the Wairau Valley, where the New Zealand Company claimed to have purchased land. Ngāti Toa disagreed, obstructing surveyors and destroying their huts. The chief Te Rauparaha insisted on an investigation by William Spain, who was looking into pre-1840 land purchases. Instead, warrants were issued for the arrest of Te Rauparaha and his nephew Te Rangihaeata, and an armed but untrained posse set out from Nelson to detain them. When the two groups met at Tuamarina, fighting broke out — possibly accidentally — and several people were killed on both sides. Many of the surviving Europeans were surrounded and forced to surrender. After Te Rangihaeata demanded revenge for the death of his wife, Te Rongo, the prisoners were killed — most by Te Rangihaeata using his mere (club). Pākehā fears of a Māori insurrection proved groundless. The incoming governor, Robert FitzRoy, enraged settlers by arguing that the Europeans had provoked Ngāti Toa.

When the two groups met at Tuamarina, fighting broke out — possibly accidentally — and several people were killed on both sides.

Scene of the Wairau Massacre, painted by Charles Gold, c. 1851.

LONG-DISTANCE WALKER ESTHER JAMES REACHES BLUFF

The Aucklander, a well-connected former model, had left Spirits Bay in the far north on 3 December to walk the length of the country to promote New Zealand-made goods during the Depression. She had government patronage and support from the Manufacturers' Federation.

Having trained for six months, James was well prepared. Her walking boots also proved up to the challenge, with periodic resoling. Her progress was fairly leisurely and she took a Christmas/New Year break in Whāngārei. Her only serious mishap was a sprained ankle suffered when she was blown into a gully while crossing the Remutaka Range, which necessitated a week's rest in Wellington.

Such was the generosity of her overnight hosts — usually prominent farmers or businesspeople — that James claimed to have gained a stone (6 kilograms) in weight during the 2000-kilometre walk. Consuming only New Zealand produce, she most missed cups of tea. The following year James walked from Brisbane to Melbourne to promote New Zealand as a tourist destination. A subsequent planned walk through Great Britain publicising New Zealand exports did not come about.

Esther James walks on, 1932.

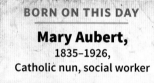

NIAGARA STRIKES MINE OFF NORTHLAND COAST
19 June 1940

The Second World War arrived in New Zealand with a bang when German mines sank the trans-Pacific liner *Niagara* off Northland's Bream Head. The sinking shocked the public and shattered any illusions that distance would protect these islands from enemy attack. On the night of 13/14 June 1940 the *Orion*, a German raider disguised as a merchant ship, had slipped undetected into New Zealand waters and laid 228 contact mines in the approaches to the Hauraki Gulf. At 3.40 a.m. on the 19th, the 13,415-ton *Niagara*, which had just left Auckland on its regular run to Suva and Vancouver, struck two mines and sank quickly by the bow. Fortunately, all 349 passengers and crew got away safely in 18 lifeboats; the only casualty was the ship's cat, 'Aussie'. Also lost was the ship's secret cargo of small-arms ammunition and gold ingots worth £2.5 million (equivalent to more than $230 million today). In late 1941, an epic salvage effort recovered almost all of the gold from the wreck, which lay at a depth of 60 fathoms (110 metres).

Survivors from the *Niagara*.

US NAVY TRAGEDY AT PAEKĀKĀRIKI

20 June 1943

Ten United States Navy personnel drowned off the Kāpiti Coast, north of Wellington, during a training exercise in bad weather. As wartime censorship prevented newspapers from publicising the American presence in New Zealand, the incident was shrouded in mystery for decades.

On the morning of 20 June, more than 30 landing craft carrying Marines from the troop transport USS *American Legion* went ashore at Whareroa Beach, Paekākāriki, an area where US troops had major camps. One vessel carried a naval 'beach party' whose role was to establish landing positions and handle communications. After suffering engine trouble, this craft was being towed back out to sea late that night when it was hit by a huge wave. One of the survivors later recalled: 'After about 5–7 minutes of being pulled through the pounding waves, we encountered the breaker that capsized our boat and dumped us into the cold, angry sea.' An officer and nine enlisted men died. A memorial to the drowned men was unveiled during a Memorial Day ceremony at nearby Queen Elizabeth Park in 2012.

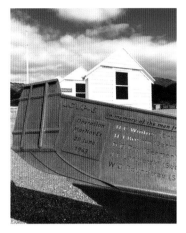

The US memorial near Paekākāriki.

ALL BLACKS WIN THE FIRST RUGBY WORLD CUP

20 June 1987

With Michael Jones, John Kirwan and David Kirk scoring tries, the All Blacks defeated France 29–9 at Eden Park, Auckland. Kirk became the first captain to lift the Webb Ellis Cup.

The first Rugby World Cup was hosted jointly by New Zealand and Australia. Rugby powerhouse South Africa was excluded because of an international sports boycott in opposition to its apartheid policies. Winger Kirwan opened the tournament by running almost the length of the field, beating most of the Italian team to score a memorable try. The All Blacks won 70–6 before comfortably beating Fiji and Argentina. In the knockout phase, Scotland was defeated 30–3 and Wales 49–6. The Webb Ellis Cup subsequently proved elusive. Despite usually heading the world rankings, the All Blacks did not win the trophy again until 2011, when New Zealand hosted the tournament.

The final — a rematch of 1987 — was a near thing as the All Blacks hung on to win 8–7. In 2015, the All Blacks became the first team to win consecutive titles and the first to win the cup three times.

All Black captain David Kirk with the Webb Ellis Cup at Eden Park, Auckland.

THE BEATLES LAND IN NEW ZEALAND

Beatlemania hit New Zealand when 7000 hysterical fans greeted the Fab Four in Wellington during their 'Far East' tour. After concerts in the United States, Europe, Hong Kong and Australia, the lads from Liverpool finally touched down in New Zealand. The Beatles' fame preceded them and our teenagers were ready for action. At Wellington Airport police struggled to keep crowds behind a wire fence, and rapturous fans besieged the Beatles' hotel.

On 22 June the Beatles played their first New Zealand concerts, repeating a 30-minute 11-song set as fans screamed and punctured the seats of the Wellington Town Hall with their stiletto heels. Audiences in Auckland, Christchurch and Dunedin followed suit. Perhaps the most dangerous moment of the tour occurred in Auckland, where several thousand people swarmed around the band; John Lennon lost a clump of hair. The tour had a huge impact on New Zealand's rock 'n' roll and pop music scene. Local artists such as Ray Columbus, Howard Morrison, and Max Merritt and the Meteors benefited from a surge of interest in the Beatles' wake.

The Beatles at Wellington Airport during their New Zealand tour, June 1964.

PARKER-HULME MURDER IN CHRISTCHURCH
22 June 1954

Armed with a brick in a stocking, 16-year-old Pauline Parker and her best friend Juliet Hulme, 15, became two of New Zealand's most notorious murderers when they killed Pauline's mother, Honora, in Victoria Park, Christchurch. The girls' trial was a sensation. Much of the evidence presented by witnesses focused on the close relationship between Parker and Hulme, their absorption with each other, and their fantasies about becoming famous novelists. When their parents, concerned that the girls' friendship had become obsessive and co-dependent, threatened to separate them, they had reacted violently. Parker and Hulme were found guilty, sentenced to indefinite imprisonment, and ordered never to contact one another again. The case remains one of New Zealand's most infamous murders and lives on in popular culture, having inspired a play, Michelanne Forster's *Daughters of Heaven*, and Peter Jackson's Academy Award-nominated film *Heavenly Creatures*. The two young women were released after serving about five years in prison. Juliet Hulme later changed her name to Anne Perry and became a successful writer. Both she and Parker now live in the United Kingdom.

Juliet Hulme (top) and Pauline Parker.

ANTARCTIC TREATY COMES INTO FORCE

As claimant to the Ross Dependency, New Zealand took part in the 1959 conference in Washington DC about the political and international status of Antarctica. The resulting Antarctic Treaty was agreed to by the 12 participating states.

In the midst of the Cold War, the treaty declared that 'Antarctica shall continue forever to be used exclusively for peaceful purposes and shall not become the scene or object of international discord'. Any measures of a military nature were outlawed, and nuclear explosions and the disposal of radioactive waste were entirely prohibited. Antarctica effectively became the world's first nuclear-free zone.

The treaty shelved the problem of territorial claims and the even more vexing problem of overlapping claims. It stated that nothing in the treaty could be interpreted as a denial 'of previously asserted rights of or claims to territorial sovereignty', and that activities which took place while the treaty was in force would not constitute a basis for claiming sovereignty. In addition, no new claims (or enlargements of existing claims) were permitted to be made during the life of the treaty.

First meeting of Antarctic Treaty countries at Canberra, 10–24 July 1961.

NZ TRUTH HITS THE NEWS STANDS
24 June 1905

At its peak in the 1950s and 1960s, *NZ Truth* prided itself on being 'the champion of the little person and the scourge of corruption and scandal in high places'. The weekly newspaper, founded by Australian John Norton, was modelled on populist papers across the Tasman. In its first decades, *Truth* took a markedly left-wing stance on many issues. It regularly attacked fat-cat businessmen, hypocritical politicians and prudish 'wowsers', a term popularised by Norton in Australia. By the 1950s, one in every two New Zealand households bought it. Although the paper relied on crime and deviance for much of its news, it also had a deep concern for conformity, morality, and law and order. In the 1960s and 1970s *Truth* became increasingly conservative, railing against 'Reds under the bed', unionists, bludgers and long-haired students. By the time its office moved from Wellington to Auckland in the early 1980s, both the paper's readership and its influence were on the wane. Sustained in its last years by sex industry advertising, it ceased publication in mid-2013.

Earthquake-damaged window of *NZ Truth*'s registered office, Wellington, January 1950.

PARLIAMENT VOTES FOR PROSTITUTION REFORM

The Prostitution Reform Act was passed on a tumultuous night in Parliament, with the public galleries filled with supporters from both sides. Christchurch Central Labour MP Tim Barnett had promoted the legislation as a private member's bill. It passed by just one vote.

Previous laws relating to soliciting, brothel-keeping and living off the earnings of prostitution were repealed, as was the Massage Parlours Act 1978.

The key aims of the act were to safeguard the human rights of sex workers, protect them from exploitation, and to promote their welfare and occupational health and safety. It was an offence to coerce another person to provide sexual services or to pay for sexual services from a person aged under 18. It also became illegal for a client to have sex with a worker without using a condom.

A committee set up to evaluate the act's operation reported in 2008 that the number of people working in the sex industry had not increased. More sex workers were operating privately, with fewer in managed premises. However, negative attitudes to sex work remained.

Tom Scott cartoon about prostitution reform, 2003.

A.J. HACKETT BUNGY JUMPS FROM EIFFEL TOWER
26 June 1987

The speed skier and bungy pioneer planned the 110-metre leap meticulously. His dozen-strong team hid on the tower overnight and Hackett jumped at dawn. He described it as 'one small step for a man, a bloody great leap for the adventure tourism industry'. Alan ('A.J.') Hackett's friend Chris Sigglekow had made the first bungy jump in New Zealand in January 1980, from Marlborough's Pelorus Bridge. The idea of jumping from a height with a sturdy elasticised band attached to the ankles had come from the vine jumpers of Pentecost Island, Vanuatu, via Oxford University students. Hackett made his first jump in November 1986, refined his equipment and six months later was ready to go public. On a quiet news day, the Eiffel Tower jump was televised around the world. In November 1988, A.J. Hackett Bungy opened the world's first commercial bungy operation at the Kawarau Gorge Suspension Bridge, near Queenstown. The company later opened sites elsewhere in the country and overseas.

A.J. Hackett is led away from the Eiffel Tower by French police.

MĀUI PŌMARE MEMORIAL UNVEILED

An estimated crowd of 1200 Māori and Pākehā from around the country converged on Manukorihi Pā in Waitara, Taranaki, to attend the unveiling of a memorial to 'one of New Zealand's greatest men', Sir Māui Pōmare.

During the ceremony, Governor-General Galway unveiled an imposing white Sicilian marble statue of Pōmare and opened a beautiful newly carved wharenui (meeting house). The statue, created by Christchurch sculptor W.T. Trethewey, depicts Pōmare delivering an oration. The students of the School of Māori Art at Rotorua carved the wharenui, under the supervision of Sir Āpirana Ngata.

Also in attendance were nearly 40 Members of Parliament, including Prime Minister Michael Joseph Savage and two of his predecessors, J.G. Coates and G.W. Forbes. Other significant guests included the Māori King Korokī Te Rata Mahuta, who had travelled with a large contingent from Waikato and King Country to help open the new meeting house.

The students of the School of Māori Art at Rotorua carved the wharenui . . .

Hera Retimana beside the statue of Māui Pōmare at Manukorihi Pā, Waitara, 1936.

HMNZS *OTAGO* SAILS FOR MURUROA TEST ZONE
28 June 1973

Prime Minister Norman Kirk told the 242 crew of the *Otago* that their Mururoa mission was an 'honourable' one — they were to be 'silent witness[es] with the power to bring alive the conscience of the world'. France had conducted atmospheric nuclear tests at Mururoa (or Moruroa), an atoll 1250 kilometres south-east of Tahiti in French Polynesia, since 1966. When the French refused to accept an International Court of Justice injunction against atmospheric testing, New Zealand's Labour government decided to station a frigate in international waters outside the test area. A Cabinet minister would accompany this daring protest. Kirk put all the names into a hat and drew out that of Fraser Colman, the minister of immigration and mines. The protests had some success. In 1974, by which time 41 atmospheric tests had been conducted at Mururoa, the new French president, Valéry Giscard d'Estaing, decided that future testing would be held underground. Even so, the atoll remained a focus of anti-nuclear protest. The test site at Mururoa was dismantled following France's last underground explosion in 1996.

HMNZS *Otago*.

FIRST FEMALE ANGLICAN DIOCESAN BISHOP APPOINTED

BORN ON THIS DAY

James K. Baxter,
1926–1972,
poet

Dr Penny Jamieson's rise through church ranks was rapid. The first women were ordained to the Anglican priesthood in New Zealand in 1977. Jamieson was ordained and appointed to a Wellington parish in 1985.

Her appointment as Bishop of Dunedin in June 1990 did not meet with universal approval. Bishop Whakahuihui Vercoe refused to attend the ceremony, believing that it was not culturally appropriate to have a female bishop. He still held this opinion when he was appointed Anglican Archbishop of New Zealand in 2004.

For her part, Jamieson saw her appointment as giving 'enormous encouragement' to women in all areas of society. She felt that 'the glass ceiling' had been broken. At her investiture as a Distinguished Companion of the New Zealand Order of Merit in 2004, however, she expressed disappointment that no women had yet followed in her footsteps.

Jamieson retired in June 2004. In August 2008, Victoria Matthews became New Zealand's second woman bishop when she was elected Bishop of Christchurch.

Penny Jamieson during her ordination ceremony, 1990.

FIRST ISSUE OF *NEW ZEALAND LISTENER* PUBLISHED

The *New Zealand Listener* soon expanded beyond its original brief to publicise radio programmes. Today it is the country's only national weekly current affairs and entertainment magazine.

From major investigative stories to crosswords, the *Listener* has published the serious, the trivial and everything in between. Features such as a 1939 war diary about clothes for the well-dressed soldier, Aunt Daisy's instructions for cooking a swan, and the recent 'Power Lists' of influential New Zealanders have traced changing preoccupations over the years.

From the outset, the arts were a major focus for the *Listener*, which has published works by leading literary figures such as James K. Baxter, Janet Frame and Maurice Shadbolt.

The *Listener*'s paid circulation peaked at 375,885 in 1982. Some feared its demise when it lost its monopoly on programme schedules in the free-market 1980s, but it adapted and survived. In 1990 the *Listener* was sold to New Zealand Magazines, and it is now published by the Hamburg-based Bauer Media Group. In the 2010s it remains one of New Zealand's top-selling magazines.

From the outset, the arts were a major focus for the Listener, *which has published works by leading literary figures such as James K. Baxter, Janet Frame and Maurice Shadbolt.*

Cover of the first issue of the *New Zealand Listener*.

BASTION POINT LAND RETURNED

The government announced that it had agreed to the Waitangi Tribunal's recommendation that Takaparawhā (Bastion Point) on the southern shore of Auckland's Waitematā Harbour be returned to local iwi Ngāti Whātua.

Protesters had occupied Bastion Point in early 1977 (see 5 January) after the government revealed that expensive houses would be built on former Ngāti Whātua reserve land. The reserve had been gradually reduced in size by compulsory acquisition, leaving Ngāti Whātua ki Ōrākei tribal group holding less than 1 hectare. The protesters, under the banner of the Ōrākei Māori Action Committee, refused to leave their ancestral lands and occupied Bastion Point for 506 days.

On 25 May 1978, when the government sent in a massive force of police and army personnel to evict the occupiers, 222 protesters were arrested and their temporary meeting house, buildings and gardens were demolished. The Bastion Point occupation became one of the most famous protest actions in New Zealand history. Nine years later the Waitangi Tribunal supported Māori claims to the land, and the government accepted this finding the following year.

Ngāti Whātua leader Joe Hawke addresses a crowd at Bastion Point.

ELECTRIC TRAINS COME TO WELLINGTON
2 July 1938

On 2 July 1938, Minister of Railways Dan Sullivan and Wellington Mayor Thomas Hislop officially opened the electrified rail line between central Wellington and the northern suburb of Johnsonville. The Wellington and Manawatu Railway Company had originally built this steep, winding line in 1886, and, until 1937, it was part of the main trunk route out of the capital. Following the completion of the Tawa Flat deviation that year, the bypassed Johnsonville section was truncated and converted into a suburban route. The line was served by sleek, modern English Electric DM-class multiple units, the first of their kind in New Zealand. As the city's electrified rail network expanded during and after the Second World War, DM units were used on the Kāpiti and Hutt Valley lines. Most were replaced in the 1980s following the introduction of Hungarian-built EM-class units, but a number of refurbished DMs continued to serve the Johnsonville line. These units, some of which had been in service since 1949, were finally retired in 2012 when new South Korean-built Matangi units took over the route.

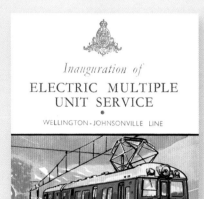

Invitation to the opening of the electric Wellington–Johnsonville line, 1938.

DC-3 CRASHES IN KAIMAI RANGE

The 1963 crash of a National Airways Corporation DC-3, with the loss of all 23 people on board, remains the worst air accident within New Zealand.

The flight from Auckland was bound for Wellington via Tauranga, Gisborne and Napier. The weather was stormy, but forecasts underestimated the force of the wind. During its descent into Tauranga, the plane was caught in a turbulent downdraught, slamming into a ridge on the Kaimai Range. Insufficient altitude and navigational problems contributed to the crash, but the ferocious winds were the deciding factor. It took rescuers two days to locate and reach the crash site.

A Court of Inquiry noted that there was no distance-measuring equipment at Tauranga airport, which would have given the pilot an accurate indication of how far he was from his destination. It recommended that this equipment be installed at all commercial airports, minimum safe altitudes for flights be reviewed, and that aircraft carry locator beacons so they could be found quickly if they crashed.

BORN ON THIS DAY

Āpirana Ngata,
1874–1950,
Māori politician

Wreckage of the National Airways Corporation DC-3 in the Kaimai Range.

TE KOOTI ESCAPES FROM CHATHAM ISLANDS
4 July 1868

Te Kooti Arikirangi Te Tūruki of Rongowhakaata was arrested near Gisborne in 1865 after allegedly helping a 'rebel' Pai Mārire force. Released and then re-arrested, he became one of hundreds exiled to the remote Chatham Islands. Here Te Kooti established the Ringatū faith, which was adopted by many of his fellow exiles. In July 1868, he masterminded an uprising by 300 prisoners who overpowered their guards, captured the schooner *Rifleman* and sailed for New Zealand, landing near Poverty Bay six days later. When the government refused to negotiate with them, the whakarau (exiles) fought their way inland. In November, they raided Poverty Bay, killing many people — Māori and Pākehā — who had crossed Te Kooti over the years (see 10 November). Te Kooti was an effective guerrilla leader, but no military genius. After defeat at Ngātapa in early 1869, he retreated to the remote Urewera Ranges. For three years, he was pursued across the central North Island by Pākehā and Māori forces. When his Tūhoe hosts were forced to surrender, Te Kooti sought the protection of King Tāwhiao. The government pardoned him in 1883.

Sketch of Te Kooti probably drawn by Thomas Ryan, 1880s.

1881

POLL TAX IMPOSED ON CHINESE

Parliament passed the Chinese Immigrants Act, which introduced a 'poll tax' of £10 (equivalent to about $1650 today) on Chinese migrants and restricted the number allowed to land from each ship arriving in New Zealand (only one Chinese passenger was allowed for every 10 tons of cargo). In 1896 this was changed to one passenger for every 200 tons, and the tax was increased to £100 ($18,660).

As employment on the goldfields had dwindled, anti-Chinese prejudice intensified, with calls for Chinese immigration to be restricted. In 1881 New Zealand followed Canada and the Australian colonies in imposing entry taxes on Chinese immigrants.

Numerous organisations opposed to Chinese immigration emerged during the late 19th and early 20th centuries, including the Anti-Chinese Association, the Anti-Chinese League, the Anti-Asiatic League and the White New Zealand League. The minister of customs waived the poll tax from 1934, but it was not repealed until 1944, after other countries had abandoned it. In 2002 the New Zealand government officially apologised to the Chinese community for the injustice of the tax.

BORN ON THIS DAY

Len Lye,
1901–1980,
sculptor, artist

CERTIFICATE.

Under Section 7 of "The Chinese Immigrants Act, 1881," and Section 2 of "The Chinese Immigrants Act Amendment Act, 1896."

No. 1615   £100.

Date of issue : 16 · 11 · 04.

Name : Yee Nam

Born at Canton.

Apparent age : 27.

Former place of residence : Canton.

Arrived by ship Moeraki

From Sydney

Collector of Customs at Whn.

[This part to be retained in the office of the Collector who issues the Certificate.]

[10 bks./4/1904— 3128

Poll tax certificate.

MAIN TRUNK LINE EXPRESS TRAIN DISASTER

The Auckland–Wellington express ploughed into a huge slip that had slumped across the tracks at Ōngarue, north of Taumarunui in the King Country. Seventeen people were killed and 28 injured. This was the first accident to claim more than four lives since the beginning of New Zealand's railway history 60 years earlier.

The disaster occurred just before 6 a.m. There was no chance to stop as the train was rounding a sharp bend. Locomotive A^B 748, its tender and the following postal van were thrown off the track. Further back in the train, the force of the impact telescoped three wooden carriages. At least 12 passengers were killed instantly. The engine driver and fireman both survived, but were badly injured. Most of those in the sleeping cars at the rear of the train only learned of the accident when they were woken so that their bedsheets could be used as bandages. Ōngarue remains the country's third-deadliest rail disaster, behind the Tangiwai (see 24 December) and Hyde (see 4 June) tragedies, which killed 151 and 21 people respectively.

The Auckland–Wellington express after it ploughed into a landslide at Ōngarue.

BORN ON THIS DAY

Arthur Lydiard,
1917–2004,
running coach

1916

NEW ZEALAND LABOUR PARTY FOUNDED

What is now New Zealand's oldest political party emerged from a joint conference in Wellington of the United Federation of Labour, the Social Democratic Party (SDP) and local Labour Representation Committees (LRCs).

Since the early 1900s a number of candidates had stood for Parliament under various 'labour' banners, including those of the Socialist Party, the Independent Political Labour League, local LRCs, the first New Zealand Labour Party (1910–12), the United Labour Party (ULP) and the SDP, which had been formed at a 1913 Unity Conference in Wellington.

By 1916 there were six 'labour' members in Parliament — three elected as members of the now-defunct ULP, two as SDP candidates and one as an independent. They operated as a de facto opposition to the wartime Reform–Liberal coalition government. This grouping formed the basis of the second New Zealand Labour Party. Although the party's name was a concession to the moderates, members of the more radical SDP held 11 of the 13 positions on its founding executive.

Members of the Parliamentary Labour Party, 1922. Left to right, back row: Ted Howard, Bill Parry, James Munro, Dan Sullivan, Michael Joseph Savage; front row: James McCombs, Harry Holland, Peter Fraser, Fred Bartram.

NEW ZEALAND'S FIRST PRIZE FIGHT?

The boxing bout was fought in an improvised ring on the banks of the Waimakariri River near Kaiapoi after police were ejected from the scene. London prizefighter Harry Jones defeated 'navvie' George Barton over 30 bloody bare-knuckle rounds for a purse of £100 (worth more than $11,000 today).

The pugilists were subsequently charged with making an affray and assault, and the officials and handlers with aiding and abetting. The case had farcical elements — the 500 spectators had allegedly included one of the magistrates who committed Jones and Barton for trial, as well as Christchurch's Crown Prosecutor, who mysteriously stepped aside on this occasion.

After the bit players were discharged, each boxer had his day in court. The jury acquitted them of the affray charges but found them guilty of assault, for which both served a month in jail.

Jones enlivened proceedings by claiming that a magistrate had put up part of the purse, and that Police Sub-Inspector Revell had enjoyed a dram or three at ringside while watching the fight he had failed to stop.

Cartoon showing a bare-knuckle boxing bout, 1889.

Jones enlivened proceedings by claiming that a magistrate had put up part of the purse . . .

HOMOSEXUAL LAW REFORM BILL PASSED
9 July 1986

Wellington Central MP Fran Wilde's private member's bill, which removed criminal sanctions against consensual male homosexual practices, was passed by 49 votes to 44. The legislation was signed by the governor-general on 11 July 1986 and came into effect on 8 August. It decriminalised sexual relations between men aged 16 and over. No longer would men having consensual sex be liable to prosecution and a term of imprisonment. Though sex between women had never been illegal, many lesbians suffered the same social discrimination as gay men and were staunch supporters of the reform movement. The campaign to reform the law aroused bitter public and political debate. The Coalition of Concerned Citizens organised a petition opposing Wilde's bill and claimed to have gathered more than 800,000 signatures (although many of these were later discredited). The group believed that decriminalising gay sex would lead to moral decline and the spread of HIV/AIDS. In 1993 reforms to the Human Rights Act finally prohibited discrimination on the grounds of sexual orientation.

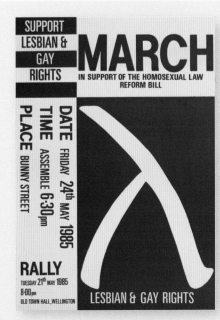

SUPPORT LESBIAN & GAY RIGHTS

MARCH IN SUPPORT OF THE HOMOSEXUAL LAW REFORM BILL

DATE FRIDAY 24th MAY 1985
TIME ASSEMBLE 6·30pm
PLACE BUNNY STREET

RALLY
TUESDAY 21st MAY 1985
8·00pm
OLD TOWN HALL, WELLINGTON

LESBIAN & GAY RIGHTS

Poster advertising a march in support of the Homosexual Law Reform Bill, 1985.

10 July 1967

NEW ZEALAND ADOPTS DECIMAL CURRENCY

E.D. Vallence of the Reserve Bank feeds obsolete banknotes into a furnace, 19 July 1968.

Pounds, shillings and pence were replaced by dollars and cents — 27 million new banknotes and 165 million new coins. The New Zealand government decided to decimalise in 1963, and set the date for 10 July 1967. There was much public discussion over what to call the new currency. Names suggested included 'crown', 'fern', 'tūī', 'Kiwi' and 'zeal'. In the end, both Australia and New Zealand settled on 'dollar'. The new coins were in denominations of 1, 2, 5, 10, 20 and 50 cents. Designs for the coins publicised in early 1966 were revised after being criticised. The notes — the first New Zealand paper money to show the reigning monarch — were kept under wraps until June 1967 to thwart counterfeiters.

The new $1, $2, $5, $10, $20 and $100 banknotes each had different native birds and plants on the reverse, and were distinguishable by colour. Their design featured complicated geometric patterns, including Māori iconography. A $50 note was introduced in 1981, and in 1990 the $1 and $2 notes were replaced by coins.

10 July 1985

RAINBOW WARRIOR SUNK IN AUCKLAND

Sinking of the *Rainbow Warrior*.

One crew member died when French secret agents blew up the Greenpeace vessel *Rainbow Warrior* in Auckland Harbour. The ship had been involved in protests against French nuclear testing in the Pacific. French Secret Service (DGSE) agents were sent to prevent it from leaving for another protest campaign at Mururoa Atoll in French Polynesia. They attached two limpet mines to the hull of the ship, the first of which blew a massive hole in its side. Photographer Fernando Pereira was killed in the second explosion. DGSE officers Dominique Prieur and Alain Mafart were subsequently arrested and charged with murder. After pleading guilty to manslaughter, they each received a 10-year prison sentence. Within a year, the pair were sent to French Polynesia, and from there they soon returned to France. The case caused the French government considerable embarrassment. While the attack was on an international organisation and not New Zealand as such, most Kiwis did not make this distinction. The fact that it was carried out on New Zealand territory by a supposedly friendly nation caused outrage and compromised relations between New Zealand and France for some years.

FIRST WOMAN GRADUATES FROM A NEW ZEALAND UNIVERSITY

Kate Edger became the first woman in New Zealand to gain a university degree and the first woman in the British Empire to earn a Bachelor of Arts (BA).

She was soon joined by other pioneering New Zealand women graduates. Helen Connon, Canterbury College's first female student, graduated with a BA in 1880, and became the first woman to graduate with an honours degree in 1881. New Zealand's first woman lawyer, Ethel Benjamin, graduated from the University of Otago's law school in 1898. Stella Henderson achieved unusual academic distinction for a 19th-century woman, gaining a BA with a special focus on political science, a Master of Arts (MA) with first-class honours in English and Latin, and completing the requirements for a Bachelor of Laws during the 1890s.

Elizabeth Gregory graduated Doctor of Philosophy (PhD) in biochemistry at University College, London, in 1932. She received an honorary Doctorate of Laws (LLD) degree in 1967 — the first New Zealand woman graduate to be so honoured.

Kate Edger.

The gunboat *Pioneer* at anchor off Meremere, on the Waikato River, *Illustrated London News*, c. 1864.

BRITISH FORCES INVADE WAIKATO
12 July 1863

British troops invaded Waikato by crossing the Mangatāwhiri Stream, which the Kīngitanga (Māori King Movement) had declared an aukati (a line not to be crossed). The Kīngitanga had been formally established in 1858. The government saw its refusal to sell land as an impediment to European settlement. Kīngitanga warriors fought in Taranaki in 1860–61, fuelling fears that the movement posed a challenge to British sovereignty. In January 1863, Governor George Grey announced his intention to 'dig around' the Kīngitanga until it fell. Amid rumours of an imminent Māori attack on Auckland from Waikato, settlers and missionaries fled north. Grey exploited the situation to persuade the British authorities to send him thousands more soldiers. When fighting resumed in Taranaki in 1863, the alleged involvement of Kīngitanga forces gave Grey the excuse he needed. In July, he gave Māori living between Auckland and the Waikato River an ultimatum: swear allegiance to the Queen or be deemed rebels. Within days, Lieutenant-General Duncan Cameron crossed the Mangatāwhiri Stream with the declared intention of establishing military posts on the Waikato River.

13 July
1916

VIVIAN WALSH OBTAINS NEW ZEALAND'S FIRST PILOT'S CERTIFICATE

Vivian Walsh in later life.

Following the establishment of the New Zealand Flying School at Ōrākei on Auckland's Waitematā Harbour, Vivian Walsh became the first pilot to obtain an aviator's certificate in New Zealand (several New Zealanders had earlier qualified as pilots in England).

The pioneering brothers Vivian and Leo Walsh built their first aircraft, a British-designed Howard Wright biplane, from imported plans, and, on 5 February 1911, Vivian completed New Zealand's first controlled powered flight.

After the outbreak of the First World War, many would-be pilots wrote to the Defence Department asking how they could qualify to join Britain's Royal Flying Corps (RFC). Eager to set up a training school, the Walshes persuaded the government to approach the British authorities. The RFC agreed to cable an aviator's certificate to each trained pilot, provided military observers witnessed their qualifying flight. Vivian was first in line, and by the war's end more than 100 pilots had been trained at Ōrākei. Most of them, including New Zealand's leading fighter 'ace', Keith Caldwell, saw combat with the RFC or the Royal Air Force, which was formed in 1918.

NEW ZEALAND'S FIRST GENERAL ELECTION BEGINS
14 July 1853

BORN ON THIS DAY

Rangitīaria Dennan
(Guide Rangi),
1897–1970,
Rotorua tourist guide

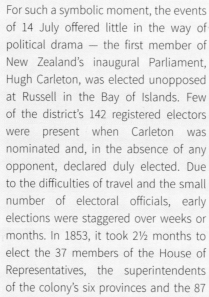

For such a symbolic moment, the events of 14 July offered little in the way of political drama — the first member of New Zealand's inaugural Parliament, Hugh Carleton, was elected unopposed at Russell in the Bay of Islands. Few of the district's 142 registered electors were present when Carleton was nominated and, in the absence of any opponent, declared duly elected. Due to the difficulties of travel and the small number of electoral officials, early elections were staggered over weeks or months. In 1853, it took 2½ months to elect the 37 members of the House of Representatives, the superintendents of the colony's six provinces and the 87 members of the provincial councils. The level of popular interest and participation varied widely around the colony. In a number of electorates, like the Bay of Islands, the elections aroused little excitement. Other contests, especially in the capital, Auckland, were fiercely fought and tainted by allegations of corruption and drunkenness. The Members of Parliament elected in 1853 would assemble for the first time in Auckland the following year (see 24 May).

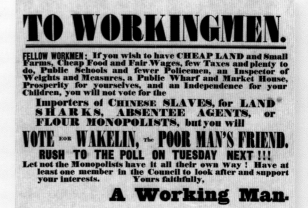

TO WORKINGMEN.

FELLOW WORKMEN; If you wish to have CHEAP LAND and Small Farms, Cheap Food and Fair Wages, few Taxes and plenty to do, Public Schools and fewer Policemen, an Inspector of Weights and Measures, a Public Wharf and Market House, Prosperity for yourselves, and an Independence for your Children, you will not vote for the Importers of CHINESE SLAVES, for LAND SHARKS, ABSENTEE AGENTS, or FLOUR MONOPOLISTS, but you will VOTE for WAKELIN, the POOR MAN'S FRIEND. RUSH TO THE POLL ON TUESDAY NEXT !!! Let not the Monopolists have it all their own Way ! Have at least one member in the Council to look after and support your interests. Yours faithfully,

A Working Man.

Election advertisement, 1853.

FIRST GALLIPOLI WOUNDED ARRIVE HOME

The first large group of Gallipoli wounded to return to New Zealand arrived in Wellington on the *Willochra* as part of a draft of around 300 men. The ship arrived around midnight on the 14th and anchored in the harbour. In the morning, various dignitaries and journalists went aboard. Some relatives took boats out to welcome the ship. Most people caught their first glimpse of the returning men as the ship arrived at Glasgow Wharf in the afternoon. About 2000 family, officials and journalists waited in a reserved area alongside the berth.

Authorities organised an official reception at Wellington Town Hall. Members of the public crowded the galleries, while returning soldiers, family and officials mingled on the ground floor. Men not fit enough to attend went straight to hospital or stayed on board the *Willochra*. A specially outfitted 'Red Cross train' — a New Zealand first — transported men to Auckland or other towns along the North Island main trunk line. Men bound for South Island ports left Wellington on the *Willochra* two days later.

The Homecoming from Gallipoli, Walter Armiger Bowring, 1916.

NEW ZEALAND ARTILLERY OPENS FIRE IN VIETNAM

Gunners from 161 Battery fired New Zealand's first shots of the Vietnam War from their Biên Hòa base near Saigon. Between 1963 and 1975 more than 3000 New Zealand military personnel and civilian volunteers served in Vietnam. Thirty-seven died on active service and 187 were wounded. Two civilians also died. This was the first war in which New Zealand did not fight alongside its traditional ally Britain, reflecting increasing defence ties with the United States and Australia.

The New Zealand government was cautious in its approach to Vietnam, sending a New Zealand Civilian Surgical Team in April 1963, then a team of army engineers in June 1964. The latter were engaged in road- and bridge-building projects.

The crucial decision to send combat forces was made in May 1965 and the Royal New Zealand Artillery's 161 Battery replaced the engineers in July. They served with the United States 173rd Airborne Brigade before joining an Australian task force. As New Zealand's commitment escalated, two rifle companies of the 1st Battalion, Royal New Zealand Infantry Regiment arrived in 1967.

161 Battery sign at Biên Hòa base.

DEATH OF PADDY THE WANDERER
17 July 1939

Paddy, a ginger and brown Airedale terrier, became a national celebrity because of his exploits on the Wellington waterfront (and beyond) during the 1930s. Paddy probably began life as Dash, the pet of a young girl whose father was a seaman. Dash spent a lot of time on the Wellington wharves when the family came to meet his ships. After the girl's death in 1928, Paddy, as he became known, began to wander the wharves. Paddy soon became a much-loved identity. Watersiders, Harbour Board workers, seamen and taxi drivers helped pay his annual dog licence. He became a familiar sight on Wellington's trams and taxis, and journeyed by sea to New Zealand and Australian ports. In December 1935, he even took to the air in a Gypsy Moth biplane. As he aged, Paddy wandered less. When his health deteriorated, he slept in a shed on the wharves, where he received frequent visitors. When Paddy died, notices were placed in the local papers and a radio tribute was broadcast. A drinking fountain near the Queens Wharf gates commemorates his life.

Paddy the Wanderer, 1935.

NEW ZEALAND'S FIRST POSTAGE STAMPS GO ON SALE

These adhesive, non-perforated stamps for prepaid postage were the famous 'Chalon Head' design, showing Queen Victoria in her coronation robes.

New Zealand issued its first postage stamps 15 years after they had appeared in Britain. The three stamps in the 'Full-face Queen' set — one penny (1d), two pence (2d) and one shilling (1s) — were printed in Britain. Other values were added later.

The first stamp designed in New Zealand was a halfpenny (½d) stamp issued on 1 January 1873. This had a side view of Queen Victoria's head and was known as the 'Newspaper' stamp because it was often used as payment for posting a newspaper. During the 1890s, New Zealand introduced a short-lived stamp with advertising on the back, and became one of the first countries in the world to release stamps with images of the countryside, birds and animals.

New Zealand was also one of the first countries to issue a 'penny universal' stamp in 1900. The idea was that all countries would charge a standard amount for postage, making it easier to send letters internationally.

'Full-face Queen' stamp, 1855.

These adhesive, non-perforated stamps for prepaid postage were the famous 'Chalon Head' design, showing Queen Victoria in her coronation robes.

PRIVY COUNCIL RULES ON SAMOAN CITIZENSHIP
19 July 1982

The Privy Council granted New Zealand citizenship to Western Samoans born since 1924, but the New Zealand government did not accept this decision. In response, it rushed through an act granting New Zealand citizenship only to Western Samoans living in New Zealand on 14 September 1982 or who subsequently obtained permanent residence. After Western Samoa achieved independence in 1962, the status of Samoans living in New Zealand was uncertain. In a case taken to the Privy Council, a Samoan woman living in New Zealand pressed her claim to be a New Zealand citizen. The Privy Council ruled that all Western Samoans born between 1924 and 1948 were British subjects and that in 1949 they and their descendants had become New Zealand citizens. Many Samoans felt betrayed by the government's response. The 1982 act remains a concern for Samoans in New Zealand who desire freedom of movement between the two countries. In March 2003, a petition with 90,000 signatures calling for the law's repeal was presented to Parliament, where about 2000 Samoans protested with speeches, dancing and singing.

Protesters seeking the repeal of the Citizenship (Western Samoa) Act 1982, Parliament Grounds, Wellington, March 2003.

RIOTS ROCK MT EDEN PRISON

The disturbance followed a botched escape attempt and lasted into the next day. Prisoners took several warders hostage and fire gutted part of the prison. At 2 a.m. on 20 July, two prisoners attempting to escape clubbed the unlucky warder who discovered them, took two hostages, and set about unlocking cells. Chaos ensued as prisoners lit fires and fuelled them with oil, furniture and their own belongings. Firefighters had to retreat under a barrage of bricks and other missiles.

Armed police, warders and troops stood guard around the prison, discouraging any attempts to break out with warning shots and high-powered hoses. Eventually the lack of food, fuel and shelter took its toll, and the prisoners surrendered 33 hours after the riot began.

The damage at Mt Eden was extensive. Inmates destroyed basements, storerooms, the kitchen, chapel, watch house and 61 cells, while there was extensive damage to the prison roof. Following the riot there were calls for the ageing prison, built in 1917, to be demolished. Prisoners were relocated while the gutted shell was rebuilt.

BORN ON THIS DAY

Edmund Hillary,
1919–2008,
mountaineer, explorer

An armed offenders' squad officer watches the riot inside Mt Eden Prison, 1965.

SILVER FERNS WIN NETBALL WORLD CUP
21 July 2019

New Zealand won its fifth world netball title, defeating arch-rivals Australia in the final in Liverpool. It was 16 years since a team other than Australia had been crowned world champions. Just 15 months earlier, the Silver Ferns had for the first time failed to reach the Commonwealth Games final — and then lost the bronze medal match to Jamaica. The selection of Noeline Taurua as head coach in August 2018 was the turning point in their fortunes. The hard-nosed former international was now the most successful coach in Australia's Super Netball League. She set rigorous fitness standards, refusing to select players who did not meet them. Netball New Zealand bowed to the realities of the professional era by dropping its insistence that players must be based in New Zealand to be eligible for selection. As a result, the stellar trio of Laura Langman (captain), Maria Folau and Casey Kopua were reunited for a last attempt to win the world title. A one-goal loss to Australia in pool play showed that the team were serious contenders. A 47–45 semi-final victory over hosts England set up a title rematch with the Diamonds that the Silver Ferns won 52–51.

The Silver Ferns celebrate after winning the 2019 Netball World Cup in Liverpool.

LOTTO GOES ON SALE FOR THE FIRST TIME

Outlets opened to long queues, with a first division prize in the inaugural draw of $360,000 (equivalent to $725,000 today). In the first year, Kiwis 'invested' nearly $249 million ($500 million) in the new lottery, which was based on a weekly draw of six numbers plus a bonus number. Lotto has introduced other options such as Powerball and Strike over the years.

By the early 2000s, 67 per cent of the population was regularly playing Lotto. Workmates and families formed syndicates to purchase weekly tickets. Nearly one-third of those buying tickets chose self-selected numbers rather than a computer-generated Lucky Dip.

By mid-2007 Lotto had paid out more than $3.75 billion in prize money to more than 63 million winners. The largest amount won on a single ticket is the $44 million jackpot won by a Hibiscus Coast couple in November 2016.

The profits from Lotto — about 70 cents in each dollar — are transferred to the Lottery Grants Board for distribution to sports, arts, film and community organisations. By 2015 the board had allocated $3.6 billion in grants.

By mid-2007 Lotto had paid out more than $3.75 billion in prize money to more than 63 million winners.

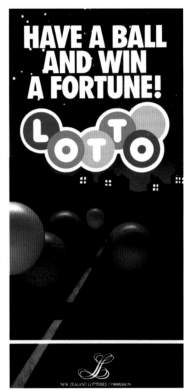

Lotto pamphlet, 1987.

Yvette Williams competes at the Helsinki Olympics.

YVETTE WILLIAMS LEAPS FOR GOLD AT HELSINKI
23 July 1952

Yvette Williams (later Corlett) won the long jump to become New Zealand's first female Olympic medallist. Thanks to amateur radio operators who were monitoring shortwave broadcasts, New Zealanders who stayed up through the night were able to follow her progress. After leading the qualifying round with a jump of 6.16 metres, Williams began the final round with two no-jumps. Facing elimination, she leaped 5.9 metres to make the top six and earn three more jumps. Her fourth jump was outstanding. At 6.24 metres (20 feet 5¾ inches), it was just 1 centimetre short of the world record. Williams had set a new Olympic record and won gold for New Zealand. International Olympic Committee member Sir Arthur Porritt presented Williams with her gold medal. The New Zealand flag was raised and the Finnish military band played both 'God Save the Queen' and 'God Defend New Zealand'. It was to be 40 years before New Zealand celebrated another female Olympic gold medallist — windsurfer Barbara Kendall at Barcelona.

NEW ZEALAND SOLDIER KILLED IN TIMOR-LESTE

Private Leonard Manning was the first New Zealander killed in combat since the Vietnam War. Manning's patrol was part of New Zealand's contribution to the United Nations (UN) peacekeeping force in the fledgling nation of Timor-Leste (East Timor). Pro-Indonesian militiamen ambushed the New Zealanders near the top of a steep hill close to the border with West Timor, which remained part of Indonesia. The ambush became the subject of a military Court of Inquiry and an Indonesian murder trial in which Manning's killer received a six-year sentence.

Violence had erupted in East Timor in September 1999 after an overwhelming majority of its people voted in favour of independence from Indonesia in a UN-supervised referendum. Pro-Indonesian militias wreaked havoc after the result, killing more than 1000 people.

With the arrival of a UN peacekeeping force, the militias fled across the border into West Timor, from where they launched sporadic armed raids such as the one that led to Manning's death. Four other New Zealand peacekeepers died while serving in East Timor.

The casket of Private Leonard Manning arrives in New Zealand, 26 July 2000.

ANTI-SPRINGBOK PROTESTERS PREVENT HAMILTON MATCH

Anti-tour demonstrators invaded Hamilton's Rugby Park, forcing the abandonment of the Springboks–Waikato match. Rugby Park was packed for the first Saturday match of the Springbok rugby team's controversial tour. More than 500 police officers were present in the city. The authorities were unaware, however, that protest organisers had bought several hundred tickets for the game. Shortly before kick-off, several hundred more invaded the pitch after ripping down a boundary fence.

Police formed a cordon around this group, which had linked arms in the middle of the pitch. They eventually arrested about 50 of them, but were concerned about their ability to hold back angry rugby fans.

Meanwhile, Pat McQuarrie had stolen a light plane from Taupō and was thought to be heading for the stadium. With his intentions unclear, the police cancelled the match. This announcement was greeted with chants of 'We want rugby!' Spectators attacked protesters as the police ushered them from the ground.

The drama was viewed live in South Africa and gave comfort to incarcerated opponents of apartheid, including Nelson Mandela.

The Reverend George Armstrong addresses police in the middle of Rugby Park, Hamilton.

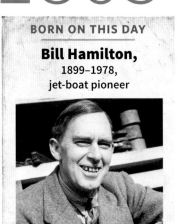

FLOODS KILL 25 MINERS IN CENTRAL OTAGO

Approximately 25 gold miners died on the Arrow diggings, north-east of Queenstown, in a series of flash floods and slips caused by 24 hours of heavy rain. It was the worst day of a brutal winter during which an estimated 100 miners were drowned, buried by mudslides or died of exposure.

The worst single tragedy occurred on the upper Shotover River, where mudslides had blocked a creek in the middle of the night. When this temporary dam burst, about 15 miners were swept away in the deluge along with their huts; 12 of them drowned. A landslip on the lower Shotover, near Moke Creek, killed seven men. Three drowned near Arthurs Point, and another three in a raging creek 3 kilometres from Arrowtown.

The floods were followed in August by snowstorms that caught out unwary travellers on high-country trails, literally freezing some in their tracks. Central Otago's rudimentary hospital facilities were soon overwhelmed, and many of the survivors lost fingers or toes to frostbite.

William Hodgkins painting of Clutha River diggings, c. 1862–63.

ARMISTICE ENDS KOREAN WAR

After lengthy negotiations, representatives of North Korea and the United Nations signed an armistice on the ceasefire line between North and South Korea. New Zealand's thousand-strong Kayforce had arrived in South Korea in December 1950 to join the UN's 'police action' against North Korean invaders. The Kiwis joined the 27th British Commonwealth Infantry Brigade in January 1951 and took part in operations in which the UN forces fought their way back across the 38th Parallel.

In April 1951 the Chinese, who had intervened to save North Korea from defeat, launched a massive offensive. The Commonwealth Brigade fought a defensive battle against a Chinese division at Kap'yong. Filling a gap in the UN line, New Zealand's 16 Field Regiment played a vital supporting role. Although Kap'yong later had to be abandoned, the Chinese offensive in this sector was checked.

About 4700 men served with Kayforce and 1300 on Royal New Zealand Navy frigates during New Zealand's seven-year involvement in Korea. Forty-five men lost their lives, 33 of them (including two naval personnel) during the war. In mid-2019 no peace treaty had been signed and the two Koreas were technically still at war.

BORN ON THIS DAY

Charles Brasch,
1909–1973,
poet, editor

New Zealand memorial in South Korea, 2010.

28 July 1893

MASSIVE WOMEN'S SUFFRAGE PETITION PRESENTED TO PARLIAMENT

The monster suffrage petition contained the signatures of more than 25,000 women. A dozen other, smaller petitions were also submitted around the same time. When pro-suffrage MP Sir John Hall presented them to the House of Representatives on 11 August, he noted that together they contained the signatures of nearly 32,000 women — almost a quarter of the adult European female population of New Zealand.

The Women's Christian Temperance Union and other organisations had campaigned for women's right to vote since the mid-1880s. In 1891 they presented to Parliament eight petitions containing more than 9000 signatures, and in 1892 six petitions containing almost 20,000. On each occasion opponents in the more conservative upper house, the Legislative Council, defeated electoral bills that would have enfranchised all adult women.

This time the outcome would be different. When the governor signed a new Electoral Act into law (see 19 September), New Zealand became the first self-governing country in the world to grant all adult women the right to vote in parliamentary elections.

Suffrage petition, 1893.

> *. . . together they contained the signatures of nearly 32,000 women — almost a quarter of the adult European female population of New Zealand.*

TASMANIA SINKS OFF MĀHIA WITH SUITCASE OF JEWELS

The Huddart-Parker Company steamer *Tasmania* left Auckland on the afternoon of 28 July bound for Dunedin via Napier, Wellington and Lyttelton. At around 11 p.m. the following night, with a strong south-east gale blowing, the ship struck rocks off Table Cape, Māhia Peninsula.

Four lifeboats and two smaller boats were launched. Five landed safely, although a seaman and a passenger were lost overboard from one; the sixth boat capsized and all nine of those on board (all crew members) were drowned. The *Tasmania* sank within an hour of striking the rocks.

The wreck of the *Tasmania* was largely unremarkable in an era when maritime accidents were commonplace. But one of the surviving passengers, jewellery merchant Isadore Jonas Rothschild, had left in his cabin a suitcase full of jewels valued at £3000 (around $560,000 today). After several unsuccessful attempts were made to retrieve the treasure, in 1973 marine archaeologist Kelly Tarlton purchased the right to salvage the jewels. Over the following years Tarlton recovered about 250 pieces, but he believed that more than half of the jewellery was still in the ship.

MOANA MACKEY JOINS MOTHER JANET IN PARLIAMENT

Twenty-nine-year-old Moana Mackey entered the House of Representatives as a Labour Party list MP, replacing Graham Kelly, who had resigned to become New Zealand's High Commissioner in Canada. She joined her mother, Janet Mackey, who had been a Labour MP since 1993, representing the seats of Gisborne, Māhia and then East Coast. They became the first mother and daughter to serve together in New Zealand's Parliament — and possibly the first to do so anywhere in the world.

Janet Mackey retired from Parliament at the 2005 election. Moana unsuccessfully contested her mother's old seat, but continued to serve as a list member until the 2014 election, when Labour's poor performance saw only five list MPs returned. By that time the Mackeys had served in the House for a combined total of 23 years.

Three pairs of fathers and sons have served in the House of Representatives at the same time: Edward Gibbon and Jerningham Wakefield in the 1850s, William and George Hutchison in the 1890s, and Norman and Roger Douglas between 1969 and 1975.

Moana Mackey, 2014.

1979

CARLESS DAYS INTRODUCED

Carless days for motor vehicles were introduced to combat the second 'oil shock' (reduced global oil supplies and increased fuel prices) of the 1970s. They did little to reduce petrol consumption and were scrapped in May 1980.

Under the legislation, all private owners of petrol-driven motor vehicles were required to select a day of the week on which they would not use their car. A coloured sticker on the windscreen indicated the chosen day. Those caught on the roads on their designated day off could be fined.

Other measures introduced to reduce petrol consumption included cutting the open-road speed limit from 100 to 80 kilometres per hour and restricting the hours during which service stations could sell petrol.

Several factors contributed to the scheme's ultimate failure. One centred on the issue of exemption — it was possible to apply for an 'X sticker' exemption if the vehicle was needed for urgent business. A black market for exemption stickers emerged, as did forgeries, making enforcement difficult. Households able to run two cars had a distinct advantage over others as they could choose different carless days for each vehicle.

This Nevile Lodge cartoon suggests one way of getting around the inconvenience of carless days.

"I SIMPLY WENT OUT AND BOUGHT A FEW MORE — NOW I HAVE ONE FOR EVERY STICKER IN THE WEEK"

FOUNDATION STONE LAID FOR NEW ZEALAND'S FIRST PURPOSE-BUILT THEATRE

Laying the foundation stone for the Royal Victoria Theatre on Manners Street, Wellington, Alderman William Lyon welcomed the new amenity — 'a theatre [was] a necessary concomitant of an advanced state of civilization'. It was a morale-boosting event six weeks after the Wairau incident (see 17 June) had shocked local settlers.

The building was erected behind the Ship Hotel by its proprietor, John Fuller. It opened on 12 September with a double bill: *Rover of the Seas* and *Crossing the Line, or the Twin Brothers*.

The Royal Victoria Theatre was a plain, rectangular wooden building, about 14 by 9 metres, with a gabled roof, a few windows along its side, and an entrance from the street next to the hotel. The interior had seating in stalls and a commodious gallery. It was brightly lit by whale oil gas, another innovation for Wellington.

Auckland's first purpose-built theatre was the Fitzroy, which opened in Shortland Street in 1844. Wellington's second theatre, the Britannia Saloon in Willis Street, forced the Royal Victoria out of business soon after it opened in 1845.

The Royal Victoria Theatre is the rectangular building adjoining the two-storey Ship Hotel at left.

1987

TE REO MĀORI RECOGNISED AS OFFICIAL LANGUAGE

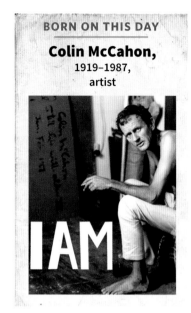

The Maori Language Act came into force, making te reo Māori an official language of New Zealand. Until the mid-19th century, te reo Māori was the predominant language spoken in Aotearoa/New Zealand. As more English speakers arrived, it was increasingly confined to Māori communities. By the mid-20th century, there were concerns that the language was dying out. In 1985 the Waitangi Tribunal heard the Te Reo Māori claim. This asserted that te reo was a taonga (treasure) that the government was obliged to protect under the Treaty of Waitangi. The Waitangi Tribunal found in favour of the claimants and recommended a number of legislative and policy remedies.

One of these was the Maori Language Act, which made Māori an official language of New Zealand and established the Maori Language Commission, renamed Te Taura Whiri i Te Reo Māori in 1991, to promote its use. According to the 2013 census there were around 125,000 speakers of Māori in New Zealand — about 21 per cent of the Māori population and 3 per cent of all New Zealanders.

Nan Bella teaching Māori at Waiwhetū School, 1991.

PROTEST AS USS *TEXAS* VISITS AUCKLAND
2 August 1983

The visit of the nuclear-powered guided missile cruiser *Texas* sparked anti-nuclear rallies on land and sea. Port visits by United States warships had been controversial for a number of years. Two nuclear-powered cruisers, USS *Truxtun* and USS *Long Beach*, had attracted protest when they visited New Zealand in 1976. On each occasion, Civil Defence established a public safety headquarters for the duration of the visit. Similar action was taken for the visits of the submarines USS *Pintado* in 1978 and USS *Haddo* in 1979. At issue was whether these ships were nuclear-armed as well as nuclear-powered. American policy was to 'neither confirm nor deny' the presence of nuclear warheads and other weapons, and most US allies chose not to ask — an arrangement that an increasing number of New Zealanders began to question. Nuclear ship visits became an election issue in 1984 and David Lange's Labour government later banned them. This policy, which led to the breakdown of the ANZUS security alliance, was later confirmed in law by the passage of anti-nuclear legislation in 1987 (see 8 June).

Protest march against the visit of USS *Texas*, Wellington, 11 August 1983.

FINNISH SAILING SHIP SEIZED AS WAR PRIZE

Five days after its arrival in Wellington, the four masted barque *Pamir* was seized in prize by the New Zealand government, which regarded Finland as 'territory in enemy occupation' (in reality, Finland had joined Nazi Germany's invasion of their mutual enemy, the Soviet Union, but was not formally a member of the Axis powers). The *Pamir* remains the only 'enemy' vessel ever to be seized by New Zealand.

Due to wartime shipping shortages, the barque was pressed into service as a New Zealand merchant vessel, mainly carrying wool and tallow to San Francisco and Vancouver. Managed by the Union Steam Ship Company and manned by a youthful, mostly New Zealand crew, the *Pamir* made 10 voyages under the New Zealand ensign. Few big square-rigged sailing ships had been seen in local ports for decades, and the barque left a lasting impression on many New Zealanders.

The *Pamir* was handed back to its Finnish owners in 1948 and later became a training vessel for the German navy. It was lost in the Atlantic during a hurricane in 1957.

The Pamir *remains the only 'enemy' vessel ever to be seized by New Zealand.*

The *Pamir* in Wellington Harbour, 1940s.

RAIL TUNNEL PIERCES THE SOUTHERN ALPS

Crowds gather for the opening of Ōtira Tunnel in 1923.

The opening of the 8.5-kilometre Ōtira Tunnel completed the long-planned transalpine railway between Christchurch and Greymouth. At the time, it was the longest tunnel in the southern hemisphere and the sixth-longest in the world.

Work had begun on the 'Midland' line 36 years before, but the original private developers' grand plans soon came unstuck. The government's Public Works Department (PWD) took over in 1895 and the West Coast section reached Ōtira by 1900. Tenders for a long tunnel through the Southern Alps to Arthur's Pass, 737 metres above sea level, were called in 1907. Contractors J.H. McLean & Sons began work the following year, but the project was plagued by engineering problems, extreme weather and labour shortages, forcing the PWD to step in again.

When the two ends of the tunnel were joined in 1918, the surveyors' centre lines were found to be less than 30 millimetres apart, impressive accuracy for the era. Due to the tunnel's length and steep gradient, electric locomotives were used to haul trains through it until 1997.

Metro cover, June 1987.

CARTWRIGHT REPORT CONDEMNS CANCER TREATMENT
5 August 1988

The report was triggered by the publication of a *Metro* magazine article by Sandra Coney and Phillida Bunkle, 'An Unfortunate Experiment', which alleged that cervical cancer patients at Auckland's National Women's Hospital were receiving inadequate treatment. Dr Herbert Green of the hospital's cervical cancer clinic had become convinced that abnormal cells in the cervix did not always progress to invasive cancer. Coney and Bunkle claimed that, from 1966, he began monitoring patients without treating them or informing them that they were taking part in an experiment. A number of women developed cervical cancer, and some died. The article caused public outrage and the government established a Committee of Inquiry, headed by Judge Silvia Cartwright, to investigate allegations of patient mistreatment. The resulting 'Cartwright Report' condemned the experiment and proposed radical new measures to ensure patients' rights, including the establishment of a National Cervical Screening Programme. A number of women received settlement packages. Charges against Dr Green did not proceed as he was deemed mentally and physically unfit to stand trial.

LOVELOCK WINS 1500 METRES GOLD AT BERLIN

Jack Lovelock won New Zealand's first Olympic athletics gold medal at the 1936 Berlin Olympics in a race witnessed by 120,000 spectators — including Adolf Hitler. Before the games, Lovelock contemplated competing in the 5000 metres instead of the 1500 metres. It seems that team manager Arthur Porritt made the final choice.

The field for the 1500 metres final included many of the top middle-distance runners against whom Lovelock had competed over the years. He ran a smart race, positioning himself inside the American Glenn Cunningham. As they approached the final lap, Swede Eric Ny was leading. When Lovelock surged to his shoulder, Cunningham followed. With 300 metres to go, Lovelock accelerated.

Lovelock's dramatic surge famously caused the BBC radio commentator, 1924 sprint gold-medallist Harold Abrahams, to forget his broadcasting etiquette: 'My God, he's done it! Jack! Come on! ... He wins! He's won! Hooray!' Lovelock's time of 3 minutes 47.8 seconds broke the world record for the 1500 metres and made the 4-minute mile seem a real possibility (another 109 metres run at the same pace would have resulted in a 4:04 mile).

Jack Lovelock won New Zealand's first Olympic athletics gold medal at the 1936 Berlin Olympics in a race witnessed by 120,000 spectators — including Adolf Hitler.

Jack Lovelock winning the 1500 metres at the Berlin Olympic Games, 1936.

1991

DEATH OF BILLY T. JAMES

The much-loved entertainer was just 43 when he died of heart failure. Born William Taitoko, the multi-talented musician toured the world with the Maori Volcanics Showband in the 1970s. He adopted the stage name Billy T. James because Australians could not pronounce his surname correctly.

James came to prominence in the television variety show *Radio Times*, but he is best remembered for the *Billy T James Show*, six series of which were screened by TVNZ between 1981 and 1986. On the show, the gifted impressionist portrayed a variety of characters in recurring sketches such as 'Te News', a parody of the Māori news show *Te Karere*. He lampooned both Māori and Pākehā quirks with affection and a trademark giggle. Later series of the show were co-written with Peter Rowley and featured more diverse material.

In 1985 James played the Tainuia Kid in an eccentric film adaptation of Ronald Hugh Morrieson's novel, *Came a Hot Friday*.

James suffered a major heart attack in 1988 and died three years later. The annual Billy T Award honours up-and-coming New Zealand comedians.

Billy T. James, 1985.

WELLINGTON BATTALION CAPTURES CHUNUK BAIR

The high point of the New Zealand effort at Gallipoli, the attack on Chunuk Bair peak highlighted the leadership of Lieutenant-Colonel William Malone.

Two columns of the New Zealand Infantry Brigade carried out the attack, which began on 6 August. The operation started well, but delays meant not all the infantrymen had reached Rhododendron Spur (which ran up to Chunuk Bair) by the time the assault on the summit started. The Auckland Battalion tried first and failed. The commander of the Wellington Battalion, Malone, argued against sacrificing his men in daylight and urged a night attack.

The Wellington Battalion occupied the summit before dawn on 8 August. With sunrise came a barrage of fire from Ottoman Turks holding higher ground to the north. A desperate struggle to hold Chunuk Bair ensued. By the time the Wellingtons were relieved that evening, only 70 of the battalion's 760 men were still standing. Malone was one of the casualties, killed by an Allied shell about 5 p.m.

Ottoman forces recaptured the position on 10 August from British troops who had relieved the New Zealanders.

By the time the Wellingtons were relieved that evening, only 70 of the battalion's 760 men were still standing.

The Battle of Chunuk Bair, 8 August 1915, painting by Ion G. Brown, 1990, commissioned to mark the 75th anniversary of the battle.

US 'GREAT WHITE FLEET' ARRIVES IN AUCKLAND

Sixteen American battleships and their escorts arrived in New Zealand with much pomp and ceremony. A feature of the six-day 'Fleet Week' stopover was a civic reception attended by most members of the New Zealand Parliament, who had travelled north from Wellington aboard the 'Parliament Special' — the first train to traverse the whole length of the still-unfinished main trunk railway (see 6 November).

The 'Great White Fleet' was a popular nickname for the US Navy battle fleet despatched on a global tour by President Theodore Roosevelt to show off the United States' growing naval capability. Between December 1907 and February 1909 the fleet covered nearly 70,000 kilometres and visited 20 ports on six continents. It travelled down the east coast of South America and through the Strait of Magellan before arriving in San Francisco in May 1908. Leaving California on 7 July, it crossed the Pacific to Auckland.

After stopovers in Australia, the Great White Fleet visited the Philippines, Japan and China before returning to America's Atlantic coast via Ceylon (Sri Lanka), the Suez Canal and the Strait of Gibraltar.

Crowd in Queen Street, Auckland, during celebrations for Fleet Week, 1908.

NEWS CORPORATION'S RIGHTS TO PROFESSIONAL RUGBY BOLSTERED

All Blacks Josh Kronfeld and Jeff Wilson signed contracts with the New Zealand Rugby Football Union (NZRFU), heralding the victory of Rupert Murdoch over Kerry Packer in a battle for the right to televise professional rugby.

The announcement of the Murdoch-backed professionalisation of southern hemisphere rugby on 23 June was the latest salvo in a war between the two Australian media magnates. Enraged by Murdoch's News Corporation's attempt to take over Australian rugby league, Packer backed the World Rugby Corporation (WRC), which lobbied the world's best players to join a global competition.

Murdoch's offer of US$555 million over 10 years for the right to televise South African, Australian and New Zealand rugby depended on the involvement of the same players. Lawyer Jock Hobbs and revered coach Brian Lochore travelled New Zealand making the NZRFU case.

In the previous few days the Springboks had disavowed their contracts with the WRC and Wallabies Tim Gavin and Jason Little had signed up with the Australian Rugby Football Union. When Wilson and Kronfeld went with the NZRFU, other All Blacks soon followed. On 27 August, the International Rugby Board declared the previously amateur game 'open'.

Jeff Wilson — shown here playing against the Wallabies — and his Otago teammate Josh Kronfeld were the first All Blacks to sign professional contracts with the NZRFU, 1995.

PICTON FERRY *ARAMOANA* ENTERS SERVICE

Few ships had as much impact on New Zealand history as the *Aramoana*, the country's first roll-on roll-off ferry, which entered service between Wellington and Picton in 1962. Cars and rail-freight wagons could now readily cross Cook Strait and be driven on and off at each end of the voyage.

The GMV *Aramoana* ('GMV' stood for 'government motor vessel') was the poster child of the Railways Department's new Cook Strait ferry service. Its influence was immediate. In its last year of service, the Union Steam Ship Company's former Wellington–Picton ferry *Tamahine* had carried 60,000 passengers, 11,000 cars and 14,000 tonnes of cargo. In its first year, the *Aramoana* carried 207,000 passengers, 46,000 cars and 181,000 tonnes of cargo.

Since the 1960s, five other Cook Strait ferries have carried the 'Ara' (meaning 'pathway') prefix: *Aranui*, *Arahanga*, *Aratika*, *Arahura* and *Aratere*. For more than half a century these ships — and more recent successors and competitors — have formed a 'floating bridge', linking the North and South Islands' road and rail networks in a truly national transport system.

The Cook Strait ferry *Aramoana* in rough seas, 1964.

WINTON 'BABY FARMER' MINNIE DEAN HANGED

In 1895 Southland's Williamina (Minnie) Dean became the first — and only — woman hanged in New Zealand. Her story exposed the stark realities of paid childcare and the lack of choice that many women faced in this period. Dean had looked after children, for a fee, since the late 1880s at her home, The Larches. In 1889 a six-month-old infant died, and two years later, a six-week-old baby. An inquest concluded that children at The Larches were well cared for, but that the premises were inadequate.

Police, concerned about Dean's activities, began watching her closely. On 2 May 1895, after she arrived home in Winton with only a heavy hatbox and without the child who had earlier been seen in her care, police searched her garden and unearthed the bodies of babies Dorothy Carter and Eva Hornsby and the skeleton of a four-year-old boy. Minnie Dean went on trial for Carter's murder in Invercargill on 18 June. Although her defence claimed the baby's death had been accidental, she was found guilty of murder and hanged at Invercargill jail two months later.

Dolls in miniature hat boxes are reputed to have been sold as souvenirs outside the Invercargill courtroom during the 1895 trial of Minnie Dean.

FIRST FATAL CASUALTY OF THE GREAT WAR
13 August 1914

Sapper Robert Arthur Hislop was guarding Parnell railway bridge in Auckland when he accidentally fell, dying from his injuries six days later. It would take a century, however, for Hislop to be officially recognised as the first New Zealand casualty of the Great War. A Railways Department employee, Hislop was a member of the North Island Railway Battalion, a territorial unit in which many railwaymen served. At the outbreak of the war, members of the battalion were mobilised to guard strategic assets such as bridges against possible sabotage. Hislop received a military funeral, his gravestone featured the battalion's badge, and his name appeared in the Railways Department roll of honour. But he had not enlisted in the New Zealand Expeditionary Force and was never assigned a service number — perhaps explaining why his name was not entered on the official national roll of honour. In 2014 Hislop was one of six servicemen added to the official roll after the New Zealand Defence Force determined that he had died as a result of his war service.

Robert Hislop's grave at Waikumete Cemetery, Auckland, 2014.

POLAR BLAST SWEEPS THE COUNTRY

Nw Zealand's heaviest snowfall in decades closed airports and schools, forced the cancellation of bus and train services, caused electricity blackouts and cut off many communities across the country. Weather watchers described the storm as 'a once in a lifetime' event. While the South Island was hardest hit, with widespread power outages and numerous school, airport and road closures, normally milder areas of the North Island were also severely affected. Power was cut to around 4000 homes in South Taranaki, Manawatū, Whanganui and Wairarapa.

Wellington saw snow down to sea level for the first time since 1976 and, remarkably, even Auckland's CBD got a dusting — for the first time since the 1930s.

Snow in the Upper Hutt suburb of Pinehaven, 16 August 2011.

TROOPSHIP *WAHINE* WRECKED EN ROUTE TO KOREA
15 August 1951

The New Zealand government chartered the TSS (Twin-Screw Steamship) *Wahine*, which had spent 38 years on the Lyttelton–Wellington ferry run and seen service in two world wars, to transport Kayforce troops to the Korean War. Shortly after leaving Darwin, the *Wahine* ran aground on Masela Island in the Arafura Sea, east of Timor. There were no fatalities but the ship became a total loss. Built in Scotland in 1913, the 4436-ton *Wahine* joined the Union Steam Ship Company's inter-island service. In 1915 the British government requisitioned the vessel as a despatch ship at Gallipoli and later as a minelayer. The *Wahine* impressed British observers with its manoeuvrability and it laid more than 11,000 mines in the North Sea during the war. During the Second World War the *Wahine* served as a troopship, mainly in the South Pacific. In April 1968, 17 years after the demise of the first *Wahine*, a much worse fate was to befall its namesake, the new TEV (Turbo-Electric Vessel) *Wahine*, which foundered near the entrance to Wellington Harbour with the loss of more than 50 lives (see 10 April 1968).

The *Wahine* leaving Wellington with troops for the Korean War, 3 August 1951.

EVERS-SWINDELL TWINS DEFEND OLYMPIC ROWING TITLE AT BEIJING

While Kiwis had high expectations of their rowing squad at the Beijing Olympics, few expected identical twins Caroline and Georgina Evers-Swindell to successfully defend the double sculls title they had won in Athens in 2004.

No duo had ever won this event twice at the Olympics. The Evers-Swindells' career seemed to have peaked with the third world championships they won in 2005 at Gifu, Japan. While they won bronze and then silver at the 2006 and 2007 worlds, by 2008 they were struggling to make the A finals (top six) at major European regattas. Victory in their heat at Beijing brought renewed hope.

Television viewers watching the final cheered as the Evers-Swindells launched a withering finishing burst, and then groaned as they apparently just failed to catch the German scullers. The British were also within centimetres and commentator Peter Montgomery called the New Zealanders in third. By next morning, he had re-recorded his commentary — the Kiwis had won gold by 1/100th of a second. New Zealand won another four medals that day, which was soon dubbed 'Super Saturday'.

Georgina and Caroline Evers-Swindell at Beijing.

NEW ZEALAND COMPANY SHIP
TORY ARRIVES

The sailing ship *Tory* dropped anchor in Queen Charlotte Sound to pick up fresh water, food and wood before proceeding to Port Nicholson (Wellington Harbour). On board were representatives of the New Zealand Company, sent to smooth the way for organised settlement. Their objectives were to purchase land, acquire information about the country and prepare settlements for the emigrants the Company was recruiting. Led by Colonel William Wakefield, brother of the Company's leading figure, Edward Gibbon Wakefield, the party also included William's nephew, Edward Jerningham Wakefield, naturalist Ernst Dieffenbach, draughtsman Charles Heaphy and interpreter Nahiti, a young Māori who had been conned by a whaling captain into working his passage to France. Dr John Dorset was Colonial Surgeon and Captain E.M. Chaffers the ship's master.

The *Tory* reached New Zealand in just 96 days. Haste was important as the New Zealand Company intended to send ships with settlers to New Zealand before receiving confirmation that the initial expedition had been successful. The first migrant ship, the *Aurora*, arrived in Wellington Harbour in January 1840 (see 22 January).

Painting of ships and waka (canoes) in Wellington Harbour, 1840, published as a supplement to the *Auckland Weekly News*, 1899.

CHAMPION ROWER DICK ARNST WINS RACE ON ZAMBEZI RIVER
18 August 1910

Former leading cyclist Dick Arnst had become world sculling champion in 1908. After two successful title defences at home, the muscular Arnst raced in a more exotic setting — on the Zambezi River. The British South Africa Company (founded by arch-imperialist Cecil Rhodes), which ruled the vast region now occupied by Zambia and Zimbabwe, sponsored his match with English champion Ernest Barry, described as 'the most scientific oarsman in the world'. It was the purse of £1000 (equivalent to $160,000 today) that lured both men so far from home. A sharpshooter deterred hippopotamuses from interfering in the race, which was rowed to the 'incessant roaring' of the nearby Victoria Falls. The umpire was Spencer Gollan, the Hawke's Bay runholder who owned the famous racehorse Moifaa. Cheered on by 'the black population, in all their finery', Arnst won easily. Arnst lost his title in a return match against Barry on the Thames in 1912. He got it back when Barry retired after the First World War, but lost it again to fellow New Zealander Darcy Hadfield in 1922.

Dick Arnst on the Whanganui River.

THREE NEW ZEALAND SOLDIERS KILLED IN AFGHANISTAN

At approximately 9.20 p.m. Afghanistan time, a Humvee (military light truck) taking a patrol member to see a doctor at the Romero base in Bamiyan province was destroyed by an improvised explosive device. Three New Zealand soldiers were killed instantly: Corporal Luke Tamatea (31) of Kawerau, medic Lance Corporal Jacinda Baker (26) of Christchurch, and Private Richard Harris (21) of Pukekohe, who was driving the Humvee.

Baker, a recipient of the Chief of Army Commendation, was the first New Zealand servicewoman killed as a result of enemy action since 10 nurses drowned when the transport ship *Marquette* was torpedoed in 1915 (see 23 October).

Tamatea and Harris were from the 2/1 Battalion while Baker was part of the 2nd Health Support Battalion. All three were deployed to Bamiyan with the Provincial Reconstruction Team in April 2012.

An emotional memorial service was held at Burnham Army Camp near Christchurch on 25 August before the bodies were released to their families for individual funeral services.

Corporal Luke Tamatea   Lance Corporal Jacinda Baker   Private Richard Harris

New Zealand soldiers killed in Afghanistan.

. . . a Humvee . . . taking a patrol member to see a doctor at the Romero base in Bamiyan province was destroyed by an improvised explosive device.

FIRST USE OF KIWI AS UNOFFICIAL NATIONAL SYMBOL

BORN ON THIS DAY

James Carroll,
1857–1926,
Māori politician

The *New Zealand Free Lance* printed a J.C. Blomfield cartoon in which a plucky kiwi morphed into a moa as the All Blacks defeated Great Britain 9–3 in the first rugby test between Motherland and colony. This may have been the first use of a kiwi to symbolise the nation in a cartoon. In 1905 Trevor Lloyd repeated this trope by depicting a kiwi unable to swallow Wales after the All Blacks' controversial loss in Cardiff. When the 'Originals' won, they were shown as a moa.

Also in 1905, the *Westminster Gazette* broadened the imagery by depicting a kiwi and a kangaroo going off to a colonial conference. By 1908 the kiwi was the dominant symbol for New Zealand in cartoons, especially sporting ones, having replaced images of moa, fern leaves, a small boy and a lion cub.

The New Zealand representative rugby league team was dubbed the Kiwis by a journalist in 1921 and has officially had this name since 1938. The 1945–46 2NZEF rugby team was also known as the Kiwis.

This may have been the first use of a kiwi to symbolise the nation in a cartoon.

THE TRIUMPH OF JOHN BULL, JUNIOR.
Episodes of Fact and Fancy in the Struggle for Rugby Supremacy.

J.C. Blomfield cartoon, 1904.

AUCKLAND PEDESTRIANS BEGIN 'BARNES DANCE'

Auckland became the first city in New Zealand to introduce the 'Barnes Dance' street-crossing system, which stopped all traffic at intersections, allowing pedestrians to cross in any direction at the same time.

Named after an American traffic engineer, Henry A. Barnes, the system was first used in the United States in the 1940s. Barnes did not claim to have invented the system, but, as traffic commissioner in Denver, Baltimore and then New York, he promoted its use in the CBDs of these cities. Despite many dire predictions, local newspapers were soon admitting that it worked well. The name was coined when a reporter wrote that 'Barnes has made the people so happy they're dancing in the streets'.

In Auckland the Barnes Dance became a feature of pedestrian traffic in Queen Street. Other New Zealand cities soon followed Auckland's lead and introduced the system. But as more vehicles clogged city streets, the Barnes Dance came under attack, with traffic engineers regarding cars as more important than pedestrians.

Queen Street, c. 1960.

FIRST YOUNG FARMER OF THE YEAR CHOSEN
22 August 1969

Held at the South Pacific Hotel in Auckland, the competition was open to all members of the Young Farmers' Club. The inaugural winner was Gary Frazer from Swannanoa, near Christchurch. The contest has since become an established part of the farming calendar. From humble beginnings in 1969, the Young Farmer of the Year competition today attracts up to 300 entrants each year. They compete at district and regional level to win the right to represent one of seven regions in the grand final. The 2016 finalists competed for more than $300,000 worth of prizes with the winner, Athol New from Aorangi, Mid Canterbury, scooping a prize package worth $80,000. By 2019 six women had made it to the final: Denise Brown in 1981, Louise Collingwood in 2003 and 2004, Katherine Tucker in 2012, Lisa Kendall in 2017, and Emma Dangen and Georgie Lindsay in 2019. The grand final involves three days of physical and intellectual challenges designed to test practical, business-management, problem-solving and social skills. The final has been televised since 1981.

Gary Frazer.

ASSISTED IMMIGRATION RESUMES AFTER WAR

The first draft of 118 British immigrants arrived in Auckland on the New Zealand Shipping Company liner *Rangitata*. They were among 77,000 men, women and children who arrived from Great Britain under the assisted immigration scheme between 1947 and 1975. Among the dignitaries waiting to greet them was Auckland's mayor, John Allum. In his speech of welcome, Allum acknowledged the differences between New Zealand and Britain, and 'asked the newcomers to be patient and take time to know New Zealand ways'.

The immigration assistance scheme, introduced in July 1947, was designed to bring skilled workers into New Zealand. Unlike earlier schemes, the focus was on attracting single people with industrial skills. There was an initial preference for 20 to 35-year-olds, but the upper age limit was extended to 45 in 1950.

While assistance went primarily to white British citizens, the country also sought other European groups who could easily assimilate into post-war New Zealand. The most favoured were the Dutch — more than 6000 arrived in the 1950s as part of an assisted passage scheme from the Netherlands.

Advertisement for the New Zealand Shipping Company, c. 1940.

WELLINGTON STEAM-TRAM SERVICE OPENED

The governor, the Marquess of Normanby, formally opened the new service, which was said to be the first in the southern hemisphere.

The Wellington Tramway Company had begun operating three days earlier, on 21 August. Its three small steam engines, *Hibernia*, *Wellington* and *Zealandia*, each hauling a passenger tramcar, ran from a terminus on Lambton Quay via Cuba and Vivian Streets to the company's depot in King Street, off Adelaide Road. The fleet later grew to eight engines, but they were not universally appreciated.

The steam trams were criticised for being noisy, dirty, frightening to horses and prone to derailment. As economic depression took hold at the end of the 1870s, the business was regularly up for public auction. Horse-drawn trams were reintroduced in 1882 and quickly proved popular. The last steam trams were withdrawn in 1892.

The city's tramway system was taken over by the Wellington City Corporation (WCC) in 1900, during the era of 'municipal socialism'. In 1904, the WCC introduced electric trams, which proved much more popular, remaining in service until 1964 (see 2 May).

The *Hibernia* and *Florence* steam trams being prepared for service outside the sheds at Adelaide Road, Newtown, Wellington, 1879.

1948

KILLER TWISTER HITS FRANKTON

Three people were killed, 80 injured and about 150 buildings destroyed or badly damaged by New Zealand's deadliest recorded tornado. The damage was estimated at more than £1 million (equivalent to about $72 million today).

Cars were smashed, concrete telephone poles snapped and trees torn up during the 10 minutes the tornado took to cut a path 100 to 200 metres wide through Frankton, on the western outskirts of Hamilton. The tornado lifted as it reached Hamilton's CBD but touched down again in Hamilton East. Here more trees were uprooted and two more houses damaged before it moved away from the city towards Tamahere.

The tornado picked up one house and turned it around before dropping it across the street. Amazingly, the occupants — a woman and her two children — escaped unharmed. The western side of the North Island is the second most tornado-prone area of the country, after Westland. On average, more than 30 tornadoes a year strike New Zealand. Most are relatively small and only about one-third of them occur near people and so are reported.

Cabinet minister Walter Nash visits a tornado-damaged house in Keddell Street, Frankton.

TELEGRAPH LINE LAID ACROSS COOK STRAIT
26 August 1866

After two bungled attempts and near disaster at sea, the installation of the first communications cable between the North and South Islands of New Zealand was completed. A simple copper telegraph cable was laid on the sea floor from Lyall Bay on Wellington's south coast to Whites Bay, north of Blenheim. The operation began off Wellington on 26 July 1866. The initial attempt failed after the cable snapped because the cable ship pulled it too quickly. A second attempt came up 32 kilometres short because the cable had drifted sideways in strong currents. Recycling cable from the first attempt helped make up the shortfall. The Cook Strait cable extended the telegraph network from Napier to Bluff. Given the large area covered, the government decided to introduce a uniform New Zealand time in September 1868. Before this, provincial centres maintained their own time according to longitude. This disrupted the telegraph system, as individual stations opened and closed at different times. New Zealand was the first jurisdiction in the world to implement a standard time nationwide.

Cross-section of telegraph cable.

PAWELKA'S LAST PRISON BREAK

POWELKA,
THE ESCAPED PRISONER.

Joseph Pawelka's escape from Wellington's Terrace Gaol was the last of the bold but seemingly effortless prison escapes he made over a period of 18 months. Pawelka's first escape was from Palmerston North's prison on 12 March 1910, when he climbed over a wall with the assistance of two upturned buckets and an inattentive guard. He rode off on a stolen bicycle, ending up 13 kilometres away at Awahuri, where he was recaptured two days later. Transferred to Wellington, he escaped again on 23 March from an unlocked police cell.

This led to what was then New Zealand's biggest manhunt as Pawelka fled north, committing burglaries and arsons along the way. Police finally caught up with him at Ashhurst on 17 April.

Pawelka received a cumulative sentence of 21 years. In August 1911 he escaped from the Terrace Gaol by removing the grille from his cell window.

Picture of Joseph Pawelka (also spelled Powelka) in the *Evening Post*, c. 1911.

Pawelka was never recaptured. While family lore suggests he fled to Canada, in 1913 *NZ Truth* published an account of his escape and new life in Mexico.

Sheep struggling in snow on Sawdon Station, Lake Tekapo, 1992.

A reported one million sheep died, at an estimated cost to farmers of $40 million . . .

CANTERBURY'S 'BIG SNOW'
28 August 1992

Cantabrians awoke to find the region blanketed in snow. The 'Big Snow', as the 1992 storm came to be known, was the region's heaviest for 30 years. From midday on 27 August weather forecasts alerted residents to the likelihood of snow, which began to fall that evening. As predicted, it snowed down to sea level. By mid-morning the next day, power was out throughout much of the region. Most of Christchurch city had electricity restored by the afternoon, but it took days for line gangs to reach some rural areas. Snow closed Christchurch Airport and many inland roads, schools and courts. Hospitals stayed open with assistance from the army and Red Cross. The rural community was hardest hit. It was the middle of the lambing season, and farmers lost newborn lambs, ewes and sheep freshly shorn in preparation for lambing. Other regions supplied hay and the government covered road-user charges incurred collecting and distributing feed. A reported one million sheep died, at an estimated cost to farmers of $40 million (equivalent to $65 million today).

NEW ZEALAND FORCE CAPTURES GERMAN SAMOA

Colonel Robert Logan led a 1400-strong expeditionary force to capture German Samoa in New Zealand's first action of the First World War. This was the second German territory, after Togoland in East Africa, to fall to the Allies in the war.

On 6 August, shortly after the outbreak of war, Britain asked the New Zealand government to capture a wireless station in German Samoa. The station, situated in the hills behind Apia, was strategically important because it was capable of sending signals to Berlin and the German fleet in the Pacific.

A small force of local constabulary protected the wireless station. They were no match for the Samoa Expeditionary Force, which achieved its objective without resistance.

New Zealand occupied the islands for the remainder of the war, then from 1920 until 1962 administered Western Samoa under mandates from the League of Nations and its successor, the United Nations. New Zealand's rule was marred by its inept handling of the deadly influenza epidemic of 1918 and suppression of the Mau nationalist movement in the 1920s (see 28 December).

Cartoon from the *Observer*, 1914.

The station, situated in the hills behind Apia, was strategically important because it was capable of sending signals to Berlin and the German fleet in the Pacific.

FOUR KILLED BY WAIMANGU GEYSER

Guide Joseph Warbrick and three tourists were killed instantly when the Waimangu Geyser, located south of Rotorua near Lake Rotomahana, erupted unexpectedly.

North Island geyser fields played an important part in the emergence of New Zealand's tourism industry during the 19th century. After the eruption of Mt Tarawera destroyed one of the major fields, Rotomahana, in 1886, geyser tourism received a boost in 1900 when the Waimangu ('black water') Geyser burst into life.

The largest known geyser in the world at the time, its activity increased in 1903, attracting more visitors. Warbrick and the party he was leading were caught out by a highly unpredictable natural phenomenon. The regularity and force of the geyser began to wane in 1904 and, in November, it stopped as suddenly and inexplicably as it had begun.

Warbrick had earlier achieved some fame as captain of the 1888/89 New Zealand Natives rugby team. The first New Zealand representative rugby team to tour beyond Australia, they played a staggering 107 matches in New Zealand, Australia and Great Britain, winning 78 of them.

BORN ON THIS DAY

Ernest Rutherford,
1871–1937,
Nobel Prize-winning scientist

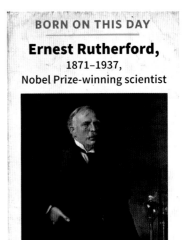

Waimangu Geyser, c. 1903–04.

ARBITRATION ACT BECOMES LAW

31 August
1894

The Industrial Conciliation and Arbitration (IC&A) Act made New Zealand the first country in the world to outlaw strikes and introduce compulsory arbitration. Following the failure of the trans-Tasman Maritime Strike of 1890, some major employers refused to recognise unions, blacklisted their members and slashed wages and conditions. The Liberal government that took office in 1891 was determined to find an alternative to industrial conflict, and to foster the union movement, which it saw as a key political ally.

The brainchild of Minister of Labour William Pember Reeves, the IC&A Act recognised trade unions and individual employers or industrial unions of employers as responsible parties in the negotiation of wages and other employment conditions. Each party would be required, if in dispute with the other, to discuss the matter at a district Board of Conciliation. If this failed to produce an agreement, the dispute would be submitted to a national Court of Arbitration. The arbitration system would remain the cornerstone of New Zealand's industrial relations system until 1973, when a new Industrial Relations Act superseded the IC&A Act.

Cartoon showing William Pember Reeves uniting Labour and Capital in the bonds of Industrial Conciliation, *New Zealand Graphic and Ladies' Journal*, 1893.

THE NEW ZEALAND GRAPHIC.   177

ARBITRARY ARBITRATION COURT.

COMPULSORY CONCILIATION.

The Hon. Mr. Reeves, as the angel of peace, uniting Labour and Capital in the silken bonds of Industrial Conciliation.

ELEANOR ROOSEVELT VISITS AUCKLAND

1 September 1943

It was near the end of the US First Lady's surprise visit to New Zealand to meet American forces based in the country, inspect the work of the US Red Cross — whose grey uniform she wore throughout her seven-day stay — and study the contribution of New Zealand women to the war effort. The most high-profile presidential spouse to that time, she was known for her concern for the downtrodden and for the rights of women. After flying in to Auckland on 27 August, Roosevelt travelled by overnight train to Wellington, where she received a heroine's welcome (a highlight was an all-women meeting in the Majestic Theatre). Next stop was Rotorua, where she was honoured by being allowed to speak on the marae at Ōhinemutu.

Arriving back in Auckland she attended a civic reception, visited the naval hospital and the Red Cross and Allied Services Clubs, and dropped in to the Red Cross dance in the Town Hall, where Artie Shaw's band was in full swing. Eleanor Roosevelt left New Zealand on 3 September for Australia and the Pacific.

Eleanor Roosevelt arrives in Auckland, 27 August 1943.

GOLDEN HOUR FOR KIWI RUNNERS IN ROME

New Zealand sport enjoyed one of its greatest days in Rome's Olympic Stadium. Peter Snell won the 800 metres and Murray Halberg won the 5000 metres. Snell was ranked 26th in the world. Cannily coached by Arthur Lydiard, the 21-year-old cruised through the three qualifying rounds, running impressive times. The final was run at a red-hot pace. The favourite, Belgian world record-holder Roger Moens, took the lead with 100 metres to go and seemed certain to win until Snell surged past him on the inside. When he realised he had won in Olympic record time, Snell was too stunned to take a victory lap. Minutes later, Halberg lined up in the 5000 metres final, for which he had qualified easily. Running to a plan set by Lydiard, he burst ahead of the field with three laps to go and hung on to the finish before collapsing on the infield, completely spent. Amid the excitement, New Zealander Valerie Sloper (later Young) narrowly missed out on a medal in the women's shot put, which was going on at the same time.

Peter Snell overtakes Roger Moens to win the 800 metres at the Rome Olympics, 1960.

FIRST OPEN-HEART SURGERY IN NEW ZEALAND
3 September 1958

Pioneering heart surgeon Brian Barratt-Boyes performed the surgery using a heart-lung bypass machine. The procedure, at Greenlane Hospital in Auckland, was performed on an 11-year-old girl with a hole in her heart. Barratt-Boyes had persuaded the Auckland Hospital Board to purchase a heart-lung machine developed in Britain during the early 1950s. It arrived with a number of parts missing and in need of significant alteration. Kiwi ingenuity saved the day. Alfred Melville of the Auckland Industrial Development Laboratory manufactured the parts required and made the machine fully functional. It was able to bypass the patient's heart for 25 minutes. Barratt-Boyes and his medical team established an international reputation for their work. He pioneered new surgical techniques to replace defective heart valves and found new ways to treat babies born with heart defects. Many of the techniques he developed became common practice worldwide. In 1971 Barratt-Boyes received a knighthood in recognition of his services to medicine. He himself suffered from heart problems, and he died in 2006 shortly after undergoing heart surgery in the United States.

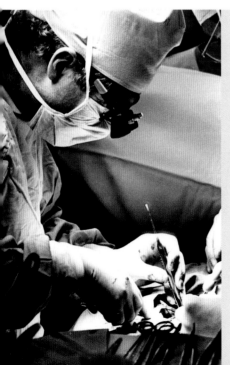

Surgeon Brian Barratt-Boyes at work.

7.1 EARTHQUAKE ROCKS CANTERBURY

The earthquake struck at 4.35 a.m. on Saturday, 4 September and was felt by many people in the South Island and the southern North Island. There was considerable damage in central Canterbury, especially in Christchurch, but no loss of life.

It was the largest earthquake to affect a major urban area since the 1931 Hawke's Bay earthquake (see 3 February). The epicentre was 37 kilometres west of Christchurch near the town of Darfield. As a relatively shallow quake — about 10 kilometres below the surface — it produced the strongest shaking recorded in New Zealand. Few people sustained serious injuries, largely because of the time the quake occurred — most were in bed and the streets were largely deserted.

The people of Christchurch would not be so lucky a few months later when a 6.3-magnitude earthquake struck (see 22 February). This event occurred in the middle of the working day at 12.51 p.m. Central Christchurch was badly damaged, 185 people were killed and several thousand injured. This time the epicentre was near Lyttelton, just 10 kilometres south-east of Christchurch's CBD.

Damaged car in Christchurch after the earthquake, September 2010.

PRIME MINISTER DECLARES NEW ZEALAND'S SUPPORT FOR BRITAIN

When New Zealand declared war on Germany on 3 September 1939, Prime Minister Michael Joseph Savage was recovering from an operation for colon cancer. Acting Prime Minister Peter Fraser issued a statement in his place.

Two days later Savage addressed the public from his sickbed at his home in Wellington. The address was broadcast on radio that evening and widely reported in newspapers in the following days. Savage's address was at once an attack on the evils of Nazism and an expression of the country's loyalty to and support for Britain:

> *Both with gratitude for the past and confidence in the future, we range ourselves without fear beside Britain. Where she goes, we go. Where she stands, we stand. We are only a small and young nation, but we are one and all a band of brothers and we march forward with union of hearts and wills to a common destiny.*

Savage died just over six months later, on 27 March 1940, and was succeeded by Fraser, who led New Zealand's government for the rest of the Second World War.

Where she goes, we go. Where she stands, we stand.

Michael Joseph Savage on the campaign trail, 1938.

NEW ZEALAND CITIZENSHIP ESTABLISHED
6 September 1948

The British Nationality and New Zealand Citizenship Act 1948 (the order of the words showed their relative importance) gave New Zealand citizenship to all current residents who had been either born or naturalised as British subjects. Until this act came into force, people born in New Zealand were British subjects but not New Zealand citizens. Almost all children subsequently born in New Zealand would become citizens. New residents who were citizens of the British Commonwealth or Ireland could become New Zealand citizens simply by registering, a regime that particularly benefited resident and arriving Indian people. 'Good character' remained necessary for those seeking naturalisation — communist leanings or affiliation ruled out some applicants in the early 1950s. Only about 10 per cent of British-born immigrants who arrived between 1948 and 1951 chose to register, as there was little practical reason for them to do so. In 1959 the registration of Commonwealth citizens as New Zealand citizens was tightened — the criteria for registration became basically the same as for naturalisation.

Passport office in Wellington, 1948.

SPRINGBOKS PLAY NEW ZEALAND MAORIS FOR THE FIRST TIME

A South African journalist was outraged when white spectators supported the New Zealand Maoris rugby team against the touring Springboks at Napier. 'Spectacle thousands Europeans frantically cheering on band of coloured men to defeat members of own race was too much for Springboks, who frankly disgusted,' he telegraphed.

The tourists held on to win 9–8. When the cable was published in *NZ Truth*, the Springboks' manager did not deny that his players had been upset by remarks from the crowd. However, the team 'had the greatest admiration for the Natives as a race'. The telegraphist found to have leaked it was later fired.

With 'the Rugby championship of the world' about to go on the line in the third test, the controversy soon blew over. But it highlighted an issue which was to fester for most of the 20th century. Opposing sporting contacts was increasingly seen as a way to exert pressure on South African racial policies. Things came to a head during the controversial 1981 Springbok tour of New Zealand (see 25 July, 12 September).

Programme cover,
Springbok tour, 1921.

8 September 1862

FIRST ALBERTLAND SETTLERS ARRIVE IN AUCKLAND

The *Matilda Wattenbach* brought 352 Nonconformist (non-Anglican Protestant) immigrants from England. Another 315 arrived on the *Hanover* a week later, and six more immigrant ships had arrived by 1865.

The newcomers were the nucleus of a model community planned by the Albertland Special Settlement Association, set up in Birmingham in 1861 and named for Queen Victoria's recently deceased husband. These idealists even brought a printing press with them. Like many of the immigrants, this stayed in Auckland for some time.

Only a few hundred of the 3000 who had signed up for the scheme eventually made a go of it on the 40 acres (16 hectares) that had been surveyed for each adult (plus 20 acres for each school-age child) around the Arapāoa, Ōtamatea and Ōruawharo 'rivers' — shallow inlets on the eastern side of Kaipara Harbour. Access via the 'Great North Road' was impossible and the Kaipara bar was dangerous to cross. Worse still, the soil was generally infertile. Most sections in the planned town of Port Albert were land-banked by speculators and it never prospered.

Sign on the foreshore at Port Albert.

PORT ALBERT

Port Albert was a centre for the non-conformist church settlement sponsored by the Albertland Special Settlement Association which was set up in Birmingham in 1861.

In October 1862 the sailing vessels *Hanover* and *Matilda Wattenbach* arrived at Auckland with the first settlers, who went by various routes to land surveyed round the Arapaoa, Otamatea and Oruawharo Rivers.

More immigrant ships followed but isolation and difficulties of access hindered progress and the original plans for a township at Port Albert were thwarted.

WANGANUI COMPUTER LEGISLATION ENACTED

The establishment of New Zealand's first centralised electronic database through the Wanganui Computer Centre Act focused attention on the state's ability to gather information on its citizens.

The National Law Enforcement Data Base — the 'Wanganui Computer' — allowed Police, Ministry of Transport and Justice officials to share information via hundreds of terminals around the country. It recorded motor vehicle registrations, driver's and firearms licences, traffic and criminal convictions, and personal information about large numbers of New Zealanders. The Serious Fraud Office and local authorities were later given access to this information.

In 1976 the Wanganui Computer was ground-breaking. Police Minister Allan McCready described it as 'the most significant crime-fighting weapon ever brought to bear . . . in this country'.

Critics were unconvinced. Civil libertarians protested, likening it to something from George Orwell's *1984*. On 18 November 1982, 22-year-old anarchist Neil Roberts was blown up by his own gelignite bomb as he tried to enter the computer centre. Eventually justice-sector agencies began to develop in-house computing capacity. The Whanganui centre closed in 1995 and the system was decommissioned in 2005.

Bomb damage to the Wanganui Computer Centre, 1982.

TE MAORI EXHIBITION OPENS IN NEW YORK

The landmark *Te Maori* exhibition was a milestone in the Māori cultural renaissance. Featuring traditional Māori artwork, it toured the United States between 1984 and 1986, before returning to New Zealand for a nationwide tour in 1987.

New Zealand and American arts professionals first discussed the idea of a Māori art exhibition touring the United States during the early 1970s. The cost proved prohibitive and the idea was shelved until the New York Metropolitan Museum of Art ('The Met') revived discussions in 1979. After securing some corporate sponsors, the government formally approved the proposal, setting up a management committee chaired by the Secretary for Maori Affairs, Kara Puketapu. A Māori sub-committee was also formed, with responsibility for deciding what role Māori would play in organising the exhibition and the traditional opening ceremonies.

This was the first time Māori were actively involved in the process of exhibiting their taonga overseas. The management committee recommended that Māori accompany the exhibition as guardians, ensured Māori were trained as guides, and helped arrange a dawn ceremony to open the exhibition at The Met. The dawn ceremony included traditional elements, such as karanga (call) and karakia (prayer) familiar to the 90-strong New Zealand party of kaumātua (elders), cultural performers, carvers, weavers and officials. The Met was the exhibition's first stop on a tour of the United States, followed by the St Louis Art Museum, the M.H. de Young Memorial Museum in San Francisco and the Field Museum in Chicago.

Te Maori made international headlines, while New Zealand's own media awoke to the nation's unique Māori point of difference. On its return to New Zealand in 1986, the exhibition was rebranded as *Te Maori: Te hokinga mai. The return home* and exhibited in Auckland, Wellington, Christchurch and Dunedin. The organising committee worked with each venue, facilitating wider Māori interaction, both as hosts and guests. Visitors were welcomed by elders and expertly guided by kaiārahi (Māori hosts) who were direct descendants of the ancestors on display.

Following the closure of *Te Maori* in September 1987, the taonga were returned to the institutions from which they had been borrowed.

Staff at the Auckland City Art Gallery just before the opening of *Te Maori*.

FIRST TRANS-TASMAN FLIGHT TOUCHES DOWN

Australian pilots Charles Kingsford Smith and Charles Ulm successfully crossed the Tasman in a Fokker tri-motor named the *Southern Cross*, covering 2670 kilometres in 14 hours 25 minutes.

New Zealander T.H. McWilliams, a teacher at the Union Steam Ship Company's radio school in Wellington, had joined the four-man crew as radio operator. Though the flight had been postponed for a week in the hope of good weather over the Tasman, they struck thunderstorms throughout the night. While McWilliams struggled to repair the radio equipment, which had failed shortly after take-off, Kingsford Smith was forced to fly blind for much of the journey as heavy rain and ice coated the windshield.

As they neared New Zealand the weather improved, and after circling over Wellington the *Southern Cross* landed at Wigram Aerodrome, Christchurch at 9.22 a.m. (New Zealand time).

The welcome in Christchurch was tremendous. About 30,000 people had made their way to Wigram, including many pupils from state schools, who were given the day off, and public servants, who were granted leave until 11 a.m.

Crowd welcoming the *Southern Cross* at Wigram, Christchurch.

12 September
1981

'FLOUR-BOMB TEST' ENDS SPRINGBOK TOUR

The third and deciding rugby test at Eden Park, Auckland, is remembered for the flares and flour bombs dropped onto the pitch. Outside the ground, violence erupted on an unprecedented scale. As was typical of this tour, the on-field action was overshadowed by events elsewhere. Fighting erupted in nearby streets and police pelted with rocks and missiles gave as good as they got. The protesters were joined by opportunists keen to fight the police.

Security around the ground was the tightest of the tour, but Marx Jones and Grant Cole took their anti-tour protest to new heights in a hired Cessna aircraft. While protesters on the ground fired flares, Jones and Cole peppered Eden Park with flour bombs in an attempt to halt the game.

Against this surreal backdrop, the rugby continued. When All Black prop Gary Knight was felled by a flour bomb, South African captain Wynand Claassen asked if New Zealand had an air force. The All Blacks won 25–22 thanks to an injury-time penalty goal by Allan Hewson.

All Black prop Gary Knight is felled by a flour bomb during the third test against the Springboks in Auckland, 1981.

NEW ZEALAND'S FIRST WOMAN MP ELECTED
13 September 1933

The Labour Party's Elizabeth McCombs became New Zealand's first woman Member of Parliament, winning a by-election in the Lyttelton seat caused by the death of her husband, James McCombs (one of the first Labour MPs, who had held the seat since 1913). Although New Zealand women had famously won the right to vote in 1893 (see 19 September), they were not allowed to stand for Parliament until 1919. A handful of women had contested elections, including the well-known Ellen Melville in Auckland, and McCombs herself in 1928 and 1931. Although James had won Lyttelton by just 32 votes in 1931, Elizabeth achieved a majority of 2600. Sadly, she died less than two years later. The McCombs family tradition continued after Elizabeth's death: she was succeeded by her and James's son Terence, who was MP for Lyttelton until 1951, and minister of education from 1947 to 1949. His defeat in the snap 'waterfront dispute' election ended his family's 38-year hold on the seat. The second woman MP was Labour's Catherine Stewart, elected for Wellington West in 1938.

Elizabeth McCombs, c. 1933.

SOCIAL SECURITY ACT PASSED

BORN ON THIS DAY

Sam Neill,
1947–,
actor

The cornerstone of the first Labour government's welfare programme, the Social Security Act overhauled the pension system and extended benefits for families, invalids and the unemployed. From the late 19th century New Zealand had gained a reputation as the 'social laboratory of the world' and a 'working man's paradise', but this status was severely challenged by the harsh economic conditions of the 1930s Great Depression. High unemployment, grim work camps and queues at soup kitchens shocked many New Zealanders.

Labour won the 1935 election arguing that every New Zealander had a right to a reasonable standard of living. The community was responsible for ensuring that people were not overwhelmed by circumstances against which they could not protect themselves. Labour's ultimate response to the Depression was the Social Security Act. The act combined the introduction of a free-at-the-point-of-use health system with a comprehensive array of welfare benefits. It was financed by a tax surcharge of one shilling in the pound, or 5 per cent. Supporters envisaged a scheme that would protect New Zealanders 'from the cradle to the grave'.

High unemployment, grim work camps and queues at soup kitchens shocked many New Zealanders.

Michael Joseph Savage opens the Social Security Building, Aotea Quay, Wellington, 27 March 1939.

1969

FIRST STEEL PRODUCED FROM LOCAL IRONSAND

BORN ON THIS DAY

Jean Batten,
1909–1982,
aviator

New Zealand Steel's Glenbrook mill, near Waiuku, south of Auckland, produced iron and steel from local ironsand (titanomagnetite) for the first time. By the 2010s ironsand and coal were used to produce about 650,000 tonnes of steel a year.

Black iron-rich sands are found along much of the western coast of the North Island. The ironsand is the product of rocks formed by volcanic activity in the Taranaki area 2.5 million years ago. In some places the ironsand deposits have formed dunes up to 90 metres high.

European settlers were fascinated by the sands' magnetic qualities. Early attempts to smelt iron from the ironsand met with little success. In the 1950s the government made renewed efforts to utilise this valuable resource. They established a New Zealand Steel Investigating Company in 1959 to determine the feasibility of manufacturing steel from local raw materials. New Zealand Steel Limited was incorporated in 1965 and the Glenbrook mill opened in 1968.

Glenbrook remains the only steel manufacturer in the world to use titanomagnetite sand as its source of iron.

New Zealand Steel mill, Glenbrook, October 1968.

'ORIGINALS' KICK OFF ALL BLACK TRADITION

The first fully representative New Zealand rugby team to tour the northern hemisphere was known as the 'Originals'. They won 34 of their 35 matches and popularised both the haka and the 'All Blacks' nickname.

Many rugby players in the 'Home Countries' believed themselves to be superior exponents of a sport they had invented and then exported to the settler colonies. But the All Blacks — named for the colour of their uniforms — hit the ground running, scoring 385 points in their first 10 games in England. Their opponents had managed a total of one dropped goal and one try.

Though scores fell off somewhat as they struck stronger opposition and injury, illness and fatigue took their toll, the All Blacks won 31 of their 32 games in the United Kingdom. The exception was a 3–0 loss to Wales (see 16 December). Welsh teams gave the All Blacks their toughest games: the three top clubs were beaten by a combined score of 20 points to 14.

A lineout during the match between the All Blacks and Midland Counties, 1905.

FLOGGING AND WHIPPING ABOLISHED
17 September 1941

As well as (temporarily) doing away with capital punishment for murder, the Crimes Amendment Act 1941 abolished judicial provision for flogging and whipping. These punishments had been introduced — initially for juveniles — from 1867 and by 1893 applied to a number of (mainly sexual) offences by adult men. In New Zealand, unlike the United Kingdom, corporal punishment was always inflicted behind prison walls. Just 17 men were flogged — receiving between 10 and 15 strokes of the 'cat' — between 1919 and 1935, when the last flogging took place. Fourteen of them had committed sexual offences. Until 1936 youths aged under 16 could be whipped for a wider variety of offences than adults. In practice, the punishment was imposed on boys mainly for theft, breaking and entering, and wilful damage. New Zealand branches of the Howard League had campaigned against both corporal and capital punishment since the 1920s. While the death penalty was reintroduced in 1950, flogging was not. It had had no apparent deterrent effect, and its removal had not been followed by increased violence in prisons.

A cat-o'-nine-tails. The label on the stick says that it was authorised for use by Minister of Justice A.L. Herdman on 6 October 1913.

FIRST STATE HOUSE OPENED IN MIRAMAR

Most of the Labour Cabinet helped the first tenants move into 12 Fife Lane in Miramar, Wellington. Even Prime Minister Michael Joseph Savage carried a cumbersome dining table through a cheering throng. The tenants, David and Mary McGregor, found themselves with such distinguished movers because their new home was the first to be completed and made available to state tenants in a new subdivision of state houses. After the opening ceremony, 300 people traipsed through the McGregors' open home, muddying floors and leaving fingerprints on freshly painted fixtures. They eventually persuaded their guests to leave, but for days afterwards, sightseers peered through the windows.

The first Labour government, elected in 1935 (see 27 November), argued that only the state could fix the housing shortage. In 1936 it drew up plans to use private enterprise to build 5000 state rental houses across New Zealand. A new Department of Housing Construction oversaw building and the State Advances Department managed the houses. The initiative formed part of a wider plan to slash unemployment and stimulate the economy.

New Zealand's first state house, pictured in 1978.

WOMEN WIN THE RIGHT TO VOTE

When the governor, Lord Glasgow, signed a new Electoral Act into law, New Zealand became the first self-governing country in the world to grant all adult women the right to vote in parliamentary elections. As women in most other democracies — including Britain and the United States — did not win the right to vote until after the First World War, New Zealand's world leadership in women's suffrage became a central part of our image as a trailblazing 'social laboratory'.

The passing of the act was the culmination of years of agitation by the Women's Christian Temperance Union (WCTU) and other organisations. As part of this campaign, a series of massive petitions were presented to Parliament; those gathered in 1893 were together signed by almost a quarter of the adult Pākehā women in New Zealand (see 28 July). As in 1891 and 1892, the House of Representatives passed an electoral bill that would grant the vote to all adult women. Once again, all eyes were on the upper house, the Legislative Council, where those two earlier attempts had foundered. Liquor interests, worried that female voters would favour their prohibitionist opponents, petitioned the Council to reject the bill. Suffragists responded with mass rallies and a flurry of telegrams to members.

New Premier Richard Seddon and other opponents of women's suffrage again tried to sabotage the bill, but this time their interference backfired. Two opposition councillors who had previously opposed women's suffrage changed their votes to embarrass Seddon. On 8 September, the bill was passed by 20 votes to 18. New Zealand women went to the polls for the first time on 28 November, when more than 90,000 of them cast votes. Despite warnings from suffrage opponents that 'lady voters' might be harassed at polling booths, election day passed off in a relaxed, festive atmosphere.

Even so, women had a long way to go to achieve political equality. They would not gain the right to stand for Parliament until 1919 and the first female MP was not elected until 1933 (see 13 September). Today women remain under-represented in Parliament, making up 42 per cent of the MPs in 2019.

. . . New Zealand became the first self-governing country in the world to grant all adult women the right to vote in parliamentary elections.

Women's suffrage memorial, Christchurch.

MAZENGARB REPORT RELEASED

The Mazengarb inquiry into 'juvenile delinquency' blamed the perceived promiscuity of the nation's youth on working mothers, easy availability of contraceptives, and young women enticing men into having sex. In July 1954 the government appointed lawyer Dr Oswald Mazengarb to chair a Special Committee on Moral Delinquency in Children and Adolescents. They established the committee after a teenage sex scandal in Lower Hutt and other high-profile incidents such as a milk-bar murder in Auckland and the Parker–Hulme killing (see 22 June).

The report, sent to every New Zealand home, blamed lack of parental supervision for juvenile delinquency and advocated a return to Christianity and traditional values. Excessive wages for teenagers, a decline in family life, and the influence of film, comics and American literature all apparently contributed to the problem. The report provided a basis for new legislation that introduced stricter censorship and restrictions on contraceptive advice to young people. Despite the public outrage it caused, the Mazengarb report and other government papers and inquiries that followed in the 1960s and 1980s had no observable impact on young people's behaviour.

Pile of envelopes containing copies of the Mazengarb report, November 1954.

RESCUE OF *HARRIET* SURVIVORS BEGINS

The family of whaler Jacky Guard were among a group of Pākehā captured by Māori in May 1834 after the barque *Harriet* was driven ashore in Taranaki. Jacky Guard and other men were released when they promised to return with gunpowder to ransom the captives. Instead, he secured the support of New South Wales Governor Bourke for a rescue mission. Meanwhile, Betty Guard lived under the protection of the chief Oaoiti. When HMS *Alligator* arrived in Taranaki with soldiers of the 50th Regiment, Ngāti Ruanui assumed they had come to negotiate. Instead, Oaoiti was bayoneted and captured on 21 September.

Four days later, Betty and her baby daughter were located at Te Namu, which was attacked and burnt. Betty and Louisa were exchanged for Oaoiti. On 8 October, John Guard junior was freed at nearby Waimate. Fighting continued for several days.

In 1835 a committee of the House of Commons condemned the level of force used during the rescue. Humanitarian groups such as the Church Missionary Society argued that unrestrained colonisation must be avoided to protect Māori.

Portrait possibly of Elizabeth (Betty) Guard, 1830.

22 September

1906

DOMESTIC WORKERS CALL FOR 68-HOUR WEEK

At a meeting in Wellington, Marianne Tasker and supporters established a domestic workers' union, hoping to use the Liberal government's Industrial Conciliation and Arbitration Act (see 31 August) to force employers to improve pay and conditions. Central to their demands was a 68-hour working week.

From the late 1880s to the 1930s, domestic service was the single largest form of paid employment for women. The 'domestics' who worked in more than 15,000 New Zealand homes often endured harsh working conditions: a 16-hour day, 6½ days a week, and all for low wages. Several earlier attempts to form unions, including one led by Tasker in 1899, had petered out. The 1906 attempt aroused much debate; the wife of Wellington's mayor sniffed that domestic workers who complained about working conditions were 'mainly those who were incompetent'.

Soon after, an administrative blunder gave opponents an opportunity to nip the union in the bud. In mid-1907, Marianne Tasker left New Zealand to visit Britain. The acting secretary failed to re-register the union and the registrar of industrial unions cancelled its registration.

New Zealand High Commission advertisement for domestic servants, c. 1912–13.

TONGARIRO MOUNTAINS PROTECTED

In February 1887 newspapers reported Ngāti Tūwharetoa's proposal to 'gift to the Crown' the mountaintops of Tongariro, Ngāuruhoe and Ruapehu as the basis of a new national park. What the iwi actually intended was that they and the government would take joint responsibility for protecting the sacred maunga. During the 1880s various claimants were seeking land around the Lake Taupō area. Because Tūwharetoa chief Horonuku had joined both Waikato and Te Kooti in fighting against the Crown, some claimants believed the Crown would treat the Taupō blocks as rebel land. Horonuku could see that he might lose the land. So on the advice of his son-in-law, politician Lawrence Marshall Grace, he signed a deed that ensured the mountaintops could never be sold.

These 6518 acres (2638 hectares) became the nucleus of the proposed Tongariro National Park — New Zealand's first and the fourth in the world. Over the next 20 years, the government sought to obtain further land with which to establish the park. Official confirmation appeared in the 1907 *New Zealand Gazette*, when sufficient land was in Crown title.

Tūwharetoa chief Horonuku Te Heuheu Tūkino IV.

RACIST KILLING IN WELLINGTON'S HAINING STREET

The murder of Joe Kum Yung in Haining Street, Te Aro highlighted the hatred some people had for New Zealand's small Chinese community. His killer, Lionel Terry, committed the brutal act to promote his crusade to rid New Zealand of the so-called 'yellow peril'. Terry had walked 1400 kilometres from Mangōnui in Northland, giving lectures and distributing copies of *The Shadow*, a book of verse with a long introduction on the need for racial purity. When he arrived in Wellington on 14 September, he tried to convince politicians and immigration officials that all non-European immigration should be stopped.

On the night of the 24th, Terry went to Haining Street and shot Joe Kum Yung with a revolver. Next morning he surrendered to police. When his case went to trial in November, he conducted his own defence. He was found guilty and sentenced to death, but this was commuted to life imprisonment on the grounds of insanity.

Later diagnosed as a paranoid schizophrenic, Terry spent the rest of his life in Lyttelton prison and Sunnyside and Seacliff mental hospitals.

Self-portrait of Lionel Terry.

NEW ZEALAND'S FIRST GRAPEVINES PLANTED

Missionary Samuel Marsden planted a vineyard at the Church Missionary Society (CMS) station at Kerikeri with various varieties brought from Sydney. He recorded the planting in his journal, noting that: 'New Zealand promises to be very favourable to the vine, as far as I can judge … Should the vine succeed, it will prove of vast importance in this part of the globe.'

Marsden's vineyard is generally considered the first planted in New Zealand, although the CMS superintendent of agriculture, Charles Gordon, may have planted vines at Rangihoua and Waitangi as early as 1817.

While Marsden may not have been New Zealand's first viticulturist, his belief that the country would prove 'favourable to the vine' was well founded. By 1840 British Resident and wine enthusiast James Busby (see 6 February, 20 March, 28 October) was producing early vintages from a vineyard he had planted at Waitangi in 1833. From 1839 Roman Catholic brothers of the Society of Mary (Marists) produced wine from their Whangaroa vineyard for sacramental purposes. When they moved south to Hawke's Bay, they established Mission Estate in 1851. This remains New Zealand's oldest surviving winery.

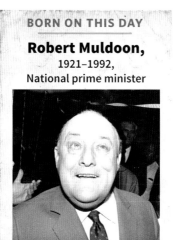

BORN ON THIS DAY
Robert Muldoon,
1921–1992,
National prime minister

CHURCH-MISSIONARY SETTLEMENT AT KIDDEEKIDDEE, NEW ZEALAND.

CMS mission station at Kerikeri, c. 1829–30.

JOSEPH WARD PROCLAIMS DOMINION STATUS

Prime Minister Ward read the proclamation to the gathered crowd from the steps of the General Assembly Library in Wellington. This first Dominion Day was a public holiday. As capital of the new dominion, Wellington put on a big show. At 11 a.m., the governor, Lord Plunket, invited Ward to read the proclamation of dominion status. He did so, and then shouted out, 'Three cheers for the King'. Cheers followed for the governor, Ward, and the new Dominion of New Zealand. Military and school cadets paraded, and Māori performed a haka. It was all over in just 15 minutes. The smallish crowd then set off for Newtown Park to watch a military review involving 1600 men.

As darkness fell, what is now the Parliamentary Library shone with bright lights spelling out 'Advance New Zealand' and the words 'Colony 1840' and 'Dominion 1907'. The change of name meant little in practice. New Zealand resisted accepting the full implications of independence from the United Kingdom until 1947; the country's subsequent change of status from 'dominion' to 'realm' was equally underwhelming.

Parliament Buildings lit up on Dominion Day, 1907.

WILLIAM SUTCH CHARGED WITH SPYING
27 September 1974

On a rainy night in Wellington's Aro Street, the Security Intelligence Service (SIS) gatecrashed a meeting between William Sutch and Dimitri Razgovorov. They believed Sutch, a prominent economist and former senior public servant, was passing information to Razgovorov, a Soviet diplomat. The pair had been under surveillance since April, after the SIS chanced upon what they interpreted as a secret meeting between them. Taken into police custody that night, Sutch initially denied knowing Razgovorov but later admitted he had met the Russian socially. He was charged with espionage under the Official Secrets Act. The trial began on 17 February 1975 and lasted five days. The Crown's case focused on the meetings between Razgovorov and Sutch, and the latter's initial denial that he knew the former. The defence argued Sutch had denied meeting with Razgovorov because he was embarrassed and confused, not because he had anything to hide. After seven hours' deliberation, the jury returned a verdict of not guilty. Despite the acquittal, the case took a toll on Sutch's health; he died in hospital on 28 September 1975.

Bill Sutch (left), his wife, Shirley Smith, and his lawyer, Mike Bungay, during Sutch's trial, 1975.

NEW ZEALAND ANSWERS THE EMPIRE'S CALL TO ARMS

28 September 1899

Premier Richard 'King Dick' Seddon asked Parliament to approve an offer to the British government of a contingent of mounted riflemen to fight in the South African War. Amid emotional scenes, the members overwhelmingly endorsed the motion — only five voted against it. Seddon was an enthusiast for New Zealand's participation in the war. He saw it as emphasising New Zealand's loyal contribution to the British Empire, and he was able to exploit the wave of public patriotism to enhance his personal popularity. His eldest son, Richard John Spotswood Seddon, served in two of the 10 New Zealand contingents.

Authorities in London accepted New Zealand's offer within days. Seddon proclaimed proudly that New Zealand's had been the first legislature in the empire to offer assistance, overlooking the fact that five other colonies had offered forces in July. Hundreds of New Zealand men applied to serve, and by the time war broke out in South Africa on 11 October 1899, the first contingent was preparing to depart. It sailed from Wellington just 10 days later, farewelled by more than 40,000 people.

Painting of a New Zealand mounted trooper during the South African War, c. 1900.

GREYMOUTH BEER BOYCOTT PROVOKED

West Coast publicans soon regretted increasing the price of a beer by 1d. During the Second World War, price controls were applied to many essential commodities, including beer. The controlled price of a 10-ounce beer had risen from 6d to 7d in 1942, but the increase had not been implemented on the West Coast.

The Licensed Victuallers' Association's decision to match beer prices with those in the rest of the country provoked determined resistance from the West Coast Trades Council, which represented most union members in the region. Within days, a boycott of the 'sevenpenny pubs' had been called and the few men who chose to drink there were ostracised. Meanwhile, business boomed in the one Greymouth hotel that had not raised its prices. With neither side willing to back down, an embattled Labour government was in an embarrassing position in the party's heartland. A solution was found with the creation of working men's clubs — co-operatively owned entities which could set their own prices. As the first three clubs opened at Christmas 1947, the hotel price quietly reverted to 6d.

Drinkers at Denniston Hotel, West Coast, 1945.

NEW CHRISTCHURCH TOWN HALL OPENS

Designed by prominent Christchurch architects Warren and Mahoney, the Brutalist (blocky, using lots of concrete) structure was officially opened by Governor-General Sir Denis Blundell. Featuring wooden panelling and beams, the complex on the north bank of the Avon River overlooking Victoria Square cost about $4 million when completely fitted out, equivalent to $50 million today. $500,000 (more than $6 million today) was raised by public subscription and the remainder contributed by local authorities.

The elliptical concert auditorium seating 2350 people benefited from pioneering acoustical research by Harold Marshall that was later applied to Wellington's Michael Fowler Centre and buildings overseas. The James Hay Theatre seated 1000 people for drama and chamber music performances. A restaurant and function rooms complemented these facilities.

The February 2011 Christchurch earthquake (see 22 February), which caused liquefaction and ground movement in the area, forced the closure of the Town Hall and the demolition of an adjoining convention centre. Work to partially demolish, repair and improve the main Town Hall building at an eventual cost of $167 million began in 2015 and was completed in early 2019.

Main auditorium of the Christchurch Town Hall.

1986

GOODS AND SERVICES TAX INTRODUCED

Adding 10 per cent to the cost of most goods and services, GST was a key part of the economic reforms of the fourth Labour government — dubbed 'Rogernomics' after Minister of Finance Roger Douglas.

Douglas implemented his 'new right' reforms after Labour won a landslide victory in the snap election of July 1984. The new government inherited an alarmingly high budget deficit and overseas debt, an overvalued dollar and rocketing inflation. Rogernomics was a ready-made solution — or so it seemed to many.

New Zealand was quickly reinvented as one of the most free-market economies in the industrialised world. Radical change came thick and fast: deregulation, corporatisation, the sale of state assets, and the removal of subsidies, tariffs and price controls. GST was added to the mix in 1986. This regressive tax hit the poorest the hardest, because people on low incomes spend a higher proportion of their money on basic goods and services than the better-off. The rate of GST was increased to 12.5 per cent in 1989 and to 15 per cent in 2010.

Roger Douglas on the steps of Parliament, November 1984.

'SLICE OF HEAVEN' HITS NO. 1

Written for the movie *Footrot Flats: the dog's tale*, based on an iconic New Zealand cartoon series, Dave Dobbyn's hit single featured reggae band Herbs. It topped the charts for eight weeks.

'Slice of Heaven' became synonymous with the film and won Song of the Year at the 1986 New Zealand Music Awards. In 2001 the Australasian Performing Right Association (APRA) invited its members and an academy to vote for New Zealand's top songs of all time. 'Slice of Heaven' made the list at number seven. In the same year Dave Dobbyn received a rare lifetime achievement award from the New Zealand recording industry in recognition of his almost 30 years as a musician and songwriter with bands such as Th' Dudes and DD Smash.

Footrot Flats was the work of cartoonist Murray Ball. The daily newspaper series featured the adventures of 'typical' New Zealand farm characters, including Dog the sheepdog, his owner Wal Footrot and their neighbour, Cooch Windgrass. *Footrot Flats: the dog's tale* was New Zealand's first full-length animated feature film.

Dave Dobbyn with Herbs, from the 'Slice of Heaven' video shoot, 1986.

NEW ZEALAND NATIVES TEAM PLAYS FIRST GAME IN UK
3 October 1888

The privately organised rugby team was the first to wear the silver fern and an all-black uniform. Originally called New Zealand Maori, their name was changed after organiser and captain Joe Warbrick (Ngāti Rangitihi) and promoter Thomas Eyton added five Pākehā to strengthen the team. The 26-man squad included six former students of Te Aute College, five Warbrick brothers, and future All Black captain Thomas Ellison. During a marathon 15-month tour of New Zealand, Australia and the United Kingdom, the Natives played 107 rugby matches — winning 78 — and another 11 under Australian rules. The team disembarked in London on 27 September after a six-week voyage from Australia. Six days later, they efficiently defeated a scratch Surrey XV 4–1. The enterprise had echoes of the Aboriginal cricket tour of 1868, but apart from performing haka before matches the Māori proved relatively unexotic. They beat Ireland, but lost to Wales and England as fatigue set in. The main legacies of the tour were Ellison's invention of the disruptive wing forward position and the adoption of more structured back play.

The Natives prepare to play in Queensland, July 1889.

MORRIS YOCK TRADEMARKS THE JANDAL

Inspired by footwear he had seen in Japan, businessman Morris Yock and his son Anthony began manufacturing this simple rubber footwear in their garage in 1957. The name 'jandal' combined the words 'Japanese' and 'sandal'.

There is some dispute about whether Yock invented the jandal. The family of John Cowie claim that he introduced the footwear from Japan in the late 1940s, coining the name 'jandal' in the process. They believe Yock only imported the jandals and applied for the trademark. Yock's son disputes this.

Jandals Ltd initially manufactured jandals using rubber imported from Hong Kong; J. Yock & Co. arranged distribution. Skellerup took over the supply of raw materials and eventually bought the business in 1987.

During the 1980s and 1990s the brand came under threat from cheap imported imitations. In response, the owners threatened legal action to protect the 'Jandal' trademark. A fresh stoush over the name broke out in 2014, when the current trademark owners, Gentex (NZ) Ltd, asked a Hamilton-based retailer to stop using the term 'jandal' to advertise their footwear.

Inspired by footwear he had seen in Japan, businessman Morris Yock and his son Anthony began manufacturing this simple rubber footwear in their garage in 1957.

Jandals.

SHIPWRECKED *RENA* SPILLS OIL INTO BAY OF PLENTY

The container ship *Rena* astonished local mariners by grounding on the clearly marked Astrolabe Reef while approaching Tauranga Harbour. Flying the Liberian flag and under charter to the Mediterranean Shipping Company, the German-built *Rena* was the largest ship ever wrecked in New Zealand waters; although no lives were lost, in financial terms it was our costliest-ever shipwreck.

Environment Minister Nick Smith described it as New Zealand's 'worst maritime environmental disaster'. About 350 tonnes of oil was spilt, and 950 tonnes of oily waste was subsequently collected from local beaches. Eighty-seven of the 1368 containers on board were washed overboard, with the contents of many fouling the coast. Thousands of birds were killed. More damage was done when the *Rena* broke in half on 8 January 2012.

The salvage operation was frequently hampered by adverse sea conditions and had cost $700 million by the time it ended in April 2016. Local iwi and others continued to battle the ship's owners and insurers over responsibility for removing what remained of the wreck.

The container ship *Rena* grounded on Astrolabe Reef.

1769

YOUNG NICK SIGHTS LAND

Ship's boy Nicholas Young received a gallon of rum and had a headland named after him for being the first aboard the *Endeavour* to spot land in the south-west Pacific. It was 127 years since Abel Tasman had made the first known European sighting of New Zealand. Lieutenant James Cook recorded in his journal that 'at 2 p.m. saw land from the mast head bearing W by N, which we stood directly for, and could but just see it of the deck at sun set'. When leaving Poverty Bay five days later, Cook wrote that the 'SW Point of Poverty Bay ... I have named *Young Nicks head*'. In fact, the land sighted by young Nick was probably inland ranges.

Aged about 12, Nicholas Young was the personal servant of the *Endeavour*'s surgeon, William Brougham Monkhouse. After the *Endeavour* returned to England, he became the servant of the botanist Joseph Banks, who had also been on the epic voyage. In 1772, Young accompanied Banks on an expedition to Iceland; nothing is known of his later life.

BORN ON THIS DAY
Valerie Adams,
1984–,
shot-putter

Young Nick's Head.

GERMAN 'SEA DEVIL' IMPRISONED IN NEW ZEALAND
7 October 1917

German Felix Graf von Luckner earned the epithet Der Seeteufel (the Sea Devil) for his exploits as captain of the raider SMS *Seeadler* in 1916–17. The *Seeadler*, a converted merchant ship, sank 14 Allied ships in the Atlantic and Pacific between January and July 1917. Von Luckner prided himself on the effectiveness, and bloodless nature, of his operations; only one person died during his raids. In August 1917 the *Seeadler* ran aground on Maupelia (Maupihaa) atoll in the Society Islands, stranding the crew. Using a salvaged open boat, von Luckner and five men sailed to Fiji in the hope of capturing another ship. When they reached a Fijian island in September, police arrested them. Sent to New Zealand, von Luckner and his crew arrived in Auckland on 7 October and were confined to a prisoner-of-war camp on Motuihe Island in the Hauraki Gulf. His escape on 13 December was a national sensation. Recaptured in the Kermadecs eight days later, von Luckner was sent to Rīpapa Island in Lyttelton Harbour before ending the war back on Motuihe.

Photograph of Felix Graf von Luckner sent to Francis Dwyer,
Assistant New Zealand Army Secretary, 1928.

STAN GRAHAM'S KILLING SPREE ON WEST COAST

Dairy farmer Stanley Graham killed seven people in Kōwhitirangi on the South Island's West Coast. One of New Zealand's largest manhunts ended when Graham was shot on the evening of 20 October. He died of his wounds the following day.

The tragedy began when Graham refused to hand over his rifle to police to assist the war effort. He felt that police were persecuting him rather than investigating his neighbours, whom he believed were poisoning his cows. On 8 October policemen Edward Best, Percy Tulloch, Frederick Jordan and William Cooper went to Kōwhitirangi after a neighbour claimed Graham had threatened him with a rifle. Cooper, Jordan and Tulloch were shot dead, while Best died later from his wounds. George Ridley, a visiting agricultural instructor, was also shot, eventually dying in 1943.

Graham fled into the bush pursued by police, soldiers and home guardsmen. On the evening of 9 October, Graham exchanged shots with home guardsmen Richard Coulson and Gregory Hutchison. Coulson died immediately and Hutchison the following day. Graham eluded capture for 12 nights until fatally wounded by police.

Cooper, Jordan and Tulloch were shot dead, while Best died later from his wounds.

Stan Graham, c. 1941.

END OF THE 'SIX O'CLOCK SWILL'
9 October 1967

Fifty years of six o'clock closing in pubs ended after a referendum convinced the government to abolish the antiquated licensing law. Introduced as a 'temporary' wartime efficiency measure in December 1917, 6 p.m. closing for pubs was made permanent the following year. The 'six o'clock swill' became part of the New Zealand way of life. In the short period between the end of the working day and closing time at the pub, men crowded together to drink as much beer as they could before bar service ended and the 'supping-up' time of 15 minutes was announced. A mood for change began to emerge in the 1960s. The growing restaurant and tourism industries questioned laws that made it difficult to sell alcohol with meals, while members of sports clubs and the Returned Services' Association also sought a change. When the government held a national referendum in late September 1967, nearly 64 per cent of voters supported a move to 10 o'clock closing.

Customers drinking at the Porirua Tavern on the last day of six o'clock closing, 1967.

WAITANGI TRIBUNAL CREATED

The government created the Tribunal to hear Māori claims of breaches of the Treaty of Waitangi. It has evolved ever since, adapting to the demands of claimants, government and public. The Tribunal was created to report on and suggest settlements for contemporary Māori claims to the government, and to ensure that future legislation was consistent with the treaty. Claims were relatively rare in its first decade, and most of the Tribunal's early inquiries addressed local environmental and planning issues.

In 1985, the government extended its jurisdiction to claims about any alleged breach of the treaty since 1840. This resulted in a huge increase in the number of claims and an expansion of the Tribunal's activities. The Tribunal concluded that governments had breached the treaty on countless occasions since 1840, and that Pākehā New Zealand had been built on many broken promises and bad deals. These conclusions were highly controversial, and a public backlash followed.

Despite these controversies, the Tribunal has made a major contribution to remedying some of the more unsettling aspects of New Zealand's colonial legacy.

Matiu Rata set up the Waitangi Tribunal during his tenure as minister of Māori affairs in the 1970s.

FIRST COBB & CO. COACH RUNS TO OTAGO GOLDFIELDS

In its first venture from Dunedin to Gabriel's Gully, Cobb & Co. reduced the time for the trip from two days to nine hours. The company was founded in Melbourne in 1854. In 1861, its proprietor, Charles Cole, arrived in Dunedin with a luxury American Concord coach, five wagons, a buggy, more than 50 horses, and a reputation for speed and reliability. One week later, the first 'Cobb & Co Telegraphic Line of Coaches' service began a new era in New Zealand transport.

New Zealand was crying out for a public transport network. Though not the first coach service in the colony, Cobb & Co. quickly became the biggest. Coach travel was not for the faint-hearted, however. At the very least, passengers had to endure a queasy rocking motion and a tendency to violent swaying. On rare occasions, passengers drowned in swollen rivers or were killed by being thrown off on steep hillsides. With the development of railways from the 1870s and later the emergence of motor transport, coach travel gradually declined. Cobb & Co. ran its last stagecoach service in 1923.

Cobb & Co. coach crossing the flooded Waimakariri River, 1875.

COBB'S COACH CROSSING THE WAIMAKARIRI, DURING A FLOOD.

1917

NEW ZEALAND'S 'BLACKEST DAY' AT PASSCHENDAELE

In terms of lives lost in a single day, the failed attack on Bellevue Spur on 12 October was probably the greatest disaster in New Zealand's history.

Ever since 1917, Passchendaele has been a byword for the horror of the Great War. In terms of lives lost in a single day, the failed attack on Bellevue Spur on 12 October was probably the greatest disaster in New Zealand's history.

Eight days earlier, 320 New Zealanders died during the capture of Gravenstafel Spur, one of two spurs on the ridge above Passchendaele in Flanders, Belgium. Although this attack was successful, it had a tragic aftermath. The British High Command mistakenly concluded that the number of German casualties meant enemy resistance was faltering and resolved to make another push immediately.

An attack on 9 October by British and Australian troops was to open the way for II Anzac Corps to capture Passchendaele on the 12th. The plan failed. Without proper preparation and in the face of strong German resistance, the 9 October attack collapsed with heavy casualties.

The New Zealanders nevertheless began their advance at 5.25 a.m. on the 12th. The preliminary artillery barrage had been largely ineffective because thick mud made it almost impossible to bring heavy guns forward, or to stabilise those that were in position. Exposed to raking German machine-gun fire from both the front and the flank, and unable to get through uncut barbed wire, the New Zealanders were pinned down in shell craters. Orders for another push at 3 p.m. were postponed and then cancelled.

The troops eventually fell back to positions close to their start line. For badly wounded soldiers lying in the mud, the aftermath of the battle was a private hell; many died before rescuers could reach them. The toll was horrendous: 843 New Zealand soldiers were either dead or lying mortally wounded between the lines.

On 18 October, Canadian troops relieved II Anzac Corps. After a series of well-prepared but costly attacks in atrocious conditions, they finally occupied the ruins of Passchendaele village on 6 November. The offensive had long since failed in its strategic purpose and the capture of Passchendaele no longer represented any significant gain.

Gater Point, on the battlefield near Zonnebeke, Ypres Sector, Belgium, 24 October 1917.

WHINA COOPER LEADS LAND MARCH INTO WELLINGTON

About 5000 marchers arrived at Parliament and presented a petition signed by 60,000 people to Prime Minister Bill Rowling. The primary aim of the hīkoi (march) was to protest against the ongoing alienation of Māori land. Te Rōpū Matakite ('Those with Foresight') was launched at a hui (meeting) convened by Te Rarawa leader Whina Cooper in South Auckland in early 1975. Its creation stemmed from concerns over the historic sale of Māori land and the control of land still in Māori hands. Fifty marchers left Te Hāpua in the far north on 14 September for the 1000-kilometre walk to Wellington. Led by 79-year-old Cooper, the hīkoi quickly grew in strength. As it approached towns and cities, local people joined to offer moral support. The marchers stopped overnight at different marae, on which Cooper led discussions about the purpose of the march.

Media interest grew and the hīkoi's arrival in Wellington was nationwide news. After a memorial of rights was presented to Rowling, about 60 protesters set up a Māori embassy in Parliament grounds.

Whina Cooper in Hamilton during the land march, 27 September 1975.

'MR ASIA' FOUND MURDERED
14 October 1979

The gangland murder of 'Mr Asia' Marty Johnstone led to the demise of one of New Zealand's largest ever drug rings. Johnstone was killed on the orders of drug lord Terry Clark. Divers found his mutilated body in a flooded quarry in England. Clark and Johnstone had begun working together in the mid-1970s, when the Mr Asia drug ring began importing large quantities of heroin into New Zealand and Australia. Gisborne-born Clark headed their operations in Australia. He became a multi-millionaire, buying properties in the Bay of Islands and Fiji, and stashing money in safes and bank accounts around the world. Clark ruthlessly protected his interests, killing a number of associates he suspected of informing. He fled to the United Kingdom in 1979 after Australian police found the bodies of two of Clark's traffickers in a shallow grave in Melbourne. Arrested in London, Clark was sentenced to life imprisonment for Johnstone's murder. He died in a British prison in 1983, supposedly of natural causes.

Mr Asia drugs boss Terry Clark (left) and associate Choo Cheng Kui in the Bay of Islands, 1979.

15 October 1942

NEW ZEALAND COASTWATCHERS EXECUTED BY THE JAPANESE

Memorial to New Zealand coastwatchers killed on Tarawa, photographed in 1951.

Seventeen New Zealand coastwatchers and five civilians captured in the Gilbert Islands (now Kiribati) during the Second World War were beheaded at Betio, Tarawa. Coastwatchers — service and civilian personnel who kept a 24-hour watch for enemy ships and aircraft — were a vital link in the intelligence chain during the Pacific War. For most, the main challenges were isolation and boredom. For those on the front line in the Gilbert Islands, however, the risk of capture by the Japanese was very real.

During August and September 1942, 17 coastwatchers (seven Post and Telegraph Department radio operators and 10 soldiers) and five European civilians were captured as Japanese forces overran the Gilbert Islands. Imprisoned on Tarawa atoll, they were all beheaded following an American air raid on the island. All those executed received a posthumous mention in despatches. The civilian coastwatchers were retrospectively given military rank in 1944 so that their dependants could claim pensions and other rights.

15 October 2007

'ANTI-TERROR' RAIDS IN UREWERA

Armed police search a vehicle near Rūātoki.

Citing the Terrorism Suppression Act, police arrested 18 people in raids linked to alleged weapons-training camps near the Bay of Plenty township of Rūātoki.

In addition to raids in Rūātoki and nearby Whakatāne, police executed search warrants in Auckland, Hamilton, Palmerston North and Wellington after 12 months of surveillance of activist groups. Among those arrested was Tūhoe activist Tame Iti. Police claimed Iti was involved in running military-style training camps in the Urewera Ranges and was planning to establish an independent state on traditional Tūhoe land. Only Iti and three others were brought to trial in February 2012, on charges of participating in a criminal group and possessing firearms. The jury could not agree on the former charge, but all four were found guilty of firearms offences. Two received nine months' home detention and the other two — including Iti — were sentenced to 2½ years in prison.

In 2013 the Independent Police Conduct Authority found that police had 'unnecessarily frightened and intimidated' people during the raids. In 2014 Police Commissioner Mike Bush apologised for mistakes made during the raids.

JEAN BATTEN REACHES AUCKLAND AFTER EPIC SOLO FLIGHT

Jean Batten left for New Zealand from Kent, England, at 4.20 a.m. on 5 October 1936. Despite the early hour, a large media contingent gathered to see her off; Batten was already famous for her successful solo flights from England to Australia in May 1934, and to South America in November 1935.

Batten had installed two extra petrol tanks in her Percival (Vega) Gull low-winged monoplane. But to reach Australia she still had to land and refuel at numerous locations across Europe, the Middle East and Asia. En route she slept little, flying day and night, sometimes in bad weather. She arrived in Darwin in 5 days 21 hours — 24 hours faster than the previous record-holder, Jimmy Broadbent.

As news of the record hit front pages around the world, Batten continued on her way, arriving in Sydney on 13 October. While she took a welcome rest and waited for the weather over the Tasman to improve, some tried to dissuade her from continuing on to New Zealand. Despite the fears expressed for her safety, Batten decided to proceed.

Before taking off from Richmond Aerodrome, Sydney, at approximately 6.30 a.m. (New Zealand time) on 16 October, she declared that no one should look for her if she went down at sea. Outwardly fearless, she later confessed that she almost 'lost her nerve' during this final leg. To her relief she finally recognised a rocky island and a few minutes later was over New Plymouth. She arrived at Auckland's Mangere Aerodrome at about 5 p.m., 10½ hours after leaving Sydney, and was greeted by a crowd of 6000.

Batten then set off to tour the country by car and train, admitting that she was weary of air travel for the time being. In fact, she was both physically and mentally exhausted by her odyssey, which had taken a total of 11 days 45 minutes. The tour was eventually called off in Christchurch and Batten spent much of November resting at Franz Josef Glacier at the government's expense. In October 1937, she made the return flight from Sydney to England — her last long-distance flight.

Jean Batten, c. 1934.

Outwardly fearless, she later confessed that she almost 'lost her nerve' during this final leg.

CHIEF JUSTICE DECLARES TREATY 'WORTHLESS' AND A 'SIMPLE NULLITY'

Chief Justice Sir James Prendergast's statements when delivering judgment in the case of *Wi Parata v The Bishop of Wellington* would influence decision-making on Treaty of Waitangi issues for decades. Prendergast was attorney-general from 1865 to 1875, and then chief justice of the Supreme Court until 1899.

The *Wi Parata* case involved a block of land at Porirua, which Ngāti Toa had given to the Anglican Church on the understanding a school would be built on it. Though no school was built, the church was later issued a Crown grant to the land.

Prendergast ruled that the courts lacked the ability to consider claims based on aboriginal or native title. The Treaty of Waitangi was 'worthless' because it had been signed 'between a civilised nation and a group of savages' who were not capable of signing a treaty. Since the treaty had not been incorporated into domestic law, it was a 'simple nullity'. Though Prendergast's ruling was essentially based on earlier Court of Appeal decisions, it would be used to justify the alienation of much more Māori land.

Sir James Prendergast, c. 1890s.

Though Prendergast's ruling was essentially based on earlier Court of Appeal decisions, it would be used to justify the alienation of much more Māori land.

FIRST TRANS-GLOBAL RADIO TRANSMISSION TO LONDON

From the family sheep station in Shag Valley, East Otago, amateur radio operator Frank Bell sent a groundbreaking Morse code transmission that was received and replied to by London-based amateur operator Cecil Goyder.

Frank and his older sister Brenda were radio pioneers. Invalided home from the Western Front in 1917, Frank revived a boyhood interest in wireless communication while recuperating. He helped pioneer the use of short radio waves to communicate over long distances, initially through Morse-code telegraphy. He achieved a number of firsts, including New Zealand's first overseas two-way radio contact with Australia and North America. But it was his radio conversation with London that made world headlines. When Frank turned his attention to running the family farm, Brenda took over the wireless station, becoming New Zealand's first female amateur radio operator. In 1927 she was the first New Zealander to contact South Africa by radio. After the Second World War, Brenda Bell moved into professional radio as a writer and broadcaster for Dunedin station 4YA.

Frank and Brenda Bell, 1974.

NEW ZEALAND'S DAY WITH LBJ
19 October 1966

President Lyndon Baines Johnson and his wife, Lady Bird, arrived at Ōhakea air base at the start of a whirlwind 24-hour visit to New Zealand. His visit, the first by a United States president, was primarily to shore up support for the war in Vietnam. Johnson's visit appeared to confirm public support for New Zealand's involvement in the war. Up to 200,000 cheering Kiwis crammed the streets of Wellington to get a glimpse of LBJ. Johnson was keen to shake hands with as many onlookers as possible, much to the consternation of his security detail. When LBJ arrived at Parliament for a state luncheon, cheering supporters outnumbered anti-Vietnam war protesters. Newspapers declared the whistle-stop tour an overwhelming success: 'the anti-Vietnam campaigners have less strength in the country than they imagined'. This conclusion was premature. Although National won the November 1966 election, in which Vietnam policy was a major point of difference with Labour, by the end of the decade thousands were marching against participation in the war.

President Johnson greets a young boy at Wellington Airport.

'BLACK TUESDAY'
SHARE-MARKET CRASH

Billions of dollars were wiped off the value of New Zealand shares in the weeks following 20 October, as the shockwaves of a sharp drop on New York's Wall Street stockmarket rippled around the world.

The 1987 Hollywood blockbuster *Wall Street* is the archetypal portrayal of the financial wheeling and dealing — not to mention excess — of the 1980s. New Zealand may not have had anyone quite as ruthless as the movie's 'corporate raider' Gordon Gekko, but many New Zealanders thrived in these deregulated times. The *National Business Review* published its first New Zealand 'rich list' the same year.

But the boom times went bust in October that year. Many investors lost everything as companies that had over-extended themselves were dragged under. Small 'mum and dad' investors were also burned by the experience; many deserted the share market, which languished until the early 2000s.

Onlookers watch hectic trading at the Wellington Stock Exchange during the crash, 1987.

Many investors lost everything as companies that had over-extended themselves were dragged under.

STOLEN MEDALS RETURNED TO NATIONAL ARMY MUSEUM

The 96 medals, including nine Victoria Crosses, two George Crosses and an Albert Medal, had been stolen from the Waiōuru museum early on the morning of 2 December 2007. The VCs included those awarded to Reginald Judson, Henry Laurent (both First World War) and Keith Elliott (Second World War).

Police recovered the medals in February 2008 after two businessmen offered a $300,000 reward. Auckland lawyer Chris Comeskey brokered their return and the thieves reportedly received some money. Television presenter John Campbell was found by the Broadcasting Standards Authority to have misled viewers by failing to make clear that an 'interview' with one of the thieves actually depicted an actor. When the police formally returned the medals to the National Army Museum, 85 descendants of the 12 men awarded the medals were present at the handover on the Waiōuru parade ground. The army's chaplain blessed the medals before they were put back on display. A week earlier, two Auckland men had appeared in court on burglary charges. One was eventually jailed for 11 years and the other for six.

BORN ON THIS DAY

Hone Tuwhare,
1922–2008,
poet

Detective Senior Sergeant Chris Bensemann and Sergeant Rangi Maniapoto carry the recovered medals into the National Army Museum, Waiōuru.

1967

DENNY HULME WINS FORMULA ONE TITLE

In 1967 Denny Hulme became the first — and so far only — New Zealander to win the Formula One World Championship. In his 10 seasons in F1, Hulme had eight victories and 33 podium finishes. He finished third in the overall standings in 1968 and 1972. After winning a Driver to Europe award in 1960, Hulme became a protégé of the legendary Australian driver, Jack Brabham, whose F1 team he joined in 1965.

The 1967 championship comprised 11 races. Hulme won at Monte Carlo and in Germany and secured enough podium finishes elsewhere to claim the championship by five points from his boss. He also finished second in the Canadian-American Challenge Cup (Can-Am) series and fourth in the Indianapolis 500. He was named New Zealand Sportsman of the Year.

In 1968 Hulme joined the team of fellow Kiwi Bruce McLaren (see 2 June). This time two victories were not enough for him to win the title. He remained with McLaren until his retirement in 1974.

Hulme turned to touring car racing and died from a heart attack during the 1992 Bathurst 1000.

Denny Hulme, 1967.

In his 10 seasons in F1, Hulme had eight victories and 33 podium finishes.

NEW ZEALAND NURSES LOST IN *MARQUETTE* SINKING
23 October 1915

Christchurch tram carrying a propaganda message about the *Marquette* sinking, 1915.

The sinking of the transport ship *Marquette* in the Aegean Sea in late 1915 added to the grief of a nation still reeling from the heavy losses at Gallipoli. Among the 167 fatalities were 32 New Zealanders, including 10 members of the New Zealand Army Nursing Service. They need not have died. As a grey-painted troop transport, the *Marquette* was fair game for the German submarine that torpedoed it. A marked hospital ship, theoretically safe from attack, had left the same port on the same day as the *Marquette*, completely empty. By putting the medical staff in an unmarked transport in a convoy carrying troops and ammunition, the authorities unnecessarily risked their lives. The New Zealand government acknowledged as much in November 1915 when the governor, Lord Liverpool, told the British War Office that New Zealand wanted future transfers of medical units completed by hospital ships where possible. The sinking caused great public outrage. The death of the nurses was felt particularly badly in the South Island, where the majority of them had lived or nursed.

VIOLENCE FLARES ON WELLINGTON WHARVES

Violent clashes between unionised waterside workers and non-union labour erupted two days after Wellington's 'wharfies' held a stopwork meeting in support of striking shipwrights.

Employers claimed the stopwork meeting breached the watersiders' collective agreement and replaced the men who attended with other (unionist) workers. The union responded by refusing to work until the dismissed men were reinstated. The employers declared that the wharfies were on strike; the wharfies claimed they had been locked out. Unionists began picketing the wharves on 23 October, and clashes broke out the following day. Negotiations between employers and union officials broke down, and unionists boarded and occupied several ships in port.

The Great Strike of 1913 — a bitter two-month strike involving 16,000 unionists around the country — had begun. The dispute saw running battles between strikers and mounted special police whom the unionists dubbed 'Massey's Cossacks' after Prime Minister William Massey. The collapse of the strike in December 1913 dealt the militant labour movement a severe blow, although many of the leading unionists later rose to prominence in the Labour Party.

Wellington unionists seek cover as mounted special constables prepare to charge them.

END OF THE LINE FOR STEAM RAILWAYS
25 October 1971

The Christchurch–Dunedin overnight express, headed by a JA-class locomotive, ran the last scheduled steam-hauled service on New Zealand Railways (NZR), bringing to an end 108 years of regular steam rail operations in this country. New Zealand's rail system was predominantly steam-powered from 1863, when the first public railway opened in Christchurch, until the 1950s, when the transition to diesel power gathered momentum. NZR operated some electric locomotives from 1923, petrol- or diesel-motored railcars from 1936, and electric multiple units from 1938. The introduction of main-line diesel-electric locomotives from 1950 spelled the end of the line for the steam engine. The dieselisation of North Island railways was complete by the late 1960s. Steam power lasted as long as it did in the South Island only because carriages on the Friday and Sunday night expresses between Christchurch and Dunedin needed steam-heating during winter. Steam has not entirely disappeared from the New Zealand rail scene: in the early 21st century, a number of rail heritage organisations run steam-hauled excursions around the country.

SOUTH ISLAND 'LIMITED' EXPRESS

FASTEST REGULAR LAND TRANSPORT SERVICE
BETWEEN
CHRISTCHURCH AND INVERCARGILL

South Island 'Limited' Express poster.

26 October 1942

WOMEN JURORS ACT ALLOWS WOMEN TO SIT ON JURIES

The Women Jurors Act provided for women aged between 25 and 60 to have their names placed on the jury list on the same basis as men — if they so desired.

New Zealand's first female juror was Elaine Kingsford, who sat on a case at the Auckland Supreme Court in 1943. Interviewed by a National Film Unit crew, she raised the possibility that one day there might even be women judges — a thoroughly radical idea at that time.

This was one of a number of important milestones for New Zealand women in the 1940s, which were in part driven by the demands of war and the absence of servicemen overseas. The first women police officers completed their training in 1941 (see 3 June). In June 1945 Mary Anderson, who had been a Justice of the Peace since 1943, became the first woman to sit on a Magistrate's Court bench. In January 1946 she and former Member of the House of Representatives Mary Dreaver were the first women to be appointed to the Legislative Council, New Zealand's upper house.

Elaine R. Kingsford, New Zealand's first female juror.

FIRST OPPOSED NEW ZEALAND LANDING SINCE GALLIPOLI

Troops from 8th Brigade, 3rd New Zealand Division, landed on Mono in the Treasury Islands (part of the Solomon Islands) to help clear it of Japanese forces. This was the first opposed landing by New Zealand troops since Gallipoli (see 25 April 1915). The 3rd New Zealand Division arrived at Guadalcanal in the Solomon Islands in mid-September 1943. A month later, it received orders to seize and hold Stirling Island and the adjacent Mono Island, where the Americans planned to establish a long-range radar station.

The New Zealanders landed on Mono Island at about 6.25 a.m. Despite enemy machine-gun fire, the New Zealand and American forces managed to establish a beachhead. By the end of the day, 21 New Zealanders had been killed and 70 wounded.

Although outnumbered, the Japanese defenders were afforded some protection by Mono's geography. The island rose steeply from the sea, and dense forest cover concealed many caves in which the enemy was able to hide. Clearing the island was a slow and difficult task. Although Mono was declared clear of Japanese forces on 7 November, isolated enemy positions held out for weeks longer.

Russell Clark, *Action, Falamai village*, c. 1944.

BORN ON THIS DAY*

James Cook,
1728–1779,
explorer

*Old Style date

1835

DECLARATION OF INDEPENDENCE SIGNED BY NORTHERN CHIEFS

Thirty-four northern chiefs signed a Declaration of Independence at a hui (meeting) called by the British Resident, James Busby. The previous year many of these chiefs had gathered to choose a national flag to fly on locally owned ships (see 20 March).

In 1835, Frenchman Charles de Thierry announced his intention to set up a 'sovereign state' in Hokianga. Concerned this might provoke intertribal conflict, Busby called a meeting of chiefs to sign a Declaration of Independence — He W[h]akaputanga o te Rangatira. This asked King William IV 'to be the parent of their infant state [and] its protector from all attempts upon its independence'. As the United Tribes of New Zealand, the signatories would meet at Waitangi annually to frame laws.

The Colonial Office in London promised that the King would protect Māori. Busby eventually acquired 52 signatures to the declaration, all but two from northern chiefs. The creation of the Confederation gave the United Kingdom influence in New Zealand that it was to exploit to the full at a third meeting of northern chiefs on 5 February 1840, the day before the signing of the Treaty of Waitangi (see 6 February).

The Declaration of Independence.

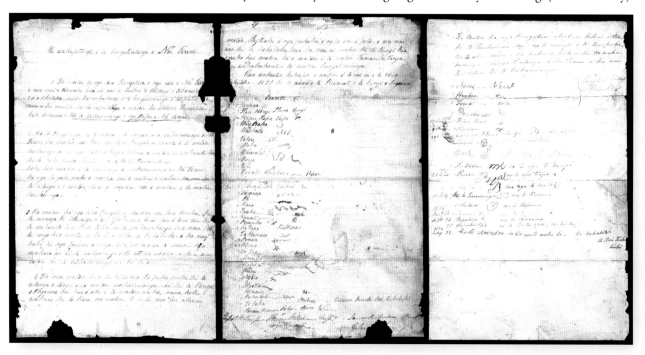

The creation of the Confederation gave the United Kingdom influence in New Zealand that it was to exploit to the full ...

SS *WAIRARAPA* WRECKED ON GREAT BARRIER ISLAND

It remains the third deadliest shipwreck ever in New Zealand waters: 121 lives were lost when the steamer *Wairarapa* struck Miners Head, on the northern tip of Great Barrier Island, 90 kilometres north-east of Auckland.

Despite thick fog, the *Wairarapa* was travelling at 13 knots (24 kph), nearly full speed, when it slammed against the cliffs of the island. Water began to flood in through a hole in the hull, and the *Wairarapa* listed to one side. Many of those on board slid off the deck into the sea; heavy seas swept others away.

Those left on board clung to the rigging or climbed to the bridge. A steward swam ashore with a line along which passengers hauled themselves through the water. Survivors huddled on the rocks for more than 30 hours before local Māori rescued them. A resulting Court of Inquiry laid the blame on the *Wairarapa*'s captain, J.S. McIntosh. As well as maintaining excessive speed, he had taken the wrong course from the Three Kings Islands and not made allowance for currents.

Wreck of the *Wairarapa*, October 1894.

MASSIVE PROHIBITION PETITION PRESENTED TO PARLIAMENT

Prohibition supporters presented Parliament with a petition containing more than 240,000 signatures demanding an end to the manufacture and sale of alcohol in New Zealand. Since the 1880s the prohibition campaign had developed into a powerful mass movement. Its supporters promoted sobriety as a 'patriotic duty' during the First World War. In 1915 and 1916 nearly 160,000 New Zealanders signed petitions calling for pubs to close at six o'clock. In 1917 the government agreed to restrict hotel opening hours to increase the efficiency of the workforce.

The 1918 petition showed that support for the prohibition lobby remained strong. Early closing hours were now made permanent. The liquor trade offered little resistance, believing that reduced opening hours had calmed the wider prohibition movement and were preferable to a total ban.

Prohibition was only narrowly defeated in a special referendum held in April 1919 (see 10 April 1919), and again at a vote held alongside the general election in December 1919. The cause continued to enjoy strong support at the polls throughout the 1920s.

Prohibition poster, early 1920s.

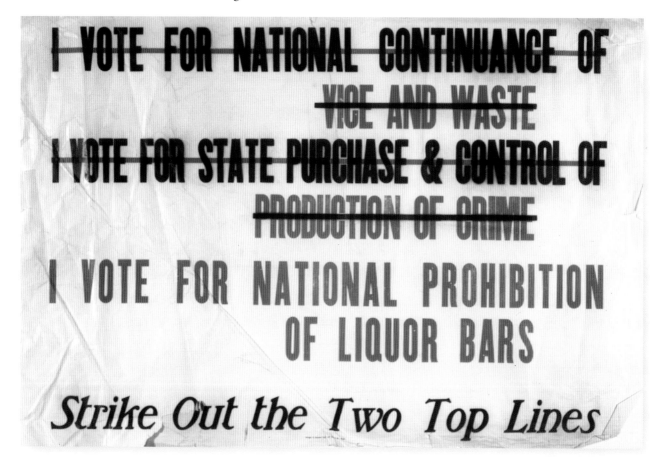

I VOTE FOR NATIONAL CONTINUANCE OF VICE AND WASTE

I VOTE FOR STATE PURCHASE & CONTROL OF PRODUCTION OF CRIME

I VOTE FOR NATIONAL PROHIBITION OF LIQUOR BARS

Strike Out the Two Top Lines

KERI HULME WINS
BOOKER PRIZE

When Keri Hulme's first novel, *the bone people*, won the prestigious Booker Prize in 1985, it was not only New Zealand's first Booker, but the first debut novel ever to win the award, made annually to the best English-language novel by a Commonwealth or Irish citizen. Hulme was up against *Illywhacker* by Peter Carey, *The Battle of Pollocks Crossing* by J.L. Carr, *The Good Terrorist* by Doris Lessing, *Last Letters from Hav* by Jan Morris, and *The Good Apprentice* by Iris Murdoch.

When told of her win, Hulme said; 'You're not pulling my leg, are you? ... Bloody hell — it's totally unbelievable!' Hulme was not able to attend the award ceremony in London, so friends and supporters accepted the award on her behalf. Spiral, a feminist publishing collective, had published the first editions of the novel after Hulme found that mainstream publishers wanted to edit the book.

In 2013 New Zealand enjoyed further success when Eleanor Catton became the youngest person ever to win the Man Booker Prize (as it had been renamed), with *The Luminaries*.

BORN ON THIS DAY

Peter Jackson,
1961–,
film-maker

1984 New Zealand Book Awards finalists, including Keri Hulme's *the bone people* (far right).

1898

OLD-AGE PENSIONS ACT BECOMES LAW

An elderly man presents his old-age pension certificate for payment, c. 1899.

A world first, the Old-age Pensions Act gave a small means-tested pension to elderly people with few assets who were 'of good moral character'. It was one of the major achievements of Richard Seddon's Liberal government. The Liberal reforms of the 1890s attracted international interest and seemed to symbolise New Zealand's egalitarian ethos. The groundbreaking legislation of 1898 was based on the principle that the state had some responsibility for elderly citizens who were not able to provide for themselves.

Funded from general taxation, the amount on offer was small. Applicants had to meet certain criteria to qualify for a pension of at most £18 per year (equivalent to $3200 today). Only those with an annual income of £34 (about $6000) or less and property valued at no more than £50 ($8800) received the full amount. Proof was required that the applicant was aged at least 65, which disadvantaged the many Māori whose births had not been registered. Applicants had to have lived in New Zealand for the previous 25 years. Chinese were specifically excluded.

1944

POLISH REFUGEES ARRIVE IN NEW ZEALAND

Peter Fraser and Countess Wodzicka (far left) with Polish refugee children on board the USS *General Randall*, 1 November 1944.

M ore than 800 Polish refugees arrived in Wellington, seeking safety from war-torn Europe. For the 732 children and 102 adults it was the end of a long and perilous journey. They had survived deportation to the Soviet Union, forced labour in Siberia and evacuation to the Middle East before reaching New Zealand. An estimated 1.7 million Poles were deported to labour camps in Siberia following the Soviet occupation of eastern Poland in 1939. Germany's invasion of the Soviet Union in 1941 prompted Joseph Stalin to send more than 120,000 Polish prisoners to Iran, where they languished in refugee camps.

The Polish government-in-exile in London appealed for help finding temporary homes for them. In 1943 Prime Minister Peter Fraser invited a group of Polish children to New Zealand for the duration of the war. A camp for the children — dubbed 'Little Poland' — was established near Pahīatua in Wairarapa. Most of the refugees chose to settle in New Zealand after the war. Relatives joined some in the late 1940s, while a small number returned to Poland.

NEW ZEALAND DIVISION LEADS BREAKTHROUGH AT EL ALAMEIN

2 November 1942

At El Alamein in Egypt, the 2nd New Zealand Division opened the way for British armour, allowing the Allies to make a breakthrough and push the Axis forces in North Africa into retreat. The North African campaign was vital to the Allied cause because of the strategic importance of the nearby Suez Canal and Middle East oilfields. The New Zealanders had been fighting German and Italian forces across the border between Egypt and Libya since late 1941.

The Second Battle of El Alamein, which began on 23 October 1942, was to determine the outcome of the Western Desert campaign. Allied infantry, including the New Zealanders, opened the attack. They seized most of their initial objectives, but battlefield congestion, poor co-ordination and cautious leadership prevented Allied armoured units from taking advantage of gains made by the infantry.

Disappointed by the lack of progress, Allied commander Lieutenant-General Sir Bernard Montgomery planned a second major attack — Operation Supercharge — further south. The New Zealand Division, boosted by two British infantry brigades, was given the responsibility of leading this attack, which began at 1.05 a.m. on 2 November. The aim was to destroy as many enemy tanks as possible and clear the way for Allied armour to break through. An air offensive preceded the advance on the ground, which was supported by an artillery barrage with nearly 350 guns firing more than 50,000 rounds. Fighting during the day was fierce, but by evening the German Afrika Korps was in a desperate position. With many of his tanks destroyed and fuel supplies low, Field Marshal Erwin Rommel began withdrawing the mobile parts of the Axis army. By 4 November it was in headlong retreat, with the British armoured divisions and the New Zealand Division in hot pursuit. Lacking transport, thousands of Italian and German troops were taken prisoner. While Rommel lived to fight another day, the Axis had suffered a decisive defeat.

BORN ON THIS DAY

Douglas Lilburn,
1915–2001,
composer

Fighting during the day was fierce, but by evening the German Afrika Korps was in a desperate position.

New Zealand war cemetery near El Alamein, Egypt, 20 August 1942.

3 November
1886

BIRTH OF ANCHOR BUTTER

From a dairy factory at Pukekura, Waikato, Henry Reynolds launched his Anchor butter. The brand name, allegedly inspired by a tattoo on the arm of one of his workers, would become one of this country's best-known trademarks.

New Zealand's dairy export industry developed following the advent of refrigerated shipping during the 1880s (see 15 February). Reynolds was one of the country's first dairy factory entrepreneurs, establishing several plants in Waikato. He built a cool store in London and sold direct to shops there, as well as exporting to Australia and Asia. The Anchor butter recipe came from an American, David Gemmell, who was farming near Hamilton. Reynolds was impressed with both the taste and the longevity of Gemmell's product. When Gemmell announced that he was moving back to the United States, Reynolds convinced him to delay his journey for six months to help him establish his dairy factory. The Anchor brand quickly established itself as a market leader and the company's butter, milk and cheese are still familiar items in households here and around the world.

The Anchor butter recipe came from an American, David Gemmell, who was farming near Hamilton.

Anchor butter advertisement, 1936.

NEW ZEALAND DIVISION LIBERATES LE QUESNOY
4 November 1918

By early November 1918 Germany stood alone against the Allies and revolution was breaking out behind the lines. But the German army was still resisting on the Western Front, and the New Zealanders' capture of the walled northern French town of Le Quesnoy was a bold feat of arms. The New Zealand artillery could not bombard Le Quesnoy heavily because of the number of civilians in the town, so General Andrew Russell decided to encircle it and hope the garrison would surrender. By midday the forward troops were well past the town and enemy fire from the ramparts had been suppressed. However, the Germans inside Le Quesnoy were not inclined to surrender. About 4 p.m. the 4th Rifle Battalion managed to place a 9-metre ladder against the town's wall, and Second Lieutenant Leslie Averill was first to scale the ramparts. About 4.30 p.m., the 2nd Rifles began entering the town through the Valenciennes Gate, and the garrison soon surrendered. Nearly 2000 prisoners and 60 field guns were captured in the Division's last major action of the war.

George Edmund Butler, *Capture of the Walls of Le Quesnoy*, **1920.**

OCCUPATION OF PACIFIST SETTLEMENT AT PARIHAKA

About 1600 government troops invaded the western Taranaki settlement of Parihaka, which had come to symbolise peaceful resistance to the confiscation of Māori land. Founded in the mid-1860s, Parihaka was soon attracting dispossessed and disillusioned Māori from around the country. Its main leaders were Te Whiti-o-Rongomai and Tohu Kākahi, both of the Taranaki and Te Ātiawa iwi.

When in May 1879 the colonial government moved to occupy fertile land in the Waimate Plains that had in theory been confiscated in the 1860s, Te Whiti and Tohu developed tactics of non-violent resistance.

Ploughmen from Parihaka fanned out across Taranaki to assert continuing Māori ownership of the land. The government responded with laws targeting the Parihaka protesters and imprisoned several hundred ploughmen without trial.

Following an election in September 1879, the new government announced an inquiry into the confiscations while sending the ploughmen to South Island jails. In 1880 the West Coast Commission recommended creating reserves for the Parihaka people. Meanwhile, the government began constructing roads through cultivated land. Men from Parihaka who rebuilt their fences soon joined the ploughmen in detention.

The prisoners were released in early 1881. After ploughing resumed in July, John Hall's government decided to act decisively while Governor Sir Arthur Gordon was out of the colony. A proclamation on 19 October gave the 'Parihaka natives' 14 days to accept the reserves offered or face the consequences.

On 5 November, 1600 volunteer and Armed Constabulary troops marched on Parihaka. Several thousand Māori sat quietly on the marae as singing children greeted the force led by Native Minister John Bryce. The Whanganui farmer had fought in the campaign against Tītokowaru (see 9 June) and viewed Parihaka as a 'headquarters of fanaticism and disaffection'. Bryce ordered the arrest of Parihaka's leaders, the destruction of much of the village and the dispersal of most of its inhabitants.

Pressmen, officially banned from the scene by Bryce, were ambivalent about the government's actions, but most colonists approved. Te Whiti and Tohu were detained without trial for 16 months. The government managed to delay for several years the publication in New Zealand of the official documents relating to these events.

Bryce ordered the arrest of Parihaka's leaders, the destruction of much of the village and the dispersal of most of its inhabitants.

Armed Constabulary units awaiting orders to advance on Parihaka, 1881.

LAST SPIKE COMPLETES NORTH ISLAND MAIN TRUNK RAILWAY

Prime Minister Sir Joseph Ward ceremonially opened the North Island main trunk railway line by driving home a final polished silver spike at Manganuioteao, between National Park and Ōhakune. According to a reporter who accompanied Ward from Wellington, the ceremony was 'as impressive as scowling weather, muddy embankments and interfering photographers would permit'.

Construction of the central section between Te Awamutu and Marton had taken 23 years of surveys, land negotiations, political wrangling and back-breaking physical effort by thousands of labourers. The first through train from Wellington to Auckland had actually run three months before the final spike ceremony when a 'Parliament Special' train carried MPs and others north to meet the US Navy's visiting 'Great White Fleet' (see 9 August). This train had crawled over a temporary section of track hastily laid between the existing railheads. Regular services between Auckland and Wellington began soon after the last spike ceremony, and an express service introduced in February 1909 made the journey in 18 hours. From 1924, a new 'Night Limited' service cut the trip to 14 hours.

Sir Joseph Ward drives the last spike in the North Island's main trunk line.

LAST UNCLIMBED FACE OF AORAKI/MT COOK CONQUERED

Long-haired Christchurch mountaineers John Glasgow and Peter Gough became the first people known to have scaled the 2000-metre Caroline Face of Aoraki/Mt Cook. They declared it a 'triumph for the hippies'. The Caroline Face was the last unclimbed face of the mountain. Four climbers lost their lives in the 1960s while trying to scale it. Two of those who died, John Cousins and Michael Goldsmith, may have achieved the feat in November 1963. Their bodies emerged from the Hooker Glacier on the other side of the mountain in 1999.

New Zealand's highest mountain at 3764 metres (it has lost 40 metres since a 1991 rockslide), Aoraki/Mt Cook became a focus of early mountaineering. Although not especially high by global standards, New Zealand peaks can be challenging to climb because of their unpredictable weather and heavy snowfall.

The first party to attempt to scale Aoraki/Mt Cook in 1882 discovered the Linda Glacier route, but turned back only 60 metres from the top. New Zealand climbers Tom Fyfe, George Graham and Jack Clarke finally reached the summit on Christmas Day 1894 via the difficult North Ridge.

BORN ON THIS DAY

Ella Yelich-O'Connor (Lorde),
1996–,
singer

John Glasgow and Peter Gough.

NEW ZEALAND CENTENNIAL EXHIBITION OPENS

More than 2.6 million people visited the New Zealand Centennial Exhibition, which ran for six months at Rongotai, Wellington. It was the centrepiece of events marking the centennial of the signing of the Treaty of the Waitangi.

The exhibition covered 55 acres (22 hectares) of land between Wellington's airport and Rongotai College. Architect Edmund Anscombe designed the centennial fair to illustrate the progress of the country. His striking art deco buildings featured a soaring central tower and masses of electric and neon lighting. There were displays of industry, transport, a large Government Court celebrating the welfare state, and Māori and women's courts. Playland, the exhibition's amusement park, was popular, with the Cyclone roller-coaster, the Crazy House and the Laughing Sailor particular highlights. But the outbreak of war affected attendance, which was lower than for the 1925–26 New Zealand and South Seas International Exhibition in Dunedin (see 17 November).

After the exhibition closed, the buildings were used for Royal New Zealand Air Force accommodation and subsequently as wool stores. They burned down in September 1946.

New Zealand Centennial
Exhibition poster, 1939.

JAMES COOK OBSERVES TRANSIT OF MERCURY

Lieutenant James Cook helped his astronomer Charles Green observe the transit of Mercury at Te Whanganui-o-Hei (Mercury Bay), Coromandel Peninsula.

When the planets Mercury and Venus pass across the Sun, they are visible as small black dots. Timing these 'transits' from different locations was the first accurate way to determine the distance between Earth and the Sun.

After observing the transit of Venus from Tahiti, Cook sailed the *Endeavour* towards the land skirted by Dutch seafarer Abel Tasman in 1642, which was sighted on 6 October 1769 (see 6 October). Tahitian navigator Tupaia was on board.

Over the next months, Cook mapped the entire coastline, establishing that this was not the fabled Great Southern Continent. Cook called Māori 'a brave, war-like people'. The Europeans were initially taken for atua (supernatural beings), ancestors, or visitors from ancestral Hawaiki. In some places, conflict broke out and several Māori were killed. Tupaia understood te reo Māori and was able to mediate. As 9 November approached, Cook sought land from which to observe the transit of Mercury with a sextant. A cairn above Cooks Beach marks the spot. The next transit of Mercury fully visible from New Zealand will occur in 2052.

Memorial above Cooks Beach erected in 1969 to commemorate the bicentennial of Cook's visit to Mercury Bay.

BORN ON THIS DAY

Te Puea Hērangi,
1883–1952,
Kīngitanga leader

TE KOOTI ATTACKS MATAWHERO

The Matawhero 'massacre' was Te Kooti's revenge for his exile to the Chatham Islands (see 4 July) and subsequent events. In the middle of the night, around 100 men, 60 on horseback, forded the Waipāoa River and moved quietly towards Matawhero. By dawn, they had killed about 60 people of all ages in the Pākehā settlement and adjacent kāinga (Māori village). Some were shot, but most were bayoneted, tomahawked or clubbed to avoid alerting their neighbours.

Most of those who escaped the slaughter ran to Tūranganui (Gisborne), 6 kilometres away, while some fled south towards Māhia. Hundreds of Māori were taken prisoner or joined Te Kooti with varying degrees of enthusiasm.

The violence was savage, but not random. Te Kooti was exacting utu for indignities heaped upon him since he had been accused of aiding Pai Mārire adherents in 1865. On his return from the Chathams, local magistrate Reginald Biggs — the man who had exiled him — rejected his request for safe passage to Waikato. Biggs and his family were among those killed at Matawhero.

Matawhero Church.

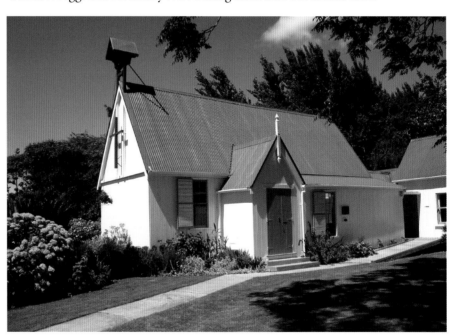

TROOPSHIP *AWATEA* GOES DOWN FIGHTING
11 November 1942

The Union Steam Ship Company of New Zealand's sleek 13,482-ton trans-Tasman liner *Awatea*, launched in 1936, was one of the fastest ships of its size in the world at the outbreak of the Second World War. Like many merchant vessels, the liner was given a coat of grey paint, fitted with defensive guns and pressed into wartime service as a troop transport — still manned by its civilian Merchant Navy crew. On 8 November 1942 the *Awatea* took part in Operation Torch, the successful Allied invasion of Morocco and Algeria, then ruled by the collaborationist Vichy French regime. After landing 3000 commandos near Algiers and ferrying other troops further to the east, on Armistice Day the Kiwi ship was attacked by German and Italian aircraft off the Algerian port of Bougie (Béjaïa). The *Awatea* was raked by bombs and holed by torpedoes. Remarkably, everyone on board escaped safely. The abandoned, burning hulk was later sunk by an Italian submarine. It was a sad end for a ship often described as the finest ever to fly the New Zealand flag.

Rescued crew from the *Awatea*.

STRIKER FATALLY WOUNDED AT WAIHĪ

12 November 1912

Striking worker Fred Evans was badly injured in the Bay of Plenty goldmining town of Waihī. He died the next day. The Australian-born stationary-engine driver belonged to the militant Waihi Trade Union of Workers, which was affiliated to the New Zealand Federation of Labour ('Red Feds') and opposed to the Waihi Goldmining Company. In May 1912 the union went on strike in protest at the formation of a company-inspired breakaway union.

Subsequent violence peaked on 'Black Tuesday', 12 November, when strike-breakers and police stormed the miners' hall, which was defended by only a few men. Both sides were armed. During a struggle, a strike-breaker was shot in the knee. As the unionists retreated, Constable Gerald Wade was shot in the stomach, allegedly by Fred Evans. Evans was struck down by a police baton and, according to some reports, savagely beaten by strike-breakers.

Left for 1½ hours in a cell before being taken to hospital, Evans never regained consciousness and died the next day. Constable Wade survived. As the strike collapsed, strikers and their families were hunted through the streets by armed mobs. Hundreds of people fled from Waihī.

Police reconstruct Frederick Evans' alleged shooting of Constable Wade, Waihī, 1912.

MT TONGARIRO ERUPTS

At 12.40 p.m. on 13 November 1896, Te Maari, a crater at the northern end of the Tongariro complex of volcanic cones and craters (see 23 September), erupted spectacularly. It continued to erupt sporadically for nearly a year.

An eruption in 1868 had formed the crater, which was named for a Māori woman of high rank who died around that time. This crater may have first erupted in November 1892, when it reportedly ejected water, sand, small stones and pumice. There was activity in other outlets in the Tongariro complex, including Ngāuruhoe, Tongariro's main active vent.

Te Maari's first 1896 eruption turned the small steam vent into a large crater 100 metres long and 150 metres wide. It lasted for about 40 minutes, emitting steam and smoke to a great height. Fine weather allowed onlookers to see the plume from some distance away. A south-westerly wind carried a cloud of red ash towards Ātiamuri, north of Taupō. A hiking party on the slopes of Tongariro made a hasty retreat. The residents of Otukou, a Māori settlement immediately beneath the crater, also evacuated the area.

DAVID GRAY KILLS 13 AT ARAMOANA

The house where David Gray was shot by police on 14 November 1990.

The small seaside township of Aramoana, near Dunedin, was the scene of the deadliest mass murder in New Zealand history when David Gray went on a shooting spree that ended with 14 people dead.

Gray, a 33-year-old unemployed Aramoana resident, went on his rampage following a verbal dispute with a neighbour. After shooting the man and his daughter, he began indiscriminately shooting at anything that moved. Armed with a scoped semi-automatic rifle, Gray eventually killed 13 people, including Sergeant Stewart Guthrie, the first policeman to respond to the emergency.

Police located Gray the next day during a careful house-by-house search. When he burst out of a house firing his weapon, members of the Anti-Terrorist Squad (now the Special Tactics Group) shot and mortally wounded him.

A number of people involved in the incident received bravery awards, including Guthrie, who was posthumously awarded the George Cross for gallantry.

The massacre sparked lengthy debate about gun control in New Zealand. The incident led to a 1992 amendment to the regulations relating to military-style semi-automatic weapons.

DPB LEGISLATION ENACTED

The passage of the Social Security Amendment Act introduced the Domestic Purposes Benefit (DPB) to New Zealand's social welfare system. The DPB was intended to help women with a dependent child or children who had lost the support of a husband, or were inadequately supported by him. It was also available to unmarried mothers and their children, and to women who were living alone and caring for incapacitated relatives. While men could also claim the DPB, the vast majority of beneficiaries were women. A new and sometimes maligned category of New Zealander was created: the 'solo mum'.

Controversy about the DPB intensified in 1976 when Minister of Social Welfare Bert Walker claimed that some solo mothers were 'ripping off the system'. Others argued that the DPB was an important right for women. It gave them and their children some protection from the potentially harmful consequences of failed relationships. Advocates also argued that as the amount paid was barely enough to cover basic necessities, it was hardly an incentive for anyone to give up paid work.

Women demonstrate outside a Social Welfare office in Wellington, 1977.

FIRST ISSUE OF *OTAGO DAILY TIMES* PUBLISHED
15 November 1861

Dunedin became the first New Zealand centre with a daily newspaper when the first issue of the *Otago Daily Times* was published. English-born Julius Vogel, a future premier (see 8 April), had been recognised as a talented journalist in Victoria before arriving in Dunedin with Otago gripped by gold fever. Vogel soon formed a partnership with William Cutten, editor of the weekly *Otago Witness*. Both men thought the soaring Otago population could support a daily newspaper, and the *Otago Daily Times* was born as a 'symbol of the progress of Otago'. Vogel became a key figure in a movement to separate the North and South Islands, and the *ODT* became a strong advocate for Otago Province. To this day, the newspaper provides comprehensive coverage of the region and advocates regional causes. Cutten terminated his partnership with Vogel after three years, and in 1866 Vogel sold the *ODT* on condition he remained as editor. Vogel left the newspaper in 1868, by which time he had been elected to Parliament. Since 1976 the *ODT*, still independently owned by Allied Press, has been Dunedin's only daily newspaper.

First edition of the *Otago Daily Times*.

1916

FIRST CONSCRIPTION BALLOT

The Military Service Act passed on 1 August 1916 had made all healthy New Zealand men of military age (20 to 45) liable for active service overseas. Conscription was introduced because after two years of war too few men were volunteering to fill reinforcement drafts for the New Zealand Expeditionary Force.

Government Statistician Malcolm Fraser supervised the first ballot of about 4140 men. The process took more than 20 hours. Choosing each man involved rotating two drums containing marbles. The marble Fraser chose from the first drum directed him to a drawer, and the marble from the second drum denoted a card in this drawer. Each card was turned upright and a magistrate attested that it had been fairly balloted. The mayor of Wellington and a representative of the local Trades and Labour Council were present as observers.

The men had to be delivered their call-up notices in time to appeal within 10 days if they so wished. The Recruiting Branch of the Defence Department worked in shifts through weekends to complete the necessary clerical work.

The Military Service Act passed on 1 August 1916 had made all healthy New Zealand men of military age (20 to 45) liable for active service overseas.

First conscription ballot, 1916.

NEW ZEALAND AND SOUTH SEAS INTERNATIONAL EXHIBITION OPENS

Governor-General Sir Charles Fergusson opened Dunedin's New Zealand and South Seas International Exhibition in November 1925. By the time the exhibition closed in May 1926, it had attracted over 3.2 million visitors, more than double New Zealand's total population at the time.

Promoted by the Otago Expansion League in response to the population and economic drift north, the exhibition was sited on reclaimed land at Lake Logan. Edmund Anscombe, the architect, designed seven pavilions linked by covered walkways around a grand court of reflecting pools leading to the domed Festival Hall. The buildings occupied approximately 16 acres (6.5 hectares). There was an art gallery, a fernery (with a waterfall and streams), and an amusement area with seven major rides and a fun factory featuring a large comic-face entrance. It seems people never tired of the exhibition in the 24 weeks it was running — the closing Saturday had a record attendance of 83,935. The next exhibition on a similar scale was the Centennial Exhibition held in Wellington in 1939–40 (see 8 November).

Postcard of New Zealand and South Seas International Exhibition site in Dunedin, 1925.

41 DIE IN BALLANTYNE'S FIRE

The fire in Christchurch's prestigious department store was one of the worst in New Zealand's history. When it began in a basement about 3.30 p.m., 250–300 people were shopping at Ballantyne's, which had a staff of 458. The staff member who saw smoke coming from a stairwell asked a colleague to call the fire brigade.

Tragically, the brigade did not log this call. By the time firefighters arrived at 3.48 — ill-equipped to tackle anything more than a fire in a cellar — the blaze was out of control.

However, staff on the ground floor assumed the fire could be contained and no general evacuation was ordered. Staff returning from a tea break were told to go back to work, and customers entered the store as late as 3.56.

As the smoke increased, individual staff members cleared their areas, and all customers and most staff escaped. But the 'millinery girls' and those working in credit and accounts were trapped. Thirty-eight staff and two auditors perished in the fire, and a pregnant staff member jumped to her death.

Fighting the fire at Ballantyne's department store, Christchurch.

PIKE RIVER MINE EXPLOSION KILLS 29

The Pike River underground coal mine was high in the rugged Paparoa Range, on the West Coast of the South Island. The only access to the mine workings was through a 2.3-kilometre tunnel that intersected with the Brunner coal seam.

At 3.45 p.m. on 19 November 2010 an explosion ripped through the mine, probably instantly killing all 29 men working underground. Two men in the tunnel, some distance from the mine workings, managed to escape. Over the next nine days, there were three more explosions before the mine was sealed.

In November 2014 the National-led government accepted a decision by Solid Energy, the new owners of the mine, that it was too dangerous to re-enter the mine to attempt to recover the bodies. The Labour-led government which took office in 2017 reversed this decision. In mid-2019 the Pike River Recovery Agency expected to 'recover the tunnel' during 2020.

This was the ninth major explosion in a New Zealand underground coal mine, accidents in which more than 200 men have lost their lives (see 21 February, 26 March). All the deaths have resulted from the explosion of methane gas or from asphyxiation by carbon monoxide and other gases formed after a fire or explosion.

BORN ON THIS DAY

Elizabeth McCombs,
1873–1935,
first woman MP

Flames burst from a ventilation shaft at the Pike River mine, 30 November 2010.

1937

PARACHUTING SANTA CRASHES IN AUCKLAND

George Sellars.

George Sellars narrowly escaped serious injury when he was able to swing his parachute away from the glass roof of the Winter Gardens during a Farmers' Christmas event in Auckland.

Organisers had planned for Sellars to land on the outer Auckland Domain disguised as Father Christmas and distribute toys to waiting children. The plane he parachuted from was flying just 300 metres above the Domain — low enough for the spectators below to see him standing on the wing waiting to jump.

According to a report on the incident, Sellars was only a few seconds from smashing into the Gardens' roof when he was able to alter the parachute's trajectory. He fell heavily into a garden patch between two hothouses, almost hitting two gardeners. As he watched Sellars head off course towards the Gardens, the manager of Farmers' Trading Company, Robert Laidlaw, thought, 'I'm going to be the first man to kill Santa Claus'.

Sellars managed to limp to a shelter and adjust his beard before bravely returning to assist with the distribution of gifts.

BRITISH CAPTURE RANGIRIRI
21 November 1863

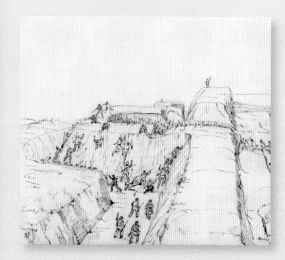

Charles Heaphy sketch of the naval brigade's attack on the central redoubt at Rangiriri, 1863.

More British soldiers were killed at 'Bloody Rangiriri' than in any other battle of the New Zealand Wars, but their victory opened the Waikato basin to the imperial forces. Following the invasion of Waikato (see 12 July), Māori had built a defensive line across a narrow strip of land between the Waikato River and Lake Waikare. The central redoubt, the work of the chief Te Wharepū, was a carefully hidden trap with concealed firing positions. But the formidable fortification was incomplete. It was also under-manned, with only about 500 warriors present, one-third of the British strength. The prolonged defence of Meremere had stretched Māori resources — and it was planting season. On the afternoon of the 20th, troops were landed by boat behind enemy lines and the outlying earthworks were cleared. The central position remained unbreached despite repeated frontal assaults. Forty-seven British and 35 Māori were killed in a few hours. At daybreak the 180 Māori still in the pā raised a white flag, possibly in an attempt to negotiate. Instead, the British took them captive.

FREYBERG GIVEN COMMAND OF 2NZEF

British-born but New Zealand-raised, Lieutenant-General Sir Bernard Freyberg was a charismatic and popular military leader who later served as governor-general. Freyberg was awarded numerous honours, including the Victoria Cross, during the First World War. He retired from the British Army in 1937 because of a heart problem, but offered his services to the New Zealand government when the Second World War began.

Appointed to command the 2nd New Zealand Expeditionary Force (2NZEF), he led its fighting arm, the 2nd New Zealand Division, through campaigns in Greece and Crete, North Africa and Italy. While criticised for his role in the fall of Crete in May 1941, and the destruction of the Benedictine Monastery above Cassino in 1944, Freyberg was admired at home and abroad, revered by his men for his concern for their welfare and readiness to be at the forefront of any action.

Following the war, Freyberg was invited to be New Zealand's governor-general. A popular choice for the post, he was the first person with a New Zealand upbringing to hold the position.

General Freyberg (at right) with New Zealand soldiers.

BORN ON THIS DAY

Annie Schnackenberg,
1835–1905,
suffragist

POPE JOHN PAUL II CELEBRATES MASS IN WINDY WELLINGTON

The first and so far only visit to New Zealand by a Bishop of Rome was significant for Catholics and the wider community. The Polish-born Pontiff had arrived in Auckland the previous afternoon. He received a state welcome at the airport before celebrating Mass in the Auckland Domain. The Pope flew to Wellington that evening and stayed at the Apostolic Nunciature (Vatican embassy) in Lyall Bay.

On Sunday, 23 November, the Pope had several meetings with dignitaries before presiding over a 2½-hour Mass for 25,000 people at Athletic Park. 'Only Wellington's wind marred proceedings, making microphones roar, billowing the Pope's vestments and blowing over a crucifix, a microphone stand and a music stand,' the *Dominion* reported.

Next morning the Pope flew to Christchurch, where he held an ecumenical liturgy at the Catholic cathedral and celebrated Mass at another sacred New Zealand venue, Lancaster Park, before flying to Canberra.

The 66-year-old John Paul II made a circuit of each outdoor venue in a specially designed 'Popemobile', a vehicle with armoured glass created after an assassination attempt in 1981.

Marilyn Pryor receives communion from Pope John Paul II at Athletic Park, Wellington.

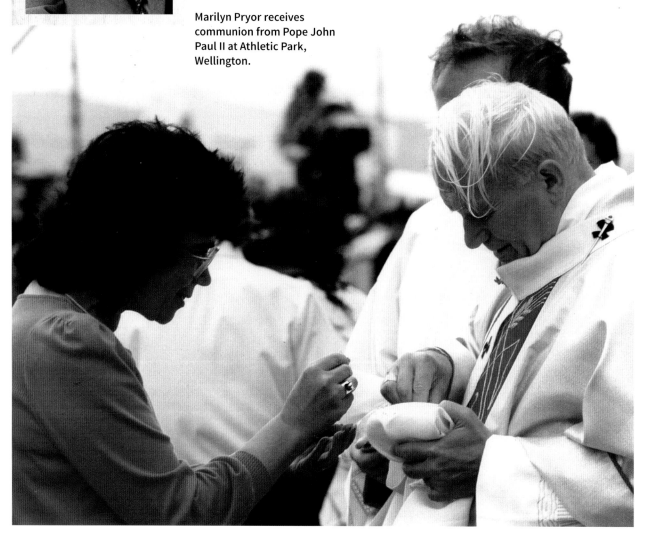

15 DIE IN MYSTERIOUS SHIPWRECK

All hands were lost when the modern coastal freighter *Holmglen* foundered off the South Canterbury coast. The cause of the tragedy was never established. The 485-ton Holm Company motor vessel was bound from Dunedin to Whanganui when it sank about 40 kilometres east of Timaru. A Mayday signal and a rushed radio message that the ship was heeling heavily to port were received on shore, but searchers found only a large oil slick and floating debris. Further searching led to the recovery of three bodies and an upturned lifeboat.

A Court of Inquiry was unable to establish the cause of the tragedy. The *Holmglen* was only three years old and was not overloaded. Although the weather at the time was poor, this should not have troubled a vessel of its size. There was speculation that shifting deck cargo, or some other instability, caused the ship to capsize.

An examination of the wreck by divers and a remotely operated underwater vehicle in 1999 failed to shed any further light on the loss of the ship.

The *Holmglen*.

BOB FITZSIMMONS WINS THIRD WORLD BOXING TITLE
25 November 1903

By winning the light-heavyweight championship, Timaru boxer Bob Fitzsimmons became the first man to have won world professional boxing titles in three weight divisions. Fitzsimmons came to New Zealand with his family from Cornwall as a 10-year-old. Working his father's blacksmith's forge developed the powerful arms and shoulders that made him a devastating puncher. Fitzsimmons arrived in America in 1890. The following year he became world middleweight champion by knocking out Jack Dempsey. In 1897 Fitzsimmons won the world heavyweight crown, knocking out James J. Corbett in the first fight to be filmed. In 1903, aged 40, Fitzsimmons completed a hat-trick of titles by outpointing George Gardner over 20 rounds for the light-heavyweight title. He lost this in 1905, but continued to fight until 1914. In all he won 40 bouts, drew 13 and lost 9. Fitzsimmons also fought exhibition bouts against his son, Robert, appeared in vaudeville shows and worked as an evangelist. Bob Fitzsimmons died of pneumonia in Chicago in 1917. He was inducted into the New Zealand Sports Hall of Fame in 1995.

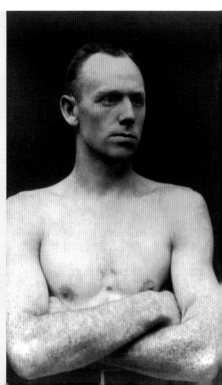

Bob Fitzsimmons, 1891.

'KIWI KEITH' BEGINS 12-YEAR REIGN AS PRIME MINISTER

Keith Holyoake led the National Party to victory over Walter Nash's Labour government, and went on to become New Zealand's third-longest-serving premier or prime minister behind Richard Seddon and William Massey.

Holyoake briefly became PM when Sid Holland resigned three months before the 1957 election, but was unable to prevent a narrow Labour victory. In 1960, he led National back into power.

'Kiwi Keith', as he was known, strove to preserve economic prosperity and stability, an aim reflected in his 1963 election slogan, 'Steady Does It'. While he was criticised by some, his administration's longevity suggests that he correctly read the mood of most New Zealanders.

One of his greatest challenges was New Zealand's involvement in the Vietnam War, which became a key election issue in 1966. While the government's share of the vote fell, it retained a comfortable majority. Holyoake's fourth victory in 1969 was even more impressive, but by 1972 his administration appeared tired and out of touch. Holyoake stepped aside in February, and in November Labour's Norman Kirk defeated his successor, Jack Marshall.

Keith Holyoake with his daughter Diane Comber and twin grandchildren in 1969.

FIRST LABOUR GOVERNMENT WINS POWER

The 1935 general election has long been seen as a defining moment in New Zealand's history. Undermined by its failure to cope with the distress of the Depression, the Coalition (or 'National') government was routed by the Labour Party led by Michael Joseph Savage.

As night fell, huge crowds congregated outside newspaper offices to follow the results as they were posted on large boards. In Auckland, Labour supporters roared 'off with his head' as each government defeat was confirmed. Overall Labour won 46 per cent of the vote to the Coalition's 33 per cent. Thanks to the first-past-the-post system and a strong showing by minor parties and independents, it secured 53 of the 76 European seats.

Savage would die in office in 1940 (see 30 March) but under Peter Fraser's leadership Labour held power for a further nine years, implementing far-reaching economic and social reforms that set the political agenda for the next half-century. Labour's victory also signalled the emergence, especially from 1938, of a remarkably stable era of two-party politics.

The first Labour Cabinet, 1935.

257 KILLED IN MT EREBUS DISASTER

On the morning of 28 November 1979, Air New Zealand Flight TE901 left Mangere Airport, Auckland, for an 11-hour return sightseeing flight to Antarctica. At 12.49 p.m. (New Zealand Standard Time), the aircraft crashed into the lower slopes of Mt Erebus, killing all 257 passengers and crew. It was the worst civil disaster in New Zealand's history. Air New Zealand had begun operating one-day sightseeing flights to Antarctica in 1977. Leaving Auckland, the aircraft headed for Antarctica, where passengers enjoyed low-level views of the Ross Dependency, before returning via Christchurch. The flights had always operated smoothly and were popular with adventurous Kiwis and tourists.

When TE901 failed to arrive at Christchurch on schedule, authorities feared the worst. It was clear that the plane, if still airborne, would soon run out of fuel. Search and rescue operations began in Antarctica but it was not until midnight (NZST) that aircraft spotted wreckage on the lower slopes of Mt Erebus. Final confirmation that there were no survivors came next day.

More than 60 professionals and volunteers were involved in the gruelling tasks of recovering bodies from the crevasse-riven site and inspecting the wreckage to determine the cause of the disaster. These operations took several weeks. Against heavy odds, they retrieved all the bodies and eventually 214 were identified. Meanwhile, an air accident investigation began, using information from the aircraft's flight recorders and other sources.

Debate raged over who was at fault for the accident. The chief inspector of air accidents attributed the disaster to pilot error. Justice Peter Mahon's Royal Commission of Inquiry disagreed, placing the blame on Air New Zealand and its systems. There were clearly a number of contributing factors. But which of them was the most significant, and whether the pilots or the airline were ultimately responsible, remains a matter of intense debate. The Erebus disaster has been remembered in many ways. Memorial services for the victims were held in the immediate aftermath of the crash, and have continued, notably on significant anniversaries. In 2019 the government announced that a national Erebus memorial would be erected in Auckland's Parnell Rose Gardens.

Against heavy odds, they retrieved all the bodies and eventually 214 were identified.

Fuselage wreckage from Air New Zealand Flight TE901.

FIRST WOMAN MAYOR IN BRITISH EMPIRE ELECTED

By becoming mayor of the Auckland borough of Onehunga, Elizabeth Yates struck another blow for women's rights in local-body polls held the day after the first general election in which women could vote.

Elizabeth's husband, Captain Michael Yates, had been a member of the Onehunga Borough Council since 1885 and was mayor from 1888 until 1892, when ill health forced his retirement. The following year Elizabeth, who was a strong supporter of the women's suffrage movement (see 19 September), accepted nomination as mayor. After a 'spirited contest', she defeated her only opponent, local draper Frederick Court, by just 13 votes to become the first 'lady mayor' in the British Empire.

Yates's victory was big news in New Zealand and around the empire, and she received congratulations from both Premier Richard Seddon and Queen Victoria. But her reign was short: opponents undermined her leadership and she was soundly defeated at the next mayoral election, on 28 November 1894. Yates served as a borough councillor from 1899 to 1901 and died in 1918.

Elizabeth Yates, c. 1893.

ELECTION OF FIRST NATIONAL GOVERNMENT

The Labour government, led by Peter Fraser, was defeated by Sidney Holland's National Party after 14 years in office. The result heralded a long period of National dominance, with the party holding power for 29 of the next 35 years.

Since its landslide 1935 victory over the Depression-era Coalition (see 27 November), the Labour government had implemented sweeping economic and social reforms and led New Zealand through the Second World War. But by 1946, its grip on power was weakening. The National Party, which had been formed in 1936 by a merger of the Reform and United parties (see 13 May 1936), mounted a credible challenge under Holland's energetic leadership. Voters were growing tired of the continuation of wartime shortages and restrictions. Despite this, Labour held on for a narrow victory.

By 1949, National's promise of a new era of prosperity and freedom held even greater appeal. Voters were also reassured by its pledge to retain most of Labour's social welfare policies. National swept to power with 52 per cent of the vote and 46 seats to Labour's 34.

National Party poster, 1949.

FIRST MOVIE SHOT IN NEW ZEALAND

The first motion pictures known to have been taken in New Zealand were made by photographer W.H. Bartlett for the entrepreneur Alfred Whitehouse, who in 1895 had imported the colony's first 'kinetoscope', a Thomas Edison invention that showed moving images to one viewer at a time.

Bartlett filmed the opening of the Auckland Industrial and Mining Exhibition, including the Newton Band playing, the arrival of the governor with a cavalry escort, and the entry of crowds to the building.

The film was screened for the public using a 'Cinématographe' at Bartlett's Queen Street studio on Christmas Eve, with musical interludes provided by another Edison invention, the phonograph. On Boxing Day Bartlett filmed Uhlan winning the Auckland Cup at Ellerslie Racecourse. These films were described as 'clear and almost free of the flicker which so often mars the effect of a good picture'. After making 10 one-minute films, Whitehouse toured the North Island showing his 'Animated Pictures'. He got a mixed reception from audiences which seem to have doubted that the local product could match up to imports.

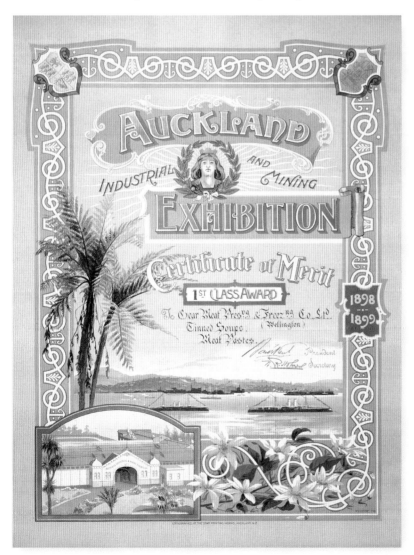

The opening of the 1898 Auckland Industrial and Mining Exhibition was shown in the first motion picture shot in New Zealand.

FIRST BISHOP OF AOTEAROA CONSECRATED

Frederick Bennett, who had a Ngāti Whakaue mother and an Irish father, was ordained as an Anglican priest in 1897. He spent 13 years as superintendent of the Māori mission in Rotorua before moving to Hastings for mission work in Hawke's Bay.

The idea of a Māori diocese with its own bishop was a response to the formation of the Rātana Church, which threatened to draw Māori away from established churches. For three years, there was deadlock between Pākehā bishops, who insisted that the first bishop be Pākehā, and Māori Anglicans led by Āpirana Ngata who were adamant that he be Māori.

The eventual solution was a classic Anglican compromise: the creation of a titular bishopric with no territorial jurisdiction. On 2 December 1928 Frederick Bennett was consecrated as Bishop of Aotearoa in Napier Cathedral. As assistant to the Bishop of Waiapu, he ministered to Māori throughout the country under licence from diocesan bishops, many of whom opposed this arrangement.

The awkward system lasted until 1978, when the Archbishop of New Zealand took over the licensing process.

Frederick Bennett, 1928.

LAND CONFISCATION LAW PASSED

Parliament passed legislation for the confiscation (raupatu) of Māori land to punish tribes deemed to have 'engaged in open rebellion against Her Majesty's authority' in the early 1860s. Pākehā settlers would occupy the confiscated land.

Three days before the British invasion of Waikato in July 1863 (see 12 July), the government ordered all Māori living in the Manukau district and on the Waikato frontier north of the Mangatāwhiri Stream to take an oath of allegiance to the Queen and give up their weapons. Those who refused would 'forfeit the right to the possession of their lands guaranteed to them by the Treaty of Waitangi'.

Under the New Zealand Settlements Act, Waikato lost almost all their land and Ngāti Hauā about a third of theirs. But pro-government and neutral Māori also lost land as the yardstick rapidly changed from guilt to convenience. Ngāti Maniapoto territory was untouched as it was still under Kīngitanga (King Movement) control. In the long term, Taranaki Māori suffered most from confiscation in terms of land actually occupied.

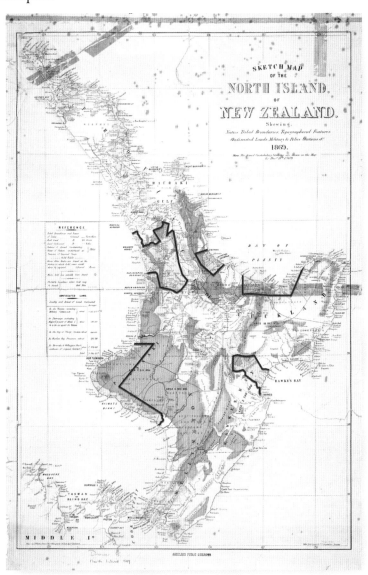

Map of the North Island, with the major areas of confiscated land outlined in blue, 1869.

RADIO HAURAKI RULES THE WAVES

Pirate station Radio Hauraki broadcast its first scheduled transmission from the vessel *Tiri* in the Colville Channel between Great Barrier Island and Coromandel Peninsula. The brainchild of journalist David Gapes, Hauraki challenged the monopoly of the conservative New Zealand Broadcasting Corporation, which held little appeal to 1960s teenagers. When attempts to secure a private broadcasting licence failed, Hauraki decided to broadcast from outside the 3-mile limit.

Test transmissions from the *Tiri* began in earnest on 1 December. The first song played three days later was Matt Monro's somewhat symbolic 'Born Free'.

Over the next 3½ years, legal challenges and incidents at sea tested the resolve of those involved. In January 1968 the *Tiri* hit rocks on Great Barrier Island. A replacement vessel, the *Kapuni* (dubbed *Tiri II*), also ran aground. In March 1970 the Broadcasting Authority awarded licences for the Auckland area to Radio Hauraki, which made its last pirate broadcast on 1 June 1970. 'Born Free' closed the transmission. Hauraki's triumph was tinged with tragedy when announcer Rick Grant was lost overboard during the return voyage to Auckland that evening.

Radio Hauraki supporters outside the Auckland Town Hall, 1966.

FIRST 'ONE MAN, ONE VOTE' ELECTION

New Zealand's electoral law had been changed so that no one could vote in more than one general electoral district. This ended the long-standing practice of 'plural voting' by those who owned property in more than one electorate.

The 1890 election has long been seen as one of the most significant in New Zealand's history. Although the result was not clear until Parliament met in early 1891, the Liberal government that ultimately took power was to dominate the political landscape for the next two decades.

Electoral rights were still in transition. Property-owners could enrol in each district in which they qualified, but come election day they had to choose where to cast their solitary vote. This 'plural registration', and a dual vote for Māori property-owners (which had existed since the Māori seats were introduced in 1867), were both abolished in 1893. The introduction of New Zealand's landmark women's suffrage legislation that year (see 19 September) established the 'one person, one vote' principle, which was to become a fundamental feature of democratic electoral systems in the 20th century.

The first Liberal Cabinet, January 1891. From left, standing: Richard Seddon, A.J. Cadman, John McKenzie, Joseph Ward, William Pember Reeves; seated: Patrick Buckley, John Ballance (Premier).

SPECIAL VOTES CAST IN GENERAL ELECTION

For the first time in New Zealand's electoral history, registered voters who were away from their electorate on polling day were able to cast a 'special' absentee vote at any polling booth in the country; this would then be posted to their local returning officer for counting. Prior to election day in 1905, 3586 electors applied for the necessary absent voter's permit, and 2781 votes were cast this way.

This innovation extended the concept of absentee voting rights, which had first been introduced for merchant seafarers in 1890, and then extended to commercial travellers and shearers. But the provision did not apply to voters in the Māori seats, who continued to vote without registration (Māori electoral rolls were not used until 1949). The wait for special votes to be counted has occasionally added drama to tight electoral or referendum contests, including, for example, the 1919 prohibition poll (see 10 April 1919). In 1999 special votes not only tipped the Green Party over the 5 per cent threshold needed to enter Parliament, but also saw them win the Coromandel seat.

Casting a special vote in the general election, 2008.

BASSETT ROAD MACHINE-GUN MURDERS

The bullet-riddled bodies of Frederick George Walker and Kevin James Speight were found in a house on Bassett Road in Remuera, Auckland. A team of 32 detectives began an immediate search that led to the arrest of Ron Jorgensen and John Gillies.

The fact that the victims were sly-groggers — traders in illegal alcohol — seemed to be a motive for the murders. The Coroner concluded that the murder weapon was probably a .45-calibre machine gun. On New Year's Eve, police arrested Jorgensen and Gillies, career criminals who had spent time in prison in New Zealand and Australia. Their trial began on 24 February 1964. Although both denied the charges, Gillies did admit in court to having purchased a machine gun. They were found guilty and sentenced to life imprisonment.

Jorgensen came to public attention again in 1984, following his release from prison, when his abandoned car was found at the bottom of a cliff near Kaikōura. Despite rumours he had faked his own death and fled to Australia, Jorgensen was declared dead in 1998.

QUEEN STREET CONCERT ENDS IN RIOT

'Tears, terror at the concert that made history' was one of the newspaper headlines the day after the Queen Street riot of December 1984. The 'Thank God it's over' concert at Auckland's Aotea Square was meant to be a summer celebration of the end of the university year. But shortly after headline act DD Smash took the stage, the power went off.

As the 10,000-strong audience waited impatiently, a drunk man urinated on the crowd from above; when police attempted to arrest him, some of the audience obstructed them and started throwing bottles. There were a few arrests, and more police arrived, ominously outfitted in riot gear. Dave Dobbyn, DD Smash's lead singer, allegedly told the crowd, 'I wish those riot squad guys would stop wanking and put their little batons away.' When the promoters announced that the concert was being called off, parts of the audience rioted. They poured onto Queen Street, smashed shop windows and left behind broken bottles, rubbish and upturned cars. Dobbyn was later charged with inciting violence and using insulting language, but was eventually cleared of all charges.

Concertgoers overturn a car during the Queen Street riot, 1984.

1942

DEADLY FIRE AT SEACLIFF MENTAL HOSPITAL

The fire that swept through a locked ward of the Seacliff Mental Hospital, north of Dunedin, killed 37 female patients. The huge, isolated hospital, opened in 1884, was built mainly of stone, but Ward 5, which housed 'difficult' women patients, was a two-storey wooden addition. This ward was always locked at night, with nearly all windows shuttered and locked. Wartime personnel shortages meant staff checked the ward only once an hour. By the time they noticed the fire it had taken hold; within an hour, the building had been reduced to ashes. Only two of the 39 female patients in Ward 5 escaped the inferno.

A commission of inquiry condemned the practice of leaving patients locked up without adequate supervision, and found that the building was a fire risk. Its ancient alarm system, which had to be unlocked before use, was virtually useless. The inquiry recommended that future institutional buildings be made of fire-resistant materials and have emergency exits, automatic monitored fire alarms and sprinkler systems. It took many years for these measures to be introduced in all institutions.

A commission of inquiry condemned the practice of leaving patients locked up without adequate supervision . . .

Aftermath of the Seacliff Mental Hospital fire.

FIRST PASSENGERS TRAVERSE LYTTELTON RAIL TUNNEL

After 6½ years of construction, it took just 6½ minutes for the first trainload of passengers to speed through the 2.6-kilometre tunnel linking the Canterbury Plains to the port of Lyttelton. Canterbury Provincial Superintendent William Moorhouse ('Railway Billy') had proposed this ambitious project as early as 1858. In July 1861, amid much fanfare, he ceremonially 'turned the first sod', but the task proved challenging. The first firm contracted to do the work withdrew. The hardness of the volcanic rock and the need to work out ways of ventilating and draining the tunnel all resulted in delays. Provincial Engineer Edward Dobson oversaw the work, and his skill was demonstrated when the Lyttelton and Heathcote ends met perfectly in May 1867. Several weeks later, the tunnel was opened to the people of Lyttelton and Christchurch for a day, and hundreds walked its length.

Temporary rails were laid to enable the passage of the first locomotive on 18 November. The first goods train followed a week later, with passenger services beginning on 9 December.

After 6½ years of construction, it took just 6½ minutes for the first trainload of passengers to speed through the 2.6-kilometre tunnel . . .

BORN ON THIS DAY

Whina Cooper,
1895–1994,
Māori leader

Lyttelton rail tunnel under construction, 1860s.

10 December 1908

RUTHERFORD WINS NOBEL PRIZE

Ernest Rutherford's discoveries about the nature of atoms shaped modern science and paved the way for nuclear physics. Albert Einstein called him a 'second Newton' who had 'tunnelled into the very material of God'.

Painting of Ernest Rutherford by Oswald Birley, 1934.

Born in 1871 near Nelson, Rutherford later claimed his inventiveness was honed on the challenges of helping out on his parents' farm: 'We haven't the money, so we've got to think.' After gaining three degrees at Canterbury College, Rutherford began his international career when he won a scholarship to the Cavendish Laboratory at the University of Cambridge, of which he was to become director many years later.

While at Cambridge, he became known for his ability to make imaginative leaps and design experiments to test them. His discovery that heavy atoms have a tendency to decay into lighter atoms heralded modern techniques of carbon dating and led to his Nobel Prize in Chemistry in 1908.

The second great discovery of his career was made at Victoria University of Manchester in 1909. With the help of experiments by assistants Hans Geiger and Ernest Marsden, Rutherford found that the atom consisted of a tiny, dense nucleus surrounded by oppositely charged electrons — a model that still forms the basis of atomic theory today.

In 1917 Rutherford made his third and perhaps most famous breakthrough. While bombarding lightweight atoms with alpha rays, he observed outgoing protons of energy larger than the incoming alpha particles. From this observation, he correctly deduced that the bombardment had converted oxygen atoms into nitrogen atoms. He had successfully 'split' the atom, ensuring his lasting scientific fame. On a final trip to New Zealand in 1925, Rutherford gave talks to packed halls around the country. His call for government support for education and research helped establish the Department of Scientific and Industrial Research (DSIR) the following year.

Public acclaim continued after his death in 1937. Buildings and streets in a number of countries bear his name, and his image has appeared on commemorative stamps and, since 1992, New Zealand's $100 banknote. He is the only New Zealander to have an element — rutherfordium — named in his honour.

PARLIAMENTARY LIBRARY ESCAPES FIRE

The country narrowly avoided a great library bonfire in 1907, when fire swept through Parliament Buildings in Wellington. At 2 a.m., Parliament's nightwatchman thought he heard rain on the roof, but when he went to check found that a substantial blaze had broken out. He sounded the alarm, threw open the gate for the fire brigade and tackled the fire with a hose. The fire, probably started by faulty electric wiring in the ceiling of the interpreters' room, spread rapidly through the old wooden parts of the buildings and then into the masonry additions of the 1880s. By 5 a.m. it had destroyed Bellamy's restaurant and fire crews were battling desperately to save the library. Staff and volunteers moved more than 15,000 volumes from the building's ground floor in case the flames broke through. The morning light revealed the scale of the devastation: the old wooden buildings were completely destroyed, but the brick walls and metal fire door had saved New Zealand's de facto national library, and the 80,000 volumes and many other treasures still inside.

Parliament Buildings on fire,
11 December 1907.

FIRST GOLDEN KIWI DRAW
12 December 1961

Tickets went on sale for New Zealand's new national Golden Kiwi lottery. All 250,000 tickets sold within 24 hours, with the £12,000 top prize (equivalent to around $500,000 today) four times that offered in previous lotteries. A national 'art union' lottery operated in New Zealand from 1932, but the prizes were small. Many people continued to take part, illegally, in overseas lotteries. In an attempt to benefit from their popularity, the government began to tax some of these lotteries in the 1950s, although the revenue was paltry. In 1961, Minister of Internal Affairs Leon Götz established a more attractive national lottery to help meet increased demands for funding from community groups. Despite criticism by some religious groups, Golden Kiwi was a huge public success. To ensure lottery funds were distributed fairly, the government established an independent committee and six specialist grants boards. Like its predecessors, the Golden Kiwi eventually lost the public's interest. It managed to survive until 1989, by which time New Zealanders had embarked on a new love affair, with Lotto (see 22 July).

Golden Kiwi poster.

13 December
1939

BATTLE OF THE RIVER PLATE

When the cruiser HMS *Achilles* opened fire on the German pocket battleship *Admiral Graf Spee* in the South Atlantic, it became the first New Zealand unit to strike a blow at the enemy in the Second World War. With the New Zealand ensign flying proudly from its mainmast, *Achilles* also became the first New Zealand warship to take part in a naval battle.

The 82-minute engagement between the *Graf Spee* and its three smaller British opponents — *Achilles*, *Ajax* and *Exeter* — was inconclusive. All four vessels were damaged, with the British ships suffering 72 fatalities (including two New Zealanders) to the *Graf Spee*'s 36. But the German warship's subsequent withdrawal to the neutral Uruguayan port of Montevideo, and its dramatic scuttling by its own crew on 17 December, turned the Battle of the River Plate into a major British victory — and a welcome morale boost for the Allied cause.

Achilles' role in the battle was a special source of pride for New Zealanders, who welcomed the crew home at huge parades in Auckland and Wellington in early 1940 (see 23 February).

Frank Norton, *HMS 'Achilles'
in the Battle of the River Plate*,
1940.

CABINET ENDORSES TINO RANGATIRATANGA FLAG

The government recognised the Māori (Tino Rangatiratanga) flag as the preferred national Māori flag. While it does not carry official status, flying it alongside the New Zealand flag on days of national significance is intended to symbolise and enhance the Crown–Māori relationship. In January 2009, Minister of Māori Affairs Pita Sharples called for a Māori flag to be flown from the Auckland Harbour Bridge on Waitangi Day. Prime Minister John Key said he would support flying the two flags together if agreement could be reached on a preferred Māori flag.

In July–August 2009, 21 public hui (meetings) were held, and written and online submissions were invited from Māori and other interested New Zealanders. Four flags were identified for consideration: the official New Zealand flag; the New Zealand Red Ensign; the United Tribes of New Zealand flag; and the Tino Rangatiratanga flag. Of the 1200 submissions received, 80 per cent opted for the Tino Rangatiratanga flag. The flag had originally been developed by members of the group Te Kawariki in 1989 and unveiled at Waitangi on 6 February 1990.

Tino Rangatiratanga flag flying on Auckland Harbour Bridge.

OMC RELEASES 'HOW BIZARRE'
15 December 1995

It may have been the mariachi trumpets, the gently rapped lyrics or that 'making-me-crazy' chorus, but whatever the cause, 'How Bizarre' by the South Auckland group OMC (Otara Millionaires Club) went on to become one of the most successful songs ever recorded in New Zealand. Produced by Alan Jansson, who co-wrote the song with singer Pauly Fuemana, 'How Bizarre' was released by huh! Records. It reached no. 1 in Australia, Austria, Canada, Ireland, New Zealand and South Africa, and spent 36 weeks on the US Billboard Mainstream Top 40, peaking at no. 4. It also won 'Single of the Year' at the 1996 New Zealand Music Awards. It is estimated that the single sold between three and four million copies worldwide. The iconic music video, which cost $7000 to make, soon followed. Shot in Auckland, it featured Fuemana and backing vocalist Sina Saipaia driving a red Chevy Impala convertible around the gardens at Ellerslie Racecourse. After Fuemana died at the age of 40 in 2010, 'How Bizarre' re-entered the New Zealand singles charts.

CD single cover for OMC's 'How Bizarre'.

ALL BLACKS' NON-TRY HANDS WALES HISTORIC WIN

A great rugby rivalry was born when a try to All Black Bob Deans was disallowed, resulting in the only loss of the 'Originals' tour (see 16 September). The incident is still debated. The only score in the match played before a crowd of 47,000 at Cardiff Arms Park was a try scored by Welsh wing Teddy Morgan 10 minutes before halftime. As the All Blacks counter-attacked in the second half, Deans was sure he grounded the ball over the line before Welsh defenders dragged him back into the field of play. Portly Scottish referee John Dallas, 30 metres behind the play, disagreed and awarded Wales a five-yard scrum.

New Zealand captain Dave Gallaher accepted defeat in what he described as a 'rattling good game, played out to the bitter end — the best team won'.

Wales won three of its first four matches against the All Blacks, the last in 1953. The All Blacks have won all 27 subsequent tests. Their narrowest winning margin has been a single point, in Cardiff in 1978 and again in 2004.

New Zealand captain Dave Gallaher accepted defeat in what he described as a 'rattling good game, played out to the bitter end — the best team won'.

The 1905–06 All Blacks touring team.

NEW ZEALAND'S OWN EIFFEL TOWER OPENS

Just 8½ months after Gustave Eiffel's famous Paris tower was officially completed in March 1889, a wooden replica Eiffel Tower opened at the 1889–90 New Zealand and South Seas Exhibition in Dunedin.

The Exhibition offered the Austral Otis Elevator Company, which built the Eiffel Tower's elevators, a chance to display its wares in New Zealand. It constructed the 40-metre wooden tower, inside which an elevator rose about 30 metres. The tower cost about £1200 (equivalent to $226,000 today). A ride cost adults sixpence ($4.60) and children threepence ($2.30).

The cabin of the elevator accommodated 16 people, who could alight on any of the four landings, each bordered by a wooden fence to prevent accidents. An Otis steam-hoisting engine provided power to the four strong wire cables. The cabin and landings were lit by electricity, and at the top, a large electric searchlight lit the sky.

The Exhibition boasted two other Eiffel Towers. A 6-metre-high wooden replica stood in the gardens, while the Auckland court featured a model built entirely of whisky barrels and bottles.

Eiffel Tower replica at the New Zealand and South Seas Exhibition, c. 1889.

BORN ON THIS DAY

Peter Snell,
1938–,
runner

1642

FIRST ENCOUNTER BETWEEN MĀORI AND EUROPEANS

Abel Tasman's Dutch East India Company expedition had the first known European contact with Māori. It did not go well. After Tasman first sighted New Zealand on 13 December, his two ships sailed up the West Coast. On the 18th they anchored north of what is now Abel Tasman National Park. The local inhabitants were Māori of Ngāti Tūmatakōkiri. Two waka (canoes) paddled out to inspect the strange vessels. The Māori challenged the intruders with ritual incantations and pūkāea or pūtātara (trumpet) blasts, possibly to frighten away dangerous spirits.

In response, the Dutch shouted and blew their own trumpets. They then fired a cannon, provoking an angry reaction. The next morning many waka came out to the Dutch ships. Four sailors were killed after a small boat was rammed by a waka. The *Heemskerck* and *Zeehaen* then weighed anchor and sailed away. Tasman named the place Moordenaers' Baij (Murderers' Bay). It is now called Golden Bay.

It would be 127 years before the next recorded encounter between European and Māori, soon after James Cook's arrival in New Zealand in 1769 (see 6 October, 9 November).

Golden Bay in December 1642, with events during the visit of Abel Tasman; sketch attributed to Isaac Gilsemans.

Four sailors were killed after a small boat was rammed by a waka.

HMS *NEPTUNE* LOST IN MEDITERRANEAN MINEFIELD

In New Zealand's worst naval tragedy, the Royal Navy cruiser HMS *Neptune* struck enemy mines and sank off Libya. Of the 764 men who lost their lives, 150 were New Zealanders. In early 1941, New Zealand provided crew for the Leander-class light cruiser HMS *Neptune*, which was to serve alongside its existing ships *Achilles* and *Leander*. The *Neptune* headed to the Mediterranean to replace naval losses suffered during the Crete campaign and joined Admiral Cunningham's Malta-based Force K.

On the night of 18 December, Force K sailed to intercept an important Italian supply convoy heading to Tripoli, Libya. At around 1 a.m. on the 19th, 30 kilometres from Tripoli, the ships sailed into an uncharted deep-water minefield. The *Neptune* triggered a mine, then exploded two more as it reversed to get clear. Several attempts were made to assist the stricken cruiser, but when the destroyer *Kandahar* also hit a mine, the *Neptune*'s Captain Rory O'Conor flashed a warning to other ships to 'Keep away'. The *Neptune* struck another mine shortly afterwards and sank within minutes. Only one crew member survived.

HMS *Neptune*.

The Neptune *triggered a mine, then exploded two more as it reversed to get clear.*

NEW ZEALAND'S FIRST CRICKET MATCH
20 December 1832

Church Missionary Society (CMS) leader Henry Williams gave the male pupils (Māori and Pākehā) of his mission school at Paihia in the Bay of Islands a rare day off. They had sat exams the previous day. Their reward was an opportunity to play cricket on the foreshore at Horotutu. They must have already had some practice, as Williams wrote in his journal that they were 'very expert, good bowlers'. Williams, who had imported the cricket equipment, had a bowl himself, conceding a run to five-year-old Edwin Fairburn. The schoolgirls were 'all fatigued', but in any case, they would not have been allowed to play alongside the boys. They had to be content with receiving prizes for their academic work. The following day 'the boys recommenced their regular work', building fences and preparing ground for cultivation. There was no summer break for an institution largely reliant on its own resources. The naturalist Charles Darwin watched the next cricket match on record, at Waimate North mission station three years later. Once again, Māori and Pākehā boys took part.

Church Missionary Society house at Paihia, c. 1843.

21 December 1964

NEW ZEALAND WHALERS HARPOON THEIR LAST VICTIM

More than 170 years of New Zealand whaling history ended when J.A. Perano and Company caught its last whale off the coast near Kaikōura. Whaling ended because of a lack of whales rather than because of public distaste for the practice. Not until 1978 would all marine mammals receive legal protection in New Zealand waters.

Dunedin-born Joe Perano had started whaling out of Tory Channel in the Marlborough Sounds in 1911, beginning a 53-year family business. He was credited with bringing many innovations to the New Zealand whaling industry: he constructed this country's first powered whale chaser, was the first operator to use explosive harpoons, introduced the electric harpoon, and in 1936 equipped his whale chasers, mother ship and shore stations with radio telephones.

Joe Perano died in 1951, aged 74. In 1964 his sons, Gilbert and Joseph, were running the business. The whale they killed on 21 December was the last harpooned in New Zealand waters from a New Zealand-owned ship. Wellington Head, a steep headland on Arapawa (now Arapaoa) Island, was renamed Perano Head in 1969.

Humpback whale being processed at J.A. Perano's factory in Tory Channel, 1953.

FUTURE PRIME MINISTER CHARGED WITH SEDITION
22 December 1916

Peter Fraser's trial in the Wellington Magistrates' Court was the sequel to a speech in which he had attacked the government's policy of military conscription. As the First World War dragged on, enlistment rates slowed after the initial rush to volunteer. The government responded with the Military Service Act passed in August 1916. This introduced conscription, initially for Pākehā men only (see 16 November). While limited exemptions were given to members of specific pacifist religious groups, no allowance was made for socialist and labour objections to the war. On 4 December 1916 the government issued new regulations to control dissent which contained a broad definition of sedition. On 20 December police arrested Fraser and charged him with inciting 'disaffection against the Government' at a meeting 10 days earlier. In court, Fraser argued that calling for the repeal of the law, rather than for disobedience or resistance to it, was legal. The judge disagreed and sentenced him to 12 months in prison. Somewhat ironically, Peter Fraser was prime minister when New Zealand reintroduced conscription during the Second World War.

Peter Fraser, 1918.

QUEEN ELIZABETH II ARRIVES FOR ROYAL TOUR

23 December 1953

For New Zealanders old enough to have experienced it, the visit of the young Queen and her dashing husband, Prince Philip, in the summer of 1953–54 was a never-to-be forgotten event. Thousands greeted the first reigning monarch to visit this country in Auckland's aptly named Queen Street. In scenes reminiscent of a modern-day rock concert, hundreds of people had camped overnight to secure a good spot for the occasion.

The Queen visited 46 towns and cities and attended 110 separate functions during her stay. It was said that three in every four New Zealanders saw her.

The country was gripped with patriotic fervour; sheep were even dyed red, white and blue. It was hard to spot a car that did not sport a Union Jack, or a building in the main cities that was not covered in bunting and flowers during the day or electric lights at night. Sadly, the Queen's triumphant arrival was swiftly followed by one of New Zealand's darkest moments, when disaster struck at Tangiwai on the following night, Christmas Eve (see 24 December).

The royal couple wave to the crowd at the Auckland Racing Club's Boxing Day meeting at Ellerslie Racecourse, 1953.

TANGIWAI RAILWAY DISASTER

The worst railway disaster in New Zealand's history occurred on Christmas Eve 1953, when the Wellington–Auckland night express plunged into the flooded Whangaehu River, just west of Tangiwai in the central North Island. Of the 285 people on board, 151 were killed.

The cause of the tragedy was a volcanic lahar from the Mt Ruapehu crater lake, which sent a huge wave of water, silt, boulders and debris surging down the Whangaehu River minutes before the express approached the bridge at Tangiwai. There was evidence that the engine driver had applied the emergency brakes, but it was too late to prevent the locomotive, its tender and the first five second-class carriages plunging off the weakened bridge into the raging torrent. The leading first-class carriage toppled moments afterwards.

The nation was stunned. New Zealand's relatively small population meant that many people had a direct relationship with someone involved. The timing of the accident added to the sense of tragedy. Most of those on the train were heading home for Christmas with presents for friends and family.

Wreckage on the banks of the
Whangaehu River at Tangiwai.

FIRST CHRISTIAN MISSION ESTABLISHED

At Hohi Beach in the Bay of Islands, Samuel Marsden preached in English to a largely Māori gathering, launching New Zealand's first Christian mission. The Ngāpuhi leader Ruatara translated Marsden's sermon. The two men had first met in Port Jackson (Sydney) in 1809. In 1814 Marsden sent Thomas Kendall to consult Ruatara about establishing a Church Missionary Society (CMS) mission at Rangihoua. Ruatara assumed the role of protector and patron of 'his Pākehā' — the CMS missionaries Kendall, John King and William Hall, who had arrived with Marsden on the brig *Active* on 22 December. A site for the mission station was chosen the following day. After cattle and horses were landed, Marsden rode along the beach to the astonishment of Māori onlookers. Following Marsden's sermon on the birth of Jesus, the *Active* left Rangihoua to obtain timber with which to build the mission station. By 13 January 1815 the missionaries, their wives and all their stores were ashore and a large hut had been erected. Ruatara's death in early March left the future of the mission uncertain.

(By courtesy of the artist, Russell Clark.)

"BEHOLD I BRING YOU GOOD TIDINGS OF GREAT JOY"

Thus was the Gospel of Jesus Christ First Proclaimed on these Shores by the Rev. Samuel Marsden at Oihi, Bay of Islands, Christmas Day, 1814

N.Z. CHURCH MISSIONARY SOCIETY

> *After cattle and horses were landed, Marsden rode along the beach to the astonishment of Māori onlookers.*

Artwork produced to commemorate the 150th anniversary of Marsden's first sermon, 1964.

SECTARIAN VIOLENCE IN CANTERBURY

Catholic patrons at Barretts Hotel, Manchester Street, Christchurch attacked Protestant Alliance Friendly Society marchers in December 1879.

In Christchurch, 30 Catholic Irishmen attacked an Orange (Protestant) procession with pick-handles, while in Timaru 150 men from Thomas O'Driscoll's Hibernian Hotel surrounded Orangemen and prevented their procession from taking place. Ireland's struggles for land reform, home rule and independence were a major issue in British politics throughout the 19th and early 20th centuries. The influx of British and Irish immigrants to New Zealand meant these debates and crises were followed closely in this country.

The trouble in Christchurch began when a group of Catholic railway workers confronted a procession of Orangemen marching down Manchester Street. Police resources were stretched because a 21-strong contingent had already left for Timaru in anticipation of the riot that occurred there the same day. The few police present, aided by a Catholic priest, managed to separate the two groups, but not before several Orangemen were injured. When the police attempted to arrest one of the Catholics, the ancient Irish battle cry 'Faugh a ballagh!' ('Clear the way!') rang out as supporters rushed to free him. The police eventually made three arrests.

When the police attempted to arrest one of the Catholics, the ancient Irish battle cry 'Faugh a ballagh!' ('Clear the way!') rang out . . .

DEATH OF REWI ALLEY
27 December 1987

The former Cantabrian died in Beijing after living in China through six tumultuous decades. After serving in the First World War and then struggling on a backblocks farm in South Taranaki, in 1927 Alley moved to Shanghai, where he was a fire officer and factory inspector before becoming involved in government-sponsored relief work. He helped establish the Industrial Co-operative movement, which advocated village-level development. Its slogan Gung Ho ('work together') entered the English language. From 1944 Alley ran the Shandan Bailie school in Gansu province. The communist victory in the Chinese civil war complicated Alley's running of the school and fundraising for it in the West. After moving to Beijing in 1953, he became an advocate for the new People's Republic and involved in the international peace movement. As well as writing many books and pamphlets, he acquired a significant collection of Chinese artefacts and artworks. Following New Zealand's recognition of the People's Republic in 1972, Alley played a significant if unofficial diplomatic role. Prime Minister David Lange eulogised him on his 90th birthday, just weeks before his death.

Rewi Alley, c. 1927.

'BLACK SATURDAY' IN SAMOA

New Zealand military police fired on Mau independence demonstrators in Apia, killing 11 Samoans, including the independence leader Tupua Tamasese Lealofi III. After the First World War, the League of Nations granted New Zealand a mandate to administer the Samoan territory which had formerly been a German colony (see 29 August). The undermining of Samoan culture by New Zealand authorities, and their inept handling of the 1918 flu epidemic, which killed 8500 in Samoa, led to the rise of an independence movement — the Mau.

In 1929 the Administrator of Western Samoa, Colonel Sir Stephen Allen, decided to crack down on mounting civil disobedience. When the Mau paraded through Apia in December, he ordered police to arrest one of their leaders. Violent clashes broke out and 11 Samoans and one policeman were killed. Mau supporters disappeared into the bush. They came out of hiding in March 1930 and agreed to disperse. Some closure regarding this dark phase of Samoan history occurred in 2002 when New Zealand Prime Minister Helen Clark apologised for wrongs committed by the colonial administration.

Tupua Tamasese Lealofi III lying in state, 1929.

FLOATING DOCK BREAKS MOORINGS IN WELLINGTON HARBOUR

Built in England, the Wellington Harbour Board's new Jubilee Dock was 178 metres long, 36 metres wide and could lift ships displacing 17,000 tons. It cost about £250,000 (equivalent to $27 million today).

Two Dutch tugs undertook the record 22,000-kilometre tow via the Suez Canal, which began on 15 July. The dock's 11-man crew lived on board.

Excitement grew as the dock neared Wellington. Locals could accompany it from the Heads by ferry for 1s 6d ($8) or view it from the air for the 'small charge' of £1 ($107). Thousands more watched from the shore.

The dock entered the harbour on the afternoon of the 28th and anchored that evening. Next morning it was moved to a purpose-built dock. Later that day it slipped its temporary moorings in a northerly gale but was secured by the Dutch tugs. Its first lift, of the *Ruahine*, was made on 2 April 1932.

Too small to take container ships, the floating dock was eventually sold. In 1989, it broke in two in the Tasman Sea while being towed to Bangkok.

Wellington's Jubilee floating dock being towed to Aotea Quay, 1988.

COLENSO ARRIVES WITH A PRINTING PRESS
30 December 1834

'Columbian'-brand printing press formerly owned by William Colenso, photographed in the 1970s.

Church Missionary Society printer William Colenso arrived in the Bay of Islands on the schooner *Blackbird* with New Zealand's first successful printing press. (Missionary William Yate's earlier efforts as a printer had borne little fruit.) Within six weeks, Colenso had produced a 16-page pamphlet containing two of Paul's epistles in Māori. Three years after his arrival he began printing 5000 copies of William Williams' 356-page Māori New Testament, then moved on to 27,000 copies of the Book of Common Prayer. Having cautioned Lieutenant-Governor William Hobson that many Māori did not understand the terms of the Treaty of Waitangi, Colenso printed a Māori-language version of the document in February 1840. Later that year he printed the first *New Zealand Government Gazette*. After he was ordained as a deacon in 1844, Colenso and his wife, Elizabeth, moved to an isolated mission station in Heretaunga (Hawke's Bay). When his relationship with a Māori member of their household was revealed by her pregnancy, Colenso was dismissed, ostracised by Pākehā and ridiculed by Māori. In later life he was an unsuccessful politician, a middling linguist, a competent historian, and made significant contributions to biology and ethnology.

FIRST GATHERING DANCE FESTIVAL HELD

On New Year's Eve around 4000 people made their way to the remote location of Canaan Downs, Takaka, to take part in the first Gathering, a two-day festival for electronic dance music fans.

Nelson DJ Murray Kingi conceived the New Year's event after becoming dissatisfied with the local Entrain parties. He worked up the idea and looked for an outdoor site to host it. With a budget of $90,000 and relying mostly on word-of-mouth advertising, the Gathering was an immediate success.

The first event featured more than 100 New Zealand DJs, with 35 acts creating live electronic music and artists performing in six separate music zones.

The 1997/98 event drew a crowd of 8000 and cost $350,000 to run, but brought an estimated $4 million into the local economy. After several successful years, the Gathering began to struggle as more dance parties were held in the South Island. The final event was held in 2002.

The 1997/98 event drew a crowd of 8000 and cost $350,000 to run, but brought an estimated $4 million into the local economy.

BORN ON THIS DAY

Richie McCaw,
1980–,
All Blacks captain

Poster for the Gathering, 1996/97.

ACKNOWLEDGEMENTS

This publication was developed as a partnership between Exisle Publishing, the Ministry for Culture and Heritage (MCH) and the Alexander Turnbull Library (ATL), under the direction of publisher Gareth St John Thomas, Chief Historian Neill Atkinson and Chief Librarian Chris Szekely respectively.

At MCH, the project was ably co-ordinated by Gareth Phipps, who shared writing duties with Neill Atkinson, David Green and Kylan McKeen. Gareth also sourced the images, with valuable assistance from Heather Mathie at ATL, which was the main image provider.

Other illustrations have been sourced from Archives New Zealand, Te Papa, Canterbury Museum, the Hocken Library, the Whanganui, Southland and Lake District regional museums, Getty, NewsPix (*New Zealand Herald*) and Photosport, as well as from private collections.

The original Today in History feature on the NZHistory website was developed and largely written by Steve Watters, supported by other staff in the Ministry for Culture and Heritage's History Group, including former Chief Historian Bronwyn Dalley, Neill Atkinson, Imelda Bargas, David Green, Megan Hutching, Joe McGee, Jamie Mackay, Gavin McLean, Alison Parr and Jean Sergent-Shadbolt.

The text was edited by Madeleine Collinge and Brian O'Flaherty, and the production process was managed by Exisle's Anouska Jones.

FURTHER READING

Web sources

Archives New Zealand, http://archives.govt.nz/

Audioculture, http://www.audioculture.co.nz/

Digital NZ, http://www.digitalnz.org/

National Library of New Zealand, http://natlib.govt.nz/

New Zealand Electronic Text Collection, Victoria University of Wellington, http://nzetc.victoria.ac.nz

New Zealand Official Yearbook Collection, Statistics NZ, http://www.stats.govt.nz/yearbooks

Ngā Taonga Sound and Vision, http://www.ngataonga.org.nz/

NZHistory (Ministry for Culture and Heritage), https://www.nzhistory.govt.nz/

NZ on Screen, https://www.nzonscreen.com/

Papers Past (National Library of New Zealand), https://paperspast.natlib.govt.nz/

Te Ara (Ministry for Culture and Heritage), http://www.teara.govt.nz/en

Te Papa, https://www.tepapa.govt.nz/

Books

Atholl Anderson, Judith Binney and Aroha Harris, *Tangata Whenua: an illustrated history*, Bridget Williams Books, Wellington, 2015

Barbara Brookes, *A History of New Zealand Women*, Bridget Williams Books, Wellington, 2016

Sandra Coney, *Standing in the Sunshine: a history of New Zealand women since they won the vote*, Viking, Auckland, 1993

Kenneth B. Cumberland, *Landmarks*, Reader's Digest, Surry Hills, New South Wales, 1981

Bronwyn Dalley, *Living in the Twentieth Century: New Zealand history in photographs, 1900–1980*, Craig Potton Publishing, Wellington, 2000

Bronwyn Dalley and Gavin McLean (eds), *Frontier of Dreams: the story of New Zealand*, Hodder Moa, Auckland, 2005

Damien Fenton with Caroline Lord, Gavin McLean and Tim Shoebridge, *New Zealand and the First World War, 1914–1919*, Penguin, Auckland, 2013

Michael King, *The Penguin History of New Zealand*, 2012 edn, Penguin, Auckland

Wendy McGuiness and Miriam White, *Nation Dates: significant events that have shaped the nation of New Zealand*, 2nd edn, McGuiness Institute, Wellington, 2012

Paul Moon, *New Zealand in the Twentieth Century: the nation, the people*, HarperCollins, Auckland, 2011

Claudia Orange, *An Illustrated History of the Treaty of Waitangi*, Bridget Williams Books, Wellington, 2004

Ranginui Walker, *Ka Whawhai Tonu Matou: struggle without end*, 2nd edn, Penguin, Auckland, 2004

Matthew Wright, *Two Peoples, One Land: the New Zealand Wars*, Reed, Auckland, 2006

PHOTOGRAPHIC CREDITS

JANUARY

1 January 1859: Alexander Turnbull Library, 1/2-136029-F

Margaret Cruickshank: Newman Coralynn Collection, Canterbury Museum, 1989.43.2

2 January 1938: Alexander Turnbull Library, 1/4-048844-G

3 January 1930: Stills Collection, Ngā Taonga Sound and Vision, courtesy of Edwin (Ted) Coubray Collection

Cyril Bassett: Alexander Turnbull Library, PAColl-6001-05

4 January 1958: Geoffrey Lee Martin © Antarctic New Zealand Pictorial Collection, 1956–1958

5 January 1977: Robin Morrison 1978, Auckland War Memorial Museum neg. RMN10-1

Gottfried Lindauer: Alexander Turnbull Library, PUBL-0092-001

6 January 1953: Alexander Turnbull Library, EP/1953/0034-G

7 January 1931: Alexander Turnbull Library, EP-Transport-Aviation-Aircraft-01

8 January 1863: Alexander Turnbull Library, A-149-011

9 January 1923: Alexander Turnbull Library, 1/4-059883-F

10 January 1928: Alexander Turnbull Library, EP-5962-1/4-G

11 January 1846: Alexander Turnbull Library, A-079-007

Fanny Howie (Te Rangi Pai): Alexander Turnbull Library, PA1-q-236-152

12 January 1954: Archives New Zealand, AAQT 6538/

13 January 1890: Alexander Turnbull Library, 1/1-007887-G

14 January 1948: Brian Donovan, Paleontology Collection, School of Environment, University of Auckland

Thomas Hocken: Alexander Turnbull Library, 1/2-004542-F

15 January 1970: Alexander Turnbull Library, MS-Papers-2511-5/1/25-9

16 January 1941: Archives New Zealand, AIR 118 Box 114/78r

Ormond Burton: Alexander Turnbull Library, 1/2-152915-F

17 January 1853: Sydney Taiwhanga, *Proposals of Mr Sydney David Taiwhanga, MHR, for the colonization and settlement of Maori lands*, Edwards & Co., Wellington, 1888

18 January 1980: Sony Music

19 January 1845: Alexander Turnbull Library, A-004-037

20 January 1957: D. Rogers © Antarctica New Zealand Pictorial Collection, 1957

21 January 1889: Harris & Ewing Collection (Library of Congress), LC-H261- 3339 [P&P]

22 January 1840: Te Ara — The Encyclopedia of New Zealand

23 January 1855: Alexander Turnbull Library, B-103-016

24 January 1980: Alexander Turnbull Library, 114/248/03-G

25 January 1974: Tom Duffy/Getty Images

26 January 1984: Alexander Turnbull Library, EP/1984/0515/7A-F

27 January 1962: Whanganui Regional Museum, Sp/Ath/17

28 January 1827: Alexander Turnbull Library, B-052-010

29 January 1842: Sir George Grey Special Collections, Auckland Libraries, 7-C1877

30 January 1911: Alexander Turnbull Library, 1/2-045407-G

31 January 1921: Alexander Turnbull Library, 1/2-070840-G

FEBRUARY

1 February 1981: www.photosport.co.nz

2 February 1974: Tony Duffy/Allsport

3 February 1931: Alexander Turnbull Library, 1/2-002952-F

4 February 1975: Alexander Turnbull Library, EP/1975/0552X/23-F

Arnold Downer: Alexander Turnbull Library, EP/1957/2460-F

5 February 1994: Ari Bakker, Flickr

6 February 1840: Alexander Turnbull Library, G-821-2

7 February 1863: Alexander Turnbull Library, PUBL-0033-1863-437

Witi Ihimaera: Alexander Turnbull Library, 1/4-089205-F

8 February 1931: Steve Lowe Collection

9 February 1900: Whanganui District Council; photographer Mark Brimblecombe

10 February 1967: Alexander Turnbull Library, 1/4-000033-F

11 February 1864: Alexander Turnbull Library, 1/2-003062-F

Fred Evans: Alexander Turnbull Library, PAColl-3736

12 February 1909: Alexander Turnbull Library, 1/1-020152-G

13 February 1983: Adrian Murrell/Getty Images

Godfrey Bowen: Alexander Turnbull Library, EP/1958/1145-F

14 February 1998: Michael Hall, Te Papa

15 February 1882: Alexander Turnbull Library, Eph-F-MEAT-Gear-018

16 February 1986: Alexander Turnbull Library, EP/1989/1713/4

17 February 1873: Alexander Turnbull Library, PA2-2506

18 February 1957: Alexander Turnbull Library, Eph-D-NEWSPAPER-NZ-TRUTH-1956-01

19 February 1938: Alexander Turnbull Library, PAColl-4431-01

20 February 1914: Te Papa, B.012165

21 February 1879: Alexander Turnbull Library, PAColl-6338-03

22 February 2011: © Gillian Needham

23 February 1940: Alexander Turnbull Library, 1/4-049251-F

24 February 1912: Lakes District Museum, EL0070

Ettie Rout: Alexander Turnbull Library, PAColl-4832

25 February 1943: Alexander Turnbull Library, 1/4-000776-F

Hester Maclean: Alexander Turnbull Library, 1/2-043492-G

26 February 1844: Hulton Archive/ Getty Images

Helen Clark: © Crown Copyright 2007

27 February 1951: Alexander Turnbull Library, Eph-A-LABOUR-1951-01

28 February 1945: National Army Museum, 1998.954

29 February 2004: Alexander Turnbull Library, DX-001-739

MARCH

1 March 1916: Alexander Turnbull Library, 1/2-066895-F

2 March 1865: Alexander Turnbull Library, PUBL-0033-1865-47-080-2

3 March 1960: Penguin New Zealand

4 March 1855: Shirley Williams, Te Ara — The Encyclopedia of New Zealand

5 March 2013: Michael Davis, Canterbury Museum, 2013.17.123

6 March 1947: Alexander Turnbull Library, Eph-B-MUSIC-NO-1947-01-front

Kiri Te Kanawa: New Zealand Herald/ Newspix

7 March 1988: New Zealand Herald/ newspix.co.nz

8 March 1929: Alexander Turnbull Library, 1/2-139949-F

9 March 1956: Te Papa, F.005006/02

10 March 1995: www.photosport.co.nz

Kate Sheppard: Canterbury Museum, S62 1/2

11 March 1884: Te Papa, C.012080

12 March 1975: Leonie Clent, New Zealand Red Cross

Rita Angus: Te Papa, CA000242/001/0001

13 March 1956: New Zealand Herald/ newspix.co.nz

14 March 1980: Warner Music

15 March 2019: Getty Images; photographer Hagen Hopkins

16 March 1940: Alexander Turnbull Library, Eph-E-COSTUME-1940-04

James Hector: Alexander Turnbull Library, MNZ-1161-1/2-F

17 March 1860: Alexander Turnbull Library, B-103-01 1

18 March 1983: Waitangi Tribunal, *Report of the Waitangi Tribunal on the Motunui–Waitara Claim (Wai 6)*, Brooker's, Wellington, 1989; artwork by Cliff Whiting

19 March 1839: William Charles Cotton, *My Bee Book*, Rivington, London, 1842, p. 358

20 March 1834: Alexander Turnbull Library, MS-Papers-0009-09-01

21 March 1994: Academy of Motion Pictures Arts and Sciences, Margaret Herrick Library, 6416_1991

22 March 1902: Adam Art Gallery Te Pātaka Toi, Victoria University of Wellington Art Collection, VUW.1933.1

23 March 1848: Alexander Turnbull Library, Ref: 1/2-003216-G

Michael Joseph Savage: Alexander Turnbull Library, 1/2-051739-F

24 March 1770: *Journal of the Polynesian Society*, University of Auckland

25 March 1940: Alexander Turnbull Library, 1/2-043306-F

26 March 1896: Christchurch City Libraries, PhotoCD 2, IMG0072

Matiu Rata: Alexander Turnbull Library, 1/4-021374-F

27 March 1984: New Zealand Police Museum Collection, 2016/325/1

28 March 2004: Wikimedia

29 March 1942: National Library of New Zealand, PapersPast, *New Zealand Herald*, 8 October 1943

30 March 1940: Alexander Turnbull Library, 1/1-021744-G

31 March 1864: Alexander Turnbull Library, C-033-004

APRIL

1 April 1965: Alexander Turnbull Library, GG-11-0760

1 April 1974: Alexander Turnbull Library, 1/2-223818-F

Frederic Truby King: Alexander Turnbull Library, PAColl-6075-16

2 April 1916: Alexander Turnbull Library, 1/2-028072-F

3 April 1943: Alexander Turnbull Library, PAColl-5936-42

4 April 2001: New Zealand Herald/ newspix.co.nz

5 April 1932: Alexander Turnbull Library, MNZ-1050-1/4

6 April 1919: Sir George Grey Special Collections, Auckland Libraries, AWNS-19190410-34-2

7 April 1856: Alexander Turnbull Library, A-109-002

8 April 1873: Alexander Turnbull Library, 1/2-053949-F

9 April 1850: Sir George Grey Special Collections, Auckland Libraries, 1052-J8-32

10 April 1919: National Library of New Zealand, PapersPast, *NZ Truth*, 19 April 1919

10 April 1968: Alexander Turnbull Library, EP/1968/1648a/1a-F

11 April 1869: Alexander Turnbull Library, 1/2-002559-F

Winston Peters: Alexander Turnbull Library, EP/1989/1300/11a-F

12 April 1913: Alexander Turnbull Library, 1/1-020101-G

13 April 1896: Alexander Turnbull Library, 1/2-041798-F

14 April 1932: Tudor Washington Collins, Auckland War Memorial Museum, PH-RES-844

Alan MacDiarmid: University of Pennsylvania Archives

15 April 1868: Alexander Turnbull Library, 1/1-019389-G

16 April 1973: Pat Booth

17 April 1820: Alexander Turnbull Library, C-082-094

18 April 1840: Alexander Turnbull Library, 1/2-038720-F

Mabel Howard: Alexander Turnbull Library, 1/2-065969-F

19 April 1893: Alexander Turnbull Library, NON-ATL-P-0083

20 April 1981: www.photosport.co.nz

21 April 1971: Court Theatre, Alexander Turnbull Library, Eph-A-COURT-1971/1975

22 April 1936: Alexander Turnbull Library, EP-NZ Obits-Ra to Rd-01

23 April 1979: Wikipedia

23 April 1983: Alexander Turnbull Library, EP Royalty Charles, Diana and William-1983 tour-01

Ngaio Marsh: Alexander Turnbull Library, 1/2-046800-F

24 April 1920: Alexander Turnbull Library, PAColl-0362-16

25 April 1915: Archives New Zealand, AAAC 898 NCWA Q388

Keith Elliott: Alexander Turnbull Library, DA-02693-F

25 April 1916: Alexander Turnbull Library, APG-0589-1/2-G

26 April 1943: Allan Wyllie Collection

27 April 1806: Alexander Turnbull Library, G-618

28 April 1888: New Zealand Rugby Museum

Frances Hodgkins: Alexander Turnbull Library, 35mm-00335-A-F

29 April 1864: Alexander Turnbull Library, 1/2-019993-G

30 April 1917: Damien Fenton Collection

MAY

1 May 1893: Alexander Turnbull Library, A-122-002

Julius von Haast: Alexander Turnbull Library, 1/4-002124-G

2 May 1964: © Chris Bradley

3 May 1897: Newman Coralynn Collection, Canterbury Museum, 1989.43.2

4 May 1772: Alexander Turnbull Library, G-824-3

5 May 1898: Alexander Turnbull Library, 1/2-018754-F

6 May 1869: Alexander Turnbull Library, 1/2-011006-F

7 May 1846: Graham Hancox, GNS Science

Tommy Solomon: Alexander Turnbull Library, PAColl-5469-048

8 May 1970: Alexander Turnbull Library, Eph-C-CABOT-Music-1970-02

9 May 1907: Sir George Grey Special Collections, Auckland Libraries, *School Journal* 10, pt 3, no. 6 (July 1916)

10 May 1960: Alexander Turnbull Library, Eph-C-RACIAL-1959-01

11 May 1945: Alexander Turnbull Library, DA-02108

12 May 1971: New Zealand Herald/ newspix.co.nz

Jonah Lomu: New Zealand Herald/ Newspix

13 May 1936: Alexander Turnbull Library, 1/1-018499-F

13 May 1995: Alexander Turnbull Library, EP/1995/1522/17-F

14 May 1907: Alexander Turnbull Library, PAColl-6075-16

15 May 1920: Alexander Turnbull Library, 1/2-029070-F

16 May 1846: Alexander Turnbull Library, B-081-002

Barry Crump: New Zealand Herald/ Newspix

17 May 1922: Sir George Grey Special Collections, Auckland Libraries, *New Zealand Observer*, 27 May 1922, p. 5

Bill Gallagher: Private Collection, Te Ara Biographies

17 May 1982: New Zealand Herald/ newspix.co.nz

18 May 1937: Alexander Turnbull Library, 1/2-C-016123-F

19 May 1987: Alexander Turnbull Library, B-136-617

20 May 1773: Alexander Turnbull Library, PUBL-0144-1-330

21 May 1840: Alexander Turnbull Library, G-826-1

22 May 1995: Alexander Turnbull Library, EP/1995/4375B/33A-F

23 May 1861: Alexander Turnbull Library, 1/2-096648-F

Elizabeth Gunn: Alexander Turnbull Library, 1/1-014009-G

24 May 1854: Andrew Robertson, *Auckland from Parnell*, 1859, Auckland Art Gallery Toi o Tāmaki

25 May 2008: Jonathan Ferrey/Getty Images

26 May 1926: Alexander Turnbull Library, 1/1-019151-F

27 May 1909: South Otago Museum

Neil Finn: Mike Walen, Wikimedia

28 May 1920: National Library of New Zealand, PapersPast, *Observer*, 5 June 1920

29 May 1953: Royal Geographical Society, S0001055

30 May 1901: Alexander Turnbull Library, J-040-008

30 May 1959: Olaf Petersen (1959), Auckland War Memorial Museum, PH-1988-9

31 May 1916: Archives New Zealand, AAAC 898 NCWA 539

JUNE

1 June 1960: Alexander Turnbull Library, A-310-078

2 June 1970: Michael Cooper Archive

3 June 1941: New Zealand Police Museum Collection, 2016/566/1.12

4 June 1943: Private Collection

5 June 1847: Alexander Turnbull Library, 1/1-002886-G

6 June 1996: Alexander Turnbull Library, EP-Energy-Wind Power-02

7 June 1976: © McDonald's

8 June 1987: Te Papa, GH011812

9 June 1868: Alexander Turnbull Library, PUBL-0047-1868-10-08

10 June 1886: Alexander Turnbull Library, C-033-002

11 June 1901: Alexander Turnbull Library, PAColl-6208-60

12 June 1942: Archives New Zealand, AAAC 898 NCWA Q392

13 June 1866: Alexander Turnbull Library, PA2-2593

14 June 1984: Alexander Turnbull Library, EP/1984/3057/12-F

15 June 1935: Alexander Turnbull Library, PAColl-8163-31

Keith Park: Alexander Turnbull Library, PICT-000173

16 June 1923: National Library of New Zealand, PapersPast, *NZ Truth*, 10 March 1923

17 June 1843: Alexander Turnbull Library, B-103-030

18 June 1932: Alexander Turnbull Library, PAColl-5744-10

19 June 1940: Alexander Turnbull Library, PAColl-8634

Mary Aubert: Alexander Turnbull Library, 1/2-197333-F

20 June 1943: Neill Atkinson

20 June 1987: Alexander Turnbull Library, EP/1987/2998/22-F

21 June 1964: Alexander Turnbull Library, 1/4-071857-F

22 June 1954: Reproduced from *So Brilliantly Clever*, courtesy of Awa Press

23 June 1961: © Antarctica New Zealand Pictorial Collection, 1961

24 June 1905: Alexander Turnbull Library, 114/103/01-G

25 June 2003: Alexander Turnbull Library, H-734-144

26 June 1987: https://www.ajhackett.com/

27 June 1936: Alexander Turnbull Library, 1/1-006789-F

28 June 1973: National Museum of the Royal New Zealand Navy

29 June 1990: Otago Daily Times

James K. Baxter: Alexander Turnbull Library, EP/1971/1098-F

30 June 1939: Alexander Turnbull Library, S-L-1249-COVER ·

JULY

1 July 1988: New Zealand Herald/newspix.co.nz

2 July 1938: Alexander Turnbull Library, Eph-A-RAIL-1938-01-front

3 July 1963: New Zealand Herald/newspix.co.nz

Āpirana Ngata: Alexander Turnbull Library, 35mm-00181-f-F

4 July 1868: Alexander Turnbull Library, A-114-004-2

5 July 1881: Archives New Zealand, LS 24/1 1615

Len Lye: Len Lye Foundation Collection, Govett-Brewster Art Gallery

6 July 1923: Geoff Conly and Graham Stewart, *Tragedy on the Track: Tangiwai & other New Zealand railway accidents*, Grantham House, Wellington, 1986

Arthur Lydiard: Alexander Turnbull Library, EP/1975/0663/7-F

7 July 1916: Alexander Turnbull Library, 1/2-044402-F

8 July 1862: National Library of New Zealand, PapersPast, *Observer*, 14 September 1889

9 July 1986: Alexander Turnbull Library, Eph-C-GAY-1985-03

10 July 1967: Alexander Turnbull Library, EP-Economy-Currency-02

10 July 1985: New Zealand Herald/newspix.co.nz

11 July 1877: Nelson College for Girls

12 July 1863: Alexander Turnbull Library, A-110-006

13 July 1916: New Zealand Herald/newspix.co.nz

14 July 1853: Alexander Turnbull Library, Eph-C-POLITICS-1853-02

Rangitīaria Dennan (Guide Rangi): Alexander Turnbull Library, PAColl-6180-06-01

15 July 1915: Archives New Zealand, AAAC 898 NCWA 532

16 July 1965: © Marie Roberts

17 July 1939: Alexander Turnbull Library, 1/2-122301-F

18 July 1855: Te Papa, PH000592

19 July 1982: Alexander Turnbull Library, PADL-000081

20 July 1965: Auckland Star/Fairfax Media New Zealand

Edmund Hillary: Royal Geographical Society, S0001055

21 July 2019: Getty Images; photographer Nigel French – PA Images

22 July 1987: New Zealand Lotteries Commission, Alexander Turnbull Library, Eph-A-LOTTERY-Lotto-1987/1988

23 July 1952: New Zealand Herald/newspix.co.nz

24 July 2000: Ross Land/Getty Images

25 July 1981: Alexander Turnbull Library, EP/1981/2598/28A-F

26 July 1863: Alexander Turnbull Library, A-253-035

Bill Hamilton: Alexander Turnbull Library, PAColl-0783-2-0327

27 July 1953: Ministry of Foreign Affairs and Trade

Charles Brasch: Alexander Turnbull Library, 1/2-049005-F

28 July 1893: Archives New Zealand, LE1, 1893/7a

29 July 2003: William Demchick, Wikipedia

30 July 1979: Alexander Turnbull Library, B-135-684

31 July 1843: *Illustrated London News*, 9 April 1859, p. 357

AUGUST

1 August 1987: Alexander Turnbull Library, EP/1991/2155/3-F

Colin McCahon: TeWheke, Wikimedia

2 August 1983: Alexander Turnbull Library, EP/1983/3124/21A-F

3 August 1941: Alexander Turnbull Library, 1/2-025572-F

4 August 1923: Alexander Turnbull Library, 1/1-008425-G

David Lange: Alexander Turnbull Library, EP/1984/3356/29-F

5 August 1988: Alexander Turnbull Library, Eph-D-SERIAL-Metro-1987-06

6 August 1936: Alexander Turnbull Library, MSX-2261-062

7 August 1991: Alexander Turnbull Library, EP/1985/3350/26-F

William Levin: Alexander Turnbull Library, PA1-q-197-18-4

8 August 1915: Alexander Turnbull Library, D-001-035

9 August 1908: Alexander Turnbull Library, 1/2-001234-G

John Key: © Crown Copyright

10 August 1995: www.photosport. co.nz

11 August 1962: Alexander Turnbull Library, PAColl-8725-1

Ralph Hotere: Alexander Turnbull Library, PAColl-6458-1-01

12 August 1895: Lynley Hood, *Minnie Dean: her life and crimes*, Penguin Books, Auckland, 1994

13 August 1914: New Zealand Defence Force

14 August 2011: frozenpuddle, Wikimedia

15 August 1951: Alexander Turnbull Library, 114/333/04-G

16 August 2008: Harry How/Getty Images

17 August 1839: Alexander Turnbull Library, C-033-005

18 August 1910: New Zealand Sports Hall of Fame

19 August 2012: New Zealand Defence Force

20 August 1904: National Library of New Zealand, PapersPast, *Free Lance*, 20 August 1904

James Carroll: Alexander Turnbull Library, 35mm-00136-d-F

21 August 1958: Alexander Turnbull Library, PAColl-7756-1-121

22 August 1969: *Farmers Weekly*

23 August 1947: Alexander Turnbull Library, Eph-G-SHIP-1940-01

24 August 1878: Alexander Turnbull Library, PAColl-D-0523

25 August 1948: Hamilton City Libraries, HCL 07046 (JAT Terry Collection)

26 August 1866: Alastair McLean, Te Ara — The Encyclopedia of New Zealand

27 August 1911: Alexander Turnbull Library, 114/356/01-G

28 August 1992: © Tony Allan

Janet Frame: Alexander Turnbull Library, EP-Honours and awards-01

29 August 1914: Alexander Turnbull Library, Eph-B-POSTCARD-Vol-1-125-top

30 August 1903: Alexander Turnbull Library, 1/2-038135-F

Ernest Rutherford: Alexander Turnbull Library, G-826-2

31 August 1894: Alexander Turnbull Library, A-312-8-005

SEPTEMBER

1 September 1943: Alexander Turnbull Library, 1/2-005368-F

2 September 1960: New Zealand Olympic Museum — He Pataka Taumahekeheke, New Zealand Olympic Committee

3 September 1958: Auckland Star/ Fairfax Media New Zealand

4 September 2010: BeckerFraserPhotos

5 September 1939: Alexander Turnbull Library, 1/2-051739-F

6 September 1948: Alexander Turnbull Library, 1/2-027793-F

7 September 1921: Alexander Turnbull Library, Eph-A-RUGBY-1921-01-front

8 September 1862: Jock Phillips, Te Ara — The Encyclopedia of New Zealand

9 September 1976: Alexander Turnbull Library, EP/1982/3990

10 September 1984: New Zealand Herald/newspix.co.nz

11 September 1928: Alexander Turnbull Library, PAColl-0813-03

12 September 1981: New Zealand Herald/newspix.co.nz

13 September 1933: Alexander Turnbull Library, 1/2-150372-F

14 September 1938: Alexander Turnbull Library, 1/4-049203-G

Sam Neill: Alexander Turnbull Library, EP/1977/3854/5-F

15 September 1969: Alexander Turnbull Library, WA-68102-G

Jean Batten: Alexander Turnbull Library, 1/2-046051-F

16 September 1905: Alexander Turnbull Library, MNZ-1012-1/4-F

17 September 1941: New Zealand Police Museum Collection, 2009/2019/5

18 September 1937: Archives New Zealand, ABVF 7484 Box 1 18

19 September 1893: Jock Phillips, Te Ara — The Encyclopedia of New Zealand

20 September 1954: Alexander Turnbull Library, PAColl-1551-1-055

21 September 1834: Te Papa, GH003416

22 September 1906: Alexander Turnbull Library, Eph-A-IMMIGRATION-1912-cover

Martin Crowe: www.photosport.co.nz

23 September 1887: Alexander Turnbull Library, 1/2-041319-F

24 September 1905: Hocken Library, 74/174

Eleanor Catton: NZ at Frankfurt, Wikimedia

25 September 1819: Alexander Turnbull Library, PUBL-0031-30

Robert Muldoon: Alexander Turnbull Library, EP/1984/3057/12-F

26 September 1907: Alexander Turnbull Library, 1/2-080522-F

27 September 1974: Alexander Turnbull Library, EP-1974-6745a

28 September 1899: Alexander Turnbull Library, A-256-002

29 September 1947: Alexander Turnbull Library, 1/4-001245-F

Anna Stout: Alexander Turnbull Library, PAColl-10309-02-08

30 September 1972: Warren and Mahoney

OCTOBER

1 October 1986: Alexander Turnbull Library, EP/1984/5279/12

Peter Blake: Alexander Turnbull Library, EP/1985/0686

2 October 1986: Sony Music

3 October 1888: Bill Brien Collection

4 October 1957: Melanie Lovell-Smith, Te Ara — The Encyclopedia of New Zealand

5 October 2011: New Zealand Defence Force

6 October 1769: Lloyd Homer, GNS Science, 12936-10

Valerie Adams: Frankie Fouganthin, Wikimedia

7 October 1917: Archives New Zealand, AAZI 19575 Dwyer2 1/1

8 October 1941: Alexander Turnbull Library, MS-Papers-2404-1-01

9 October 1967: Alexander Turnbull Library, PADL-000185

10 October 1975: Alexander Turnbull Library, 1/4-021374-F

11 October 1861: Alexander Turnbull Library, MNZ-0643-1/4-F

12 October 1917: Alexander Turnbull Library, 1/2-C-003343-F

13 October 1975: Alexander Turnbull Library, PA7-15-18

14 October 1979: New Zealand Herald/ newspix.co.nz

15 October 1942: Alexander Turnbull Library, 114/294/09-G

15 October 2007: New Zealand Herald/ newspix.co.nz

16 October 1936: Alexander Turnbull Library, 1/2-046051-F

17 October 1877: Alexander Turnbull Library, 1/2-031752-F

18 October 1924: Hocken Library, *Otago Daily Times* photograph

19 October 1966: Alexander Turnbull Library, EP/1966/4545-F

20 October 1987: Alexander Turnbull Library, EP/1987/5914/9a-F

21 October 2008: New Zealand Herald/ newspix.co.nz

Hone Tuwhare: Alexander Turnbull Library, 1/4-089310-F

22 October 1967: www.photosport. co.nz

23 October 1915: Alexander Turnbull Library, 1/1-007697-G

24 October 1913: Sir George Grey Special Collections, Auckland Libraries, 7-A10659

25 October 1971: New Zealand Railway and Locomotive Society

26 October 1942: Archives New Zealand, ARNZ 18828 Weekly Review 115

27 October 1943: Archives New Zealand, AAAC 898 NCWA 56

James Cook: Alexander Turnbull Library, A-217-010

28 October 1835: Archives New Zealand, IA9-1

29 October 1894: Alexander Turnbull Library, PA1-o-287-01

30 October 1918: Alexander Turnbull Library, Eph-D-ALCOHOL-Prohibition-01

31 October 1985: Alexander Turnbull Library, Eph-C-BOOK-AWARDS-1984-02

Peter Jackson: Alexander Turnbull Library, EP/1992/0425/6-F

NOVEMBER

1 November 1898: Sir George Grey Special Collections, Auckland Libraries, AWNS-18990929-1-3

1 November 1944: Alexander Turnbull Library, 1/2-003634-F

2 November 1942: Alexander Turnbull Library, DA-06780

Douglas Lilburn: Alexander Turnbull Library, PAColl-0675-20

3 November 1886: Alexander Turnbull Library, B-185-003

4 November 1918: Archives New Zealand, AAAC 898 NCWA 535

5 November 1881: Alexander Turnbull Library, PA1-q-183-19

6 November 1908: *Appendix to the Journals of the House of Representatives*, 1909, D-2

7 November 1970: New Zealand Alpine Club

Ella Yelich-O'Connor (Lorde): Kirk Stauffer, Wikimedia

8 November 1939: Alexander Turnbull Library, Eph-E-EXHIBITION-1939-01

9 November 1769: © Jock Phillips

Te Puea Hērangi: Alexander Turnbull Library, PAColl-5584-58

10 November 1868: David Green

11 November 1942: Wellington Museum Collection

12 November 1912: Archives New Zealand, AAAC W3529 20/1

13 November 1990: Alexander Turnbull Library, EP/1990/3989/27A-F

14 November 1973: Alexander Turnbull Library, 1/4-028276-F

15 November 1861: National Library of New Zealand, PapersPast, *Otago Daily Times*, 15 November 1861

16 November 1916: Sir George Grey Special Collections, Auckland Libraries, AWNS-19161123-35-1

17 November 1925: Alexander Turnbull Library, 1-2-002372-F

18 November 1947: Alexander Turnbull Library, PAColl-5936-48

19 November 2010: Iain McGregor-Pool/Getty Images

Elizabeth McCombs: Alexander Turnbull Library, 1/2-150372-F

20 November 1937: Hocken Library, E.A. Phillips Collection, P1968-001/7-197

21 November 1863: Alexander Turnbull Library, A-145-004

22 November 1939: Alexander Turnbull Library, PA1-q-287-0744

Annie Schnackenberg: Private Collection, Te Ara Biographies

23 November 1986: Alexander Turnbull Library, PAColl-9214-11

Ernest Adams: Private Collection, Te Ara Biographies

24 November 1959: *Holmglen* (2), painting by Wallace Trickett

25 November 1903: Library of Congress, cph 3b25739

26 November 1960: Alexander Turnbull Library, EP/1969/5344/30-F

27 November 1935: Alexander Turnbull Library, 1/1-018443-F

28 November 1979: Phil Reid © Antarctica New Zealand Pictorial Collection, 2004

29 November 1893: Enos Silvenus Pegler, Auckland War Memorial Museum, PH-NEG-C17351

30 November 1949: Alexander Turnbull Library, Eph-A-NZ-NATIONAL-1949-01-cover

Geoffrey Peren: Alexander Turnbull Library, 1/1-018848-F

DECEMBER

1 December 1898: Alexander Turnbull Library, Eph-D-MEAT-Gear-1898-01

2 December 1928: Alexander Turnbull Library, 1/1-018699-F

Rewi Alley: Alexander Turnbull Library, 1/2-036405-F

3 December 1863: Sir George Grey Special Collections, Auckland Libraries, NZ Map 471

4 December 1966: New Zealand Herald/newspix.co.nz

5 December 1890: Alexander Turnbull Library, 1/2-052824-F

6 December 1905: Nigel Roberts, Te Ara — The Encyclopedia of New Zealand

7 December 1984: Bruce Jarvis Photographic Services

8 December 1942: New Zealand Herald/newspix.co.nz

9 December 1867: Alexander Turnbull Library, MNZ-1683

Whina Cooper: Alexander Turnbull Library, PA7-15-18

10 December 1908: Alexander Turnbull Library, G-826-2

11 December 1907: Alexander Turnbull Library, 1/2-022885-F

12 December 1961: New Zealand Lotteries Commission

13 December 1939: Archives New Zealand, AAAC 898 NCWA Q223

14 December 2009: New Zealand Herald/newspix.co.nz

15 December 1995: Audioculture

16 December 1905: Alexander Turnbull Library, MNZ-1035-1/4-F

17 December 1889: Hocken Library, Box-229-001

Peter Snell: Whanganui Regional Museum, Sp/Ath/17

18 December 1642: Alexander Turnbull Library, PUBL-0086-021

19 December 1941: © IWM (FL 2929)

20 December 1832: Alexander Turnbull Library, A-048-007

21 December 1964: Alexander Turnbull Library, EP-Zoology-Whales-01

22 December 1916: Alexander Turnbull Library, PAColl-8163-51

23 December 1953: Archives New Zealand, AAQT 6538/1

24 December 1953: Alexander Turnbull Library, PAColl-4875-1-01-03

William Pickering: NASA, SPD-SLRSY-102

25 December 1814: Alexander Turnbull Library, B-077-006

26 December 1879: Zoe Roland, Heritage New Zealand

27 December 1987: Alexander Turnbull Library, 1/2-036405-F

28 December 1929: Alexander Turnbull Library, PAColl-0691-1

29 December 1931: Alexander Turnbull Library: EP/1988/4712/19

30 December 1834: Alexander Turnbull Library, 1/2-050378-F

31 December 1996: Alison Green

Richie McCaw: Steve Punter, Wikimedia

INDEX

Also by Exisle Publishing . . .

New Zealand's Worst Disasters

True Stories That Rocked a Nation

**Graham Hutchins &
Russell Young**

A full train plunges into a raging river at Tangiwai; the Wahine is tossed onto rocks at the entrance to Wellington Harbour; an Air New Zealand DC-10 plunges into Mt Erebus; an earthquake destroys Christchurch … disasters like these are known to all New Zealanders: they are part of our history. But New Zealand has experienced many less well-known disasters, some of them shocking and brutal.

Graham Hutchins and Russell Young describe some of the most extraordinary events in New Zealand history. Who knew that a fire killed 39 people at Seacliff Mental Hospital in 1942? That 10 people died in a lahar on White Island in 1914? That a yacht race between Lyttelton and Wellington in 1951 resulted in 10 fatalities? That a tornado ripped through 150 houses in Hamilton in 1948? A fire raging through Raetihi in 1918 was so fierce it destroyed houses, shops and 11 timber mills. Drownings were so common here in the 19th century that they were called 'the New Zealand death'.

These and many other remarkable stories are told in this eye-opening book. While it describes accidents and tragedies, it also reveals acts of heroism. For when human beings make mistakes, others often achieve daring feats of rescue. Some of the stories show that we underestimate Mother Nature at our peril, but many also testify to the courage of the human spirit. Few books are genuine page-turners; this one is.

ISBN 978 1 77559 270 9